Prehistoric Cheshire

Victoria B. Morgan BA (Hons), MA

and

Paul E. Morgan BSc (Hons), MSc

Published by

Landmark Publishing Ltd
Ashbourne Hall, Cokayne Ave, Ashbourne, Derbyshire DE6 1EJ England
Tel: (01335) 347349 Fax: (01335) 347303
e-mail: landmark@clara.net
website: www.landmarkpublishing.co.uk

ISBN 1 84306 140 6

Dedication: For Dorothy and James who made Cheshire our home

Print: Cromwell Press Ltd, Trowbridge
Design: Mark Titterton
Cover: James Allsopp

Front cover: The Bridestones near Congleton

Title page: The standing stone of Minn End Lane I

Back cover top: The Bullstones in Wincle

Back cover bottom: Bronze palstave found by David Bailey (in Adlington)

LANDMARK COLLECTOR'S LIBRARY

Prehistoric Cheshire

Victoria B. Morgan BA (Hons), MA
and
Paul E. Morgan BSc (Hons), MSc

Landmark Publishing

Acknowledgements

Firstly we would like to thank local Macclesfield Historian, Dorothy Bentley Smith, for her corrections to, and advice on, the text, for providing the pictures of the Oversley Farm excavations and taking some of the close-up photographs, and for the 'Introduction' to the Prehistoric Copper Mining and Metalworking section. Many thanks go also to Andy Burnham, founder of the Megalithic Portal website (www.megalithic.co.uk), who convinced us that there are other people out there interested in obscure standing stones and grassy humps; and to our friend, Gary Smith, for his help and technical advice on the diagrams and plans.

In addition, we are very grateful to Dr Jill Collens, Cheshire County Council's Archaeological Officer, for allowing us access to the *Cheshire County Sites and Monuments Record*, John Barnatt, Senior Survey Archaeologist of the Peak District National Park, for his information on The Bullstones, and the Rangers at Calderstones Park in Liverpool for arranging access to the stones in the Harthill Greenhouse.

Thanks are also due to Doug Pickford for kindly lending us the photograph of Lindow Man, Anne Hearle of The Mellor Archaeological Trust for the picture of the Mellor pot, Peter Herring for the photograph of Casthal-yn-Ard and Judy Webb for the picture of the authors. We are also very grateful to local metal detectorist, David Bailey, for allowing us to photograph the prehistoric artefacts he has found in Cheshire, and to local astronomer, Kevin Kilburn, for sharing his discoveries on the prehistoric astronomical alignments in the area.

Finally we would like to say a very big 'thank you' to our daughters, Megan and Charlotte, who have been willing participants (on most occasions) during our numerous adventures into the Cheshire countryside.

Contents

Introduction

Unlike the neighbouring county of Derbyshire, Cheshire is not famed for its prehistoric monuments. In 1940 one author commented 'in comparison with some other regions in Northern Britain, Cheshire was relatively unimportant. It has no pottery, one doubtful habitation site, no burial sites on the Plain, no monuments and no objects of precious metal; in short none of the things which suggest settlement and wealth' (Varley & Jackson, 1940).

This is what most historians have led us to believe. When reading through books on the heritage of Cheshire, prehistory is often consigned to a couple of pages or a small chapter at most. However, upon further investigation it becomes quite clear that Cheshire, particularly the east of the county on the western slopes of the Pennines and the eastern slopes of the mid-Cheshire Ridge, once possessed a rich prehistoric landscape. There is still a wealth of evidence for settlement in the area, it is just a case of knowing where to look. In order to understand why the Pre-Roman period has generally remained in obscurity, we need first to take a look at the landscape of Cheshire both in recent years and in days gone by.

The soils of Cheshire are highly suited for growing crops and keeping livestock, but while this has added to the prosperity of the county over the years, it has sadly impacted greatly upon the archaeology. In areas where the soil is rich and fertile, the land has been intensively farmed leading to the partial or even total destruction of many ancient settlement sites and ritual monuments. As amateur Macclesfield naturalist and archaeologist, Dr J.D. Sainter, once commented, 'It is generally in desolate or out-of-the-way places where archaeological remains are found to be existing' (1878). This is certainly the case in Derbyshire where most of the prehistoric monuments survive in upland regions. Today these are bleak expanses of moorland, but during the Bronze Age they were highly fertile areas of farmland. It was only when the climate became colder and wetter in the Late Bronze Age causing large areas of bog to form, that these localities were abandoned. The monuments survive because they have not been intensively farmed since. In Cheshire, however, once the forests had been cleared, the county developed into a prosperous agricultural region with a long tradition of flourishing arable and pastoral farming. Even today the symbol of Cheshire is the wheatsheaf and the area is renowned for its tasty new potatoes and crumbly white cheese.

With the invention of modern mechanised ploughing, burial mounds have been levelled and destroyed at an alarming rate. Examples from Cheshire include The Seven Lows in Delamere (three have been completely flattened and the other four remain as slight humps), the barrow cemeteries near Jodrell Bank and Old Withington, and the bowl barrow at the junction of Bonis Hall Lane and London Road in Butley near Macclesfield. Although they are now nothing more than slightly raised grassy bumps in fields, nevertheless each one has an interesting story to tell.

A typical example of a ploughed Cheshire barrow in the grounds of Swettenham Hall near Holmes Chapel.

Destruction of ancient sites is widespread, as the recent *Monuments at Risk Survey* has shown, with agriculture blamed as the main culprit. In Cheshire alone it is believed that 46% of the county's Bronze Age round barrows have been completely destroyed, and erosion of the remaining barrows is estimated at 10mm per year. This is particularly worrying when considering that many barrows are already less than one metre in height. In contrast, the process of natural erosion is infinitely slower. At Woodhouse End (a Beaker barrow in Gawsworth near Macclesfield), excavations revealed that the mound had only lost thirty or so centimetres in total height between the time of construction and modern archaeological investigation, thus averaging around 10mm per century (as opposed to 10mm per year!).

Even the largest monuments made from stone, such as the burial chambers and stone circles, have suffered. Their standing stones have been an easy source of raw materials for dry-stone walls, gateposts and lintels, while smaller stones have been used for building material and road aggregate. The Bridestones chambered tomb on the Cheshire/Staffordshire border, described as 'Cheshire's only megalith', is a prime example. During the 18th century hundreds of tons of stone were removed from the site and used to build a nearby farmhouse and turnpike road as well as to create an ornamental garden in Tunstall Park. At New Farm in Henbury near Macclesfield stones forming part of a Bronze Age stone circle, were used as a stile in a field nearby.

Given this evidence it seems a little presumptuous to say that Cheshire was obviously 'unimportant'. As the Vice President of the Macclesfield Scientific Society commented in 1877 'A roughed stone, a chipped flint, a bronze celt, an iron-spearhead, a few old bones, perhaps charred, or a few ashes and a little charcoal, are at first sight but worthless trifles, yet what a story do they tell! With them we have the skeleton history of the most civilised nation; without them, and other such trifles, history would be but a name.'

There were undoubtedly many other ancient monuments in Cheshire which have long since disappeared without a trace, but it is not all doom and gloom. For those who know where to look there remains a rich prehistoric landscape and, as already mentioned, particularly in the east of the county. From enigmatic standing stones, such as the strangely named 'Murder Stone', to the forgotten stone circle of The Bullstones near Wincle, we will take you on a fascinating journey through the county's lost past, revealing the captivating tale of Cheshire's development prior to the Roman Conquest. We shall see that the region was highly significant during prehistoric times, more than has previously been appreciated. With the Neolithic came the construction of the huge chambered long cairn of The Bridestones, possessing features found at no other site on the English mainland; with the Bronze Age, the development of the largest known surviving prehistoric copper mine in England at Alderley Edge, followed by the Iron Age, producing Lindow Man, or 'Pete Marsh' as he has come to be known, one of the most famous archaeological discoveries ever made in Britain.

Archaeological Techniques

To discover more about these ancient sites, constructed in a time long before written records existed, we are reliant almost entirely on the science of archaeology. Archaeologists must gather what information they can from the artefacts and structures that survive both above and below ground, no matter how small or apparently insignificant they may seem.

In general, the climate in the United Kingdom is not friendly to archaeology, however certain types of soil are more conducive to the preservation of certain items. Stone artefacts and structures tend to survive in most places, apart from those reused by man in later millennia, whereas organic materials are much rarer. Bone is sometimes well-preserved in dry alkaline soils like those over chalk, while items such as wood, textiles, leaves, animal skin, leather and hair tend to survive only in wet conditions, for example peat bogs, where a lack of oxygen impedes the growth of bacteria and thus prevents rotting.

Bones and teeth, both human and animal, are of particular interest. When examined closely they can tell archaeologists a great deal about how a particular creature lived and died. Human bones can show evidence of disease and injury, fatal wounds and other abnormalities as well as revealing the age and sex of an individual. In the case of animals slaughtered for meat, marks left on the bones provide clues to butchery techniques and indicate which were the favourite cuts.

Even the smallest fragments of bone, from sources such as cremations, are useful to scientists and archaeologists. Cremations in the Bronze Age were not as thorough as those of today, for now bones are ground to ash after they have been burnt. Certain ancient bones still survive and it is often possible to tell the age, sex and state of health of a person even from the tiniest pieces.

Environmental archaeologists take soil samples and analyse them to locate insects, beetles, snails, small mammal bones, pollen and seeds. By doing so they are able to establish what the environment was like and how it changed at certain times in prehistory. For example, soil samples can show the transition from natural forest through clearance to cultivation. Snails are particularly useful for a number of reasons. Certain types of snail live only in certain types of habitat, they are not capable of moving over long distances, and when they die, often their shells remain for us to find.

Dating Methods

Archaeologists use a number of dating techniques in their endeavours to ascertain a more specific time-scale in relation to the biological development of species and the anthropological evolution of man. The most widely used method is radiocarbon (or C14) dating. All living things, both plant and animal, contain atoms of two types of carbon, ordinary carbon (carbon 12) and small amounts of radioactive carbon (carbon 14). When any organism dies, the radiocarbon begins to decay and over a number of years turns into nitrogen. Thanks to American scientist William Libby, archaeologists know that after 5730 years the carbon 14 is half way to disappearing, therefore, by measuring the amount of radiocarbon that survives, scientists can work out roughly when something 'died'. This kind of dating, however, cannot produce a specific year, only a range of probable dates covering a period comprising a number of years, which are usually followed by + and -, allowing for a margin of error.

Another more precise method of dating is dendrochronology. This process, based on tree rings (oak trees in the UK), is used on sites where wooden material has survived. Each year as a tree grows, it creates a new growth ring and the climate and environmental conditions of the time determine the pattern created. Trees in the same area lay down the same rings. By gradually working backwards using ancient trees that still survive, together with timbers from old buildings and other wooden items found on archaeological sites, a master database has been created against which any new artefacts can be compared. This method of dating can be particularly precise if the outer wood, known as the sapwood, survives. Sometimes dendrochronologists can even pinpoint felling to a specific season within a particular year.

All of the dates listed in this book are quoted as BC (Before Christ) and AD (Anno Domini – after Christ), although the latter is only used where clarification is necessary. However, when reading alternative publications, you may come across the non-denominational terms BCE (Before Current Era) instead of BC and likewise CE (Current Era) in place of AD. This new method is becoming increasingly popular. Occasionally dates are also expressed as BP (Before Present) with present actually being 1950, the year to which radiocarbon dating is calibrated.

Previous Research in Cheshire

In the past several writers and historians have covered Cheshire's prehistory to varying degrees. However, the majority of these accounts are long since out of print and very difficult to get hold of. Most modern books donate only a page or two to ancient sites, preferring to concentrate on the county's Roman heritage instead. Even the museums in the area have very little on display, despite the wealth of prehistoric finds uncovered.

One of the earliest sources of Cheshire prehistory is George Ormerod's *The History of the County Palatine and City of Chester* written in the 19th century. Described as the 'first point of reference for any Cheshire Local Historian despite its age', the work is now widely available thanks to its publication on CD-Rom by the Cheshire Local History Association and the Family History Society of Cheshire. Ormerod began his *History* in 1813, personally visiting all of the townships from his home at Chorlton Hall in Backford near Sandbach. It was later revised and enlarged by Thomas Helsby in 1882. Although the work is an invaluable source of reference for Cheshire history as a whole, unfortunately the Pre-Roman period receives only a few brief mentions.

Cheshire prehistory pioneer, William Shone, taken in October 1909.

Undoubtedly one of the most important and interesting publications on the subject comes from Dr J.D. Sainter in the form of his *Jottings of some Geological, Archaeological, Botanical, Ornithological and Zoological Rambles Round Macclesfield* often shortened to *Scientific Rambles Round Macclesfield*, published in 1878. As well as being an amateur geologist, archaeologist and natural historian, Dr Sainter was also a surgeon and apothecary, practising in Macclesfield from the 1830s until his death in 1885 and was a keen member of the Macclesfield Scientific Society. Ahead of his time, Sainter's work provides a fantastic insight into the prehistory around the area of Macclesfield and the Peak District of Derbyshire. While many other antiquarians of his period were defiling the countryside in the name of archaeology, he recognised the destruction that was occurring and luckily for us carefully recorded the surviving prehistoric sites. Having said that, he did carry out some archaeological investigations of his own, the most notable being an excavation of The Bullstones in Wincle. Copies of the original publication are difficult to come by, but a reprint by The Silk Press in 1999 is available in most local bookshops.

The next work of any note is William Shone's *Prehistoric Man in Cheshire*, published in 1911. Some of the theories are out of date as one would expect, but it nevertheless provides a good overall view of Cheshire prehistory. Contained within is a comprehensive gazetteer together with many photographs of both archaeological finds and monuments, several of which have disappeared in the intervening years.

In 1940 The Cheshire Rural Community Council embarked upon a series of historical handbooks. The first, *Prehistoric Cheshire* by W.J. Varley and J.W. Jackson, endeavoured 'to give an account of early man in the area later known as Cheshire'. Unfortunately, the first volume only saw one edition and the rest of the series made no further progress because enemy bombs during the Second World War destroyed all the blocks and types from the first edition. By 1964, the Council decided to try again and W.J. Varley rewrote and updated the first work to create *Cheshire Before the Romans*. Although the titles of these works suggest an in depth look at the county, the reader is soon disappointed. The majority of the discussion covers archaeological theory and artefacts in the UK as a whole, with Cheshire once more designated an area of little consequence.

One of the more recent and comprehensive guides to prehistory in the Macclesfield area was produced by local writer Gordon Rowley (MA Cantab) in the early 1980s. Awarded a degree in Archaeology and Anthropology at the age of 55 in 1975, Rowley was involved in excavations at a number of sites, the most notable being the 'Beaker' barrow at Woodhouse End in Gawsworth. This self-published work is again very difficult to get hold of, although a copy can be found in the reference section of Macclesfield public library.

Finally in 1987, D.M. Longley published the first Cheshire volume in the *Victoria County History* Series. Edited by C.R. Elrington, it dedicates a great many pages to the prehistory of the county with full descriptions of monuments and an exhaustive gazetteer. This is, however, an academic study and difficult for the layman (or woman) to follow. Although there are many diagrams of pottery and tools, there are no photographs of the sites themselves and many of the subsequent discoveries are not, of course, included.

Numerous articles have also appeared in the county's two main archaeological journals, *The Transactions of the Historic Society of Lancashire & Cheshire (THSLC)* which later became the *Transactions of the Lancashire & Cheshire Antiquarian Society (TLCAS)* and the *Journal of the Chester Archaeological Society (JCAS)*, copies of which can be found in the reference section of the county's main libraries.

A Few Words on Maps

If you decide to visit any of the sites mentioned in this book, the following information should be considered. Whilst the maps presented here have been simplified to emphasise relevant details, initially you would be well advised to use an official map.

Britain is fortunate in having a long history of detailed, good quality mapping, which can be traced back to 1746 when a survey of the Scottish highlands was commissioned for military purposes. Through time the Ordnance Survey (OS) has evolved to provide cartographic services to a range of disciplines and for leisure purposes. The maps produced include archaeological features and the plotting of many is due to the skill of the early OS surveyors.

Not every site is shown but the most useful maps to use are those in the Landranger series (at 1:50,000 scale or $1^{1}/_{4}$ inch to the mile) or the Explorer and Outdoor Leisure maps at the 1:25,000 scale ($2^{1}/_{2}$ inches to the mile).

As mentioned in the next chapter, although the title of this book is *Prehistoric Cheshire*, included are a number of sites located in neighbouring areas due to their importance and proximity to modern boundaries.

At the 1:50,000 scale Cheshire is covered by five of the pink-covered Landranger maps – sheets 109, 117 118, 119 and 127. The latter two only contain small areas of Cheshire whilst also taking in parts of south Manchester, Derbyshire, Staffordshire and Shropshire.

Recently the Ordnance Survey has introduced a replacement for the small green-covered Pathfinder maps at the more detailed 1:25,000 scale. This comprises the Explorer series, and at least five of these orange-fronted sheets cover this study area – numbers 257, 258, 266, 267 and 268. We have found these maps most useful for navigation and location of even the smallest sites, although some are double-sided which can create handling problems.

The eastern-most area of Cheshire (the part that includes the Peak District National Park) is also covered by two of the yellow Outdoor Leisure sheets – numbers 1 (The Dark Peak) and 24 (The White Peak). This series of maps shares the same scale as the Explorer maps.

Not all the sites discussed or listed in this book are actually marked on the maps, but where they are, they can be distinguished from other named features by the use of an 'olde English' type font. In most cases a site will only be identified by the monument type (e.g. barrows will be marked as a 'tumulus' (or the plural 'tumuli') or 'cairn') but occasionally important sites will be highlighted by their name.

For those wishing to 'dig deeper' into other aspects of the stones there are the solid geology maps produced by the British Geological Survey. A good starting point is the 1:625,000 scale map (10 miles to one inch) South Sheet which covers southern Britain up to a little north of Scarborough. In addition, the British Geological Survey has also published a series of guides exploring the geology of Britain in plain English.

More recently the Ordnance Survey has developed its cartography over the internet. Its website (www.ordsvy.gov.uk) can be used to find the right map for your needs. The organisation's GetaMap feature (www.getamap.co.uk) gives you the opportunity to locate individual sites from the comfort of your own home. To obtain a different view of the countryside two websites provide aerial images, i.e. Multimap (www.multimap.com) and Getmapping (www.getmapping.com). Both have access to the aerial survey of England undertaken at the turn of the millennium. Coverage is improving all the time and now includes most of Cheshire.

Environmental and Archaeological Conservation

All of the sites discussed in this book have been in existence for thousands of years. In order to ensure that future generations can enjoy them as we do please remember the following rules:

- If a site is on private land remember to get permission – if you do not you may face court action and upset the landowner enough to deny future visitors access;

- Respect public rights of way;

- Follow the 'Country Code' – close gates, use stiles, keep to paths, control your dog and do not drop litter;

- Most of these sites have been fully excavated already and are highly unlikely to contain anything valuable, so do not dig in the ground around them;

- Do not mark any stone for any reason with anything. Do not move stones, do not light fires near them and do not place candles on them.

In most cases damage is done unwittingly, but if everyone follows these simple guidelines then access restrictions are less likely to be tightened. Should you discover any damage to archaeological sites it should be reported to the County Archaeologist in the first instance (see the useful addresses section at the back of the book).

In addition should you encounter any pollution of the watercourses or environmental crimes such as fly-tipping, then please report them to the Environment Agency on 0800 80 70 60.

Time Scale

Era	Year	Approximate construction dates of the monuments covered in this book			Other British monuments in comparison
Early Neolithic	4500BC				
	4000BC				
Middle Neolithic	3500BC	Chambered cairns and long barrows			West Kennet long barrow
	3000BC		Henge		Castlerigg stone circle
Late Neolithic	2500BC				Ring of Brodgar, Orkney Trilithons at Stonehenge Avebury
Early Bronze Age	2000BC		Stone circles	Round barrows and cremation cemeteries	Bluestones at Stonehenge Boscawen-ûn stone circle, Cornwall
Middle Bronze Age	1500BC				Men an Tol, Cornwall Uffington White Horse
Late Bronze Age	1000BC				
Iron Age	500BC			Hillforts	Maiden Castle hillfort, Dorset
	AD43				

12

2. The Landscape of Cheshire

Administrative Boundaries

Records indicate that the shire of Cheshire has been in existence for over a millennium and became a 'modern' administrative area in 1888. The present boundaries now cover an area of 2,335 square kilometres but were far larger just decades ago. The first change came in the 1930s when the boundary with Lancashire to the north adopted the line of the Manchester Ship Canal rather than the River Mersey. At this period the county boundaries extended from Wallasey on the Wirral in the west, to Tintwistle in the Etherow valley in the east, with the towns of Stockport and Altrincham extending the northern limits.

By 1974 local government reorganisation had led to the loss of the Wirral to Merseyside, Stockport and Altrincham (and their surrounding areas) to Greater Manchester and the Etherow 'spur' to Derbyshire. The county then contained the districts of Chester City, Congleton, Crewe and Nantwich, Ellesmere Port and Neston, Halton, Macclesfield, Vale Royal and Warrington. Two decades later a further change came about as Halton and Warrington became 'unitary authorities' in 1998 and Cheshire evolved into the county we know today. Who knows what further changes may lie ahead?

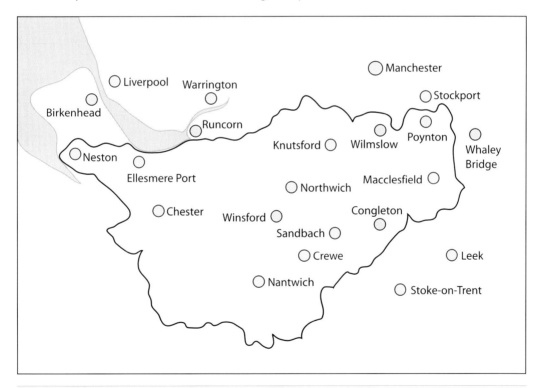

Figure 1 – The modern county of Cheshire

Although this book is entitled *Prehistoric Cheshire* our researches have not been entirely confined to the prehistory within the present boundaries of Cheshire as they exist in 2004. For much of prehistory there were no administrative regions to be concerned about. Other matters filled the thoughts of man as he strived to survive. These struggles, as you will see, often required prehistoric people to roam the countryside in search of food and land. Cheshire cannot, therefore, be viewed in isolation when it comes to studying life before the Roman invasion. Many monuments and artefacts, which contribute significantly to the story, have been found within a few miles of the modern county borders, and for this reason the most important ones are included here.

Physical Characteristics

The processes that created the land we all live on, are continuing almost unnoticed. Only spectacular volcanic eruptions or catastrophic earthquakes remind us that our planet is still far from finality. The rocks beneath our feet were created in a range of environments, subjected to massive upheavals; at the mercy of the sea, the rivers, the wind, the rain, the cold and the snow. Our planet is continually changing. Thousands of years of exposure to the elements has smoothed steep valley sides, worn down high summits, given the rivers their slow changing courses and ground down the solid rocks into soils which in turn support the plant life we rely on.

The Geology

The topography of Cheshire as we know it today has been, and continues to be, influenced by a number of factors, all of which are intertwined. The primary component is the rock beneath our feet – the 'solid' geology. Cheshire essentially comprises a basin ringed by the much older rocks of the Pennines to the east, the uplands of north-east Wales to the west and a glacial deposit, known as the Ellesmere Moraine, to the south. The upland areas provide the source for the county's two main river catchments, The Mersey and The Dee.

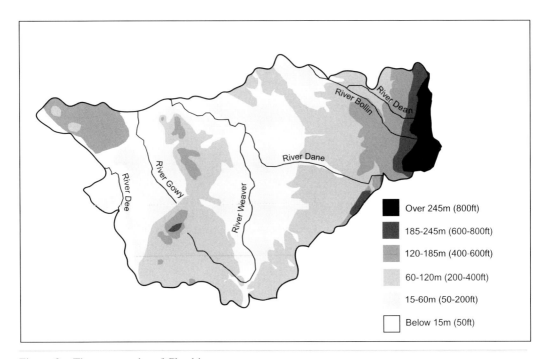

Figure 2 – The topography of Cheshire

Much of the region is a gently rolling terrain, with only slight changes in elevation of between 20 metres and 50 metres above sea level. There are, however, a number of small ridges and scarps 'puncturing' the Plain. These ridges are composed of sandstone dating to the Triassic period (formed around 250 million years ago). The most significant is the mid-Cheshire Ridge, which runs roughly north-south, neatly dividing the Plain east and west. It comprises a low, narrow, irregular 'finger' reaching heights of 141m at Helsby, 227m at Raw Head in the Peckforton Hills to the south, and 140m at Beeston. Despite being relatively low-lying, the ridge rises steeply out of the Plain and provides a prominent landmark in an otherwise flat area. It played an important role during prehistoric times when it provided a bridge of open land in an otherwise heavily forested landscape, leading from the shores of the Irish Sea to the regions around the River Severn further south. During the Iron Age a chain of heavily defended hillforts and settlements developed along its spine, from Helsby in the north to Malpas in the south.

The Delamere section of the mid-Cheshire Ridge is geologically significant as it marks the point where the so called Mouldsworth drainage channel opened out onto the east of the Plain during the last Ice Age. Here the movement of the ice had temporarily stabilised causing a glacial lake to form in the channel. Created at the end of the last Ice Age, when glacial melt waters broke through, other significant gaps, allowing access from east to west, can also be found at Beeston and Bickerton.

In the extreme east the Pennine range of hills forms the highest part of the county. Indeed the Peak District National Park extends into the Borough of Macclesfield. The county boundary here follows the line of the watershed of the southern Pennines, i.e. the source of the River Dane, the River Goyt and the River Bollin. This narrow band of uplands gives rise to a landscape that is distinctly different from the majority of Cheshire. It was created millions of years ago by a cataclysmic earth event which thrust the older Carboniferous strata against the younger Triassic rocks along the line of what is known as the Red Rock Fault. The resulting pressure led to a physical vertical rock movement of some 300 metres. Similar events created a number of smaller faults across the Plain.

The Pennine slopes rise quite steeply from the Plain and are divided into two distinct zones. The first is a 3 to 6 kilometre wide shelf at an altitude of between 60 and 90 metres. This is lined with sands and gravels, which are joined to the gravel spreads of the rivers Dane, Bollin, Goyt and Etherow flowing down from the Pennines. The second zone forms an upper slope between 90 and 180 metres above sea level. This is characteristically narrow, apart from at Alderley Edge.

The dominant rock type flanking the Pennines to the east of the Red Rock Fault, is a coarse sandstone known as Millstone Grit, formed by the deposition of delta sediments. Deeper into the Peak District this gives way to limestone on the higher plateau areas of the range. Interestingly, around the Poynton area the grits are interspersed with Carboniferous coal seams, which were mined at the surface. All of these rocks were deposited in various tropical environments in the Carboniferous period between 350 and 290 million years ago.

Through the years the geology of Cheshire has added significantly to the county's wealth, providing a number of minerals which have been exploited since prehistoric times. Of particular interest is the copper around Alderley Edge and Bickerton and the underground salt deposits between Middlewich and Nantwich. The source of this copper (and other minerals such as lead and zinc) is believed originally to have been the Carboniferous black shales that underlie the Cheshire basin. Metals dissolved in these shales migrated up into the sandstone, becoming trapped. The mineral-rich fluids then precipitated out to form the rich ore veins. In mid-Cheshire rock salt was laid down during the Triassic Period, 250 to 200 million years ago, when the area was a vast, shallow sea and dinosaurs roamed the earth. The brine fields and salt deposits around Northwich and Middlewich gave rise to the rich chemical industry across the county and were exploited as early as the Bronze Age.

The Soils

Cheshire sat under an ice sheet over a kilometre thick as little as 20,000 years ago when the Cheshire basin was filled by the eastern tongue of a stream of ice which split around the mountains of Snowdonia. Glacial activity not only affected the geology of the region, but also the overlying soils of the Plain. A variety of materials including boulder clays, sands and gravels, glacial erratic pebbles of Criffel granite and rocks from Borrowdale in the Lake District, were deposited on top of the Triassic sandstones and marls, in some places up to 100m thick. These deposits essentially comprise three distinct layers, with boulder clays top and bottom, sandwiching a layer of sand, which represents a slight lull between the two major phases of the last Ice Age when water returned for a brief span. It is these boulder clays which in turn led to the formation of heavy, easily waterlogged soils on much of the Plain. Only in the areas of sand and gravel did well-drained brown earth and sandy soils form.

The Cheshire Plain looking north-east from the hillfort of Maiden Castle in Bickerton.

This topography has significantly influenced the way in which Cheshire developed, particularly during prehistoric times. For most of prehistory the areas of boulder clay were uninhabitable, filled with dense forest from the Mesolithic to the Bronze Age, and heavily waterlogged during the climatic deterioration in the Early and Middle Iron Age. It was only in the last few centuries prior to the Roman invasion that communities began to settle and farm these areas. In general, it is only on the well-drained sand and gravels, perfect for agriculture, that most prehistoric activity occurred.

The Wetlands

One other significant feature which has shaped the landscape of Cheshire is the wetlands. The county is riddled with numerous shallow meres, peat-filled pools and mosses which have developed in hollows in the sand and gravel, and kettle holes created by the dissolving salt beds. Within the modern boundaries of Cheshire there are approximately 3,500 hectares of lowland peat deposits. The main areas are the Northern Mosses on the bank of the River Mersey including the Rixton, Risley, Woolston and Holcroft Complex; the Eastern Mosses, most notably Danes and Lindow Moss along with smaller basin mires to the west of Macclesfield; the Northern Meres, characterised by areas of open water but often fringed with peat, including Rostherne, Tatton and Tabley Meres to the north and west of Knutsford, and Pick Mere and Budworth Mere near Northwich; the wetlands of the mid-Cheshire Ridge at Delamere and Oak Mere; and the southern wetlands around Crewe and the Shropshire Border. In addition there are numerous small basin mires and larger valley mire deposits alongside the minor rivers and streams.

The infamous peat bog at Lindow Moss near Wilmslow where ancient human remains were discovered on several occasions in the 1980s.

During prehistoric times these mosses and meres would have provided a good hunting ground for fish and wild fowl, as well as offering natural protection for settlements. For example, in the Late Iron Age an enclosure was built a few metres over the Cheshire border at Great Woolden Hall in Salford, Greater Manchester. It appears to have been deliberately placed to take advantage of the protection offered by the neighbouring wetlands, bounded on three sides by Chat Moss, the Rixton/Risley Mosses and the Glazebrook, a tributary of the River Mersey.

3

The Mesolithic
(circa 10,000BC to 4500BC)

The era known as the Middle Stone Age or Mesolithic began when the last Ice Age came to an end around 12,000 years ago. People had lived in Britain prior to this in the Old Stone Age (Palaeolithic), but the advancing ice sheets (which eventually reached as far as the Midlands) had forced them southwards into what is today the Continent of Europe. Once the icecap had retreated, tundra vegetation returned to the thawing northern lands bringing with it herds of reindeer. This in turn led to a northward migration of Mesolithic hunter-gatherers who came to the area of what is Britain today via a land bridge from the area of modern Scandinavia.

At that time the land bridge, now submerged under the North Sea, was almost entirely covered with pine forests. English Heritage's chief archaeologist, David Miles, commented recently on this area, 'We know there is a prehistoric Atlantis beneath the North Sea where once an area equal to the size of present-day Britain attached us to the Continent where prehistoric people and animals roamed.' At the time of writing a significant discovery of Mesolithic flints has been made under the sea off Tynemouth. It is hoped that in years to come further discoveries of untouched artefacts will come to light in the coastal waters of the British Isles, hopefully leading to a better understanding of the Mesolithic period, which at present is rather patchy.

During the Ice Age, hunters had been able to track and kill large animals such as the mammoth and woolly rhinoceros, which would keep them in food and supplies for some months. However, as the ice retreated, the large open areas which supported these huge creatures disappeared, and with them the animals themselves. The hunter-gatherers were forced to change their entire way of life, tracking a wide variety of smaller individual species to prevent them also from becoming extinct.

Various ancient animal bones have been found in and around Cheshire over the years. Dr J.D. Sainter's *Scientific Rambles Round Macclesfield* records the discovery of bones and teeth from red deer, fallow deer, wild boar, wild horse and the extinct ox (*Bos longifrons*) during the construction of Macclesfield cemetery in the 19th century, as well as the molar tooth of a mammoth which was uncovered in some river gravel in the valley of the River Dean in Adlington. Sainter also refers to an account in the *Geological Magazine* which reported the discovery of some mammoth bones and teeth and wild horse and bison bones just over the border in Staffordshire, at Waterhouses near Leek. Another interesting find had been made at Wirksworth in Derbyshire some years earlier when 'the complete skeleton of a rhinoceros was met with in a limestone fissure laid open by mining operations'. Also in the Peak District, hundreds of bones and teeth from mammoths, woolly rhinoceros, reindeer, red deer, grisly bear, wild boar, wolf, wild horse, goat, badger, dog and cat have come to light over the years in the limestone around Castleton.

During the course of the Mesolithic as the ice retreated further northward the climate became increasingly warm, resulting in the formation of deeper soils. The tundra landscapes were eventually colonised by mixed woodland of birch and pine. Wild pigs, roe deer, red deer and elks spread northwards from southern Europe. By 6000BC seawaters had risen dramatically flooding the land bridge to Europe and creating the British Isles. Many lowland areas were completely lost under water, while in other areas free from the weight of ice, the land rose creating raised beaches. Meanwhile the climate continued to improve resulting in the appearance of a much denser deciduous woodland of oak, elm, alder and hazel over the majority of the country.

The Mesolithic era in Britain is generally divided into two phases – the Early Mesolithic (circa 8500BC to 6500BC) when we were still joined to the Continent and shared similar customs, and the Later Mesolithic (circa 6500BC to 4500BC) which saw the development of a new insular culture. The Early Mesolithic is characterised by small flint tools, known as microliths, which were pointed or triangular in shape and held in a handle of wood or bone. They are usually no more than 50mm long and 12mm wide, and are common finds across Europe. During the Later Mesolithic flint designs in Britain evolved with much narrower, more pointed blades.

The people living in post-glacial Britain were essentially mobile hunter-gatherers, occupying temporary camps and seasonal cave and rock shelters. Structures were made from organic materials and probably only erected in any one place for a brief time span; therefore, the majority of evidence for Mesolithic activity comes only from the discovery of refuse, such as midden waste and animal bones, at temporary camp sites, or scattered fragments of flint and debris from tool manufacturing spots. Environmental evidence suggests there may have been woodland clearance on a very small scale. Human burials of the period are incredibly rare, with only a handful of sites found in the UK. In a cave in the Mendips, known as Aveline's Hole, the skeletal remains of between 50 and 100 individuals were discovered in the late 18th and early 19th centuries, while at Gough's Cave in Cheddar, the complete 9,000-year-old skeleton of a young male, now known as Cheddar Man, was uncovered in 1903. Sadly no such discoveries have come to light in the Cheshire area.

During this period there is only scant evidence for semi-permanent settlement in certain areas of the country, such as the 10,000-year-old dwelling discovered recently in the sandy cliffs at Howick in Northumberland, featured on the BBC's *Meet the Ancestors*. The dwelling, known as 'Britain's oldest house', consisted of a shallow circular hollow cut into the sand, within which lay a circle of substantial postholes with charcoal stains at their bases, and a number of smaller stakeholes, some angled in from outside the hollow. The most remarkable discovery however, was of a number of hearths within the house. Each contained charcoal and burnt hazelnut shells, flecked with fragments of bone: evidence of 10,000-year-old meals. Some of the hearths appeared to have been used solely for roasting nuts, and the sheer quantity suggests a resident community who were gathering and preserving large quantities of food. Radiocarbon dating later revealed that the house was in use for over a hundred years. People had been able to settle in this location because it was one of the few places where the natural resources of both land and sea would allow all year round occupation. In general it was not until the Neolithic that humans began to build durable houses of timber and make a lasting mark on the landscape.

The Cheshire Hunter-Gatherers

In Cheshire the majority of evidence for Mesolithic activity points to a small nomadic, hunter-gatherer community. Isolated flint scatters probably representing temporary hunting forays have been found in locations such as at Tatton Mere, Alderley Edge, Oversley Farm and Mellor in the east of the county, Poulton and Alford in the west and along the edge of the mid-Cheshire Ridge near Aston and at Beeston Castle. Just outside the modern boundaries of Cheshire, in the sandstone escarpments of the North Wirral, a dense concentration of surface finds has led archaeologists to the conclusion that this area may have been used as a base camp from which the hunter-gatherers could exploit the surrounding landscape. In 1988 a shelter dating to circa 8000BC, possibly representing a tent-like structure, was excavated at Greasby. It was composed of a 21-metre-square floor made from sandstone slabs with three central poles, presumably supporting a roof of timber or skins.

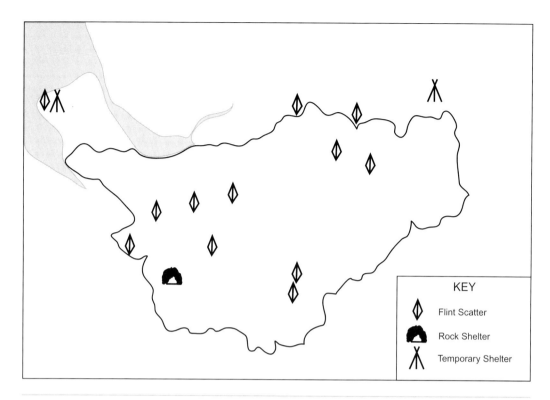

Figure 3 – Areas of current known Mesolithic activity in Cheshire

Until approximately 7000BC much of this area surrounding the North Wirral was dry land covered with forests of oak and birch, with a continuous coastline running from Anglesey to the Southern Lakes; the Dee and Mersey Estuaries were just small, wooded river channels. In the Early Mesolithic the coastline was over 8 kilometres further out than the present one but by the late 7th millennium BC the land was gradually retreating due to rapid sea-level rises. Further inland many low-lying areas became waterlogged and covered with wetland vegetation. Throughout the prehistoric period fluctuations in water levels led to a constantly changing environment with a diverse coastal landscape in the Wirral area including sand dunes, mudflats, salt marshes, marine and freshwater lagoons, swamps, mires and fens. Even in more recent times, the dredging of the Mersey channels to accommodate the growing port of Liverpool has led to erosion, with large areas of sand dunes simply washed out to sea – the coastline is now nearly half a kilometre further inland than it was in the 17th century.

A photograph taken in 1909, showing the rotting remains of the submerged Mesolithic forest at Dove Point near Hoylake on the Wirral (Shone).

A number of Early Mesolithic tools have been found near New Brighton and at Red Rocks in Hoylake in what was then a flat, wooded landscape. These areas would have been attractive with well-drained soils and strategic views to the north, an area now under Liverpool Bay. The inhabitants were within a couple of hours walking distance of the coast and close to several river channels. Other finds have come from the shores around Meols where at low tide the black remains of the rotting Mesolithic forests can occasionally be seen protruding from the sands. From 1810 onwards the inhabitants of Hoylake and Meols began retrieving artefacts from within the remains of this ancient forest on the shoreline. Luckily the respected Liverpool antiquarian, Reverend Abraham Hume, realised the importance of the discoveries and with the help of the locals and Henry Eckroyd Smith, the first curator of the Liverpool Museum, he began to amass a collection of over 3,000 artefacts dating from the Mesolithic to the medieval period.

All the evidence points to the North Wirral area being used for semi-permanent camps where family groups came together for relatively long periods within the annual cycle of following the movements of the herds of red deer. The communities may have migrated between the uplands of the Pennines and the lowlands of the Cheshire Plain in the summer, returning to the Wirral in the winter months. They almost certainly also carried out foraging trips across the region to the north, under what is now Liverpool Bay and also to the uplands of the North Wales coast where they obtained raw materials such as chert for making tools.

The area's close proximity to coastal resources and mires would undoubtedly have made it attractive for much of the year, especially during the colder months. The sea could be exploited for the fish and shellfish and also the estuaries when trout and salmon made their annual spawning visits. A number of burnt dolphin bones from the Alt near Hightown in the District of Sefton, on the other side of Liverpool Bay, indicate that communities were eating marine mammals as well as fish. Wintering birds on the estuarine mud flats would have provided a predictable hunting ground at a time when other food was scarce, whilst the wooded river channels were the ideal

habitat for wild pigs and an attractive source of edible plants, berries and hazelnuts. The fact that the area was used on a more permanent basis is further supported by pollen evidence from Bidston Moss (now part of the Birkenhead Docks complex) which has revealed the earliest evidence for the adoption of cereal cultivation in the region from between 4900BC to 4530BC (Late Mesolithic), some 500 to 1,000 years earlier than presently indicated elsewhere in the county.

The rock shelter at Carden Park, which may have been inhabited as early as 14,000 years ago. The entrance has been modified in more recent times.

One of the most important Mesolithic sites within the boundaries of modern Cheshire lies 13 kilometres to the south of Chester at Carden Park. Here evidence for temporary occupation as long ago as 14,000 years came to light when flints were discovered in a rabbit burrow in 1985. These artefacts were the first of this date to be found *in situ* in Cheshire. In 1996, a joint project between Chester Archaeology and the University of Liverpool was set up to carry out investigations. The flints were found to contain blades and core-trimming flakes of later Mesolithic type, but most interestingly, they came from a mound of soil in front of a rock overhang which had been modified to form a small cave. During excavations almost 10,000 pieces of chert and flint, mostly from the trench in front of the cave mouth, were recovered. The majority of the tools identified from amongst these fragments were dated to between circa 6800BC and 4300BC. In 1999 even earlier artefacts, made by the first communities to return to Britain after the Ice Age (between 12,800BC to 12,000BC), were also uncovered indicating that the site had been in use for thousands of years. It is unlikely that these communities settled permanently here but may have used the site sporadically, again perhaps during the colder months.

The extensive view from the rock shelter at Carden Park, looking west towards Wales.

A second site in the west of the county came to light in 1989 when a small scatter of Mesolithic flints was found by chance in a steeply sloping field overlooking the flood plain of the River Dee at Alford. Further investigations in 1991 and 1992 produced a total of twenty-five flints, the majority of which were waste fragments. The inclusion of some cores indicated that tools were made on the site from a range of flint and chert found both in the local drift deposits and perhaps further afield.

In east Cheshire another important location was turned up during fieldwalking as part of the 'Tatton Park Project', started by Cheshire County Council in the late 1970s. A scatter of flints was discovered at various sites across the park but the project really took off in 1982 when a six-year-old Knutsford schoolboy, Thomas Sprott, picked up three worked flints on the eastern edge of the Mere. A few weeks later a detailed search of the area was undertaken and dozens of flints were found in the shingle at the edge of the water. In October and November 1982 trial excavations were carried out, revealing over 8,000 pieces of worked flint most of which proved to be waste fragments dating to the Mesolithic. These were of quite low quality and may have been acquired locally. The site has since been interpreted as an Early Mesolithic temporary camp used on a hunting and gathering expedition to the Cheshire lowlands.

Understandably waterside locales seem to have been favoured by the migrating hunters as they not only provided a source of fresh water and fish, but they were also places where animals came to drink. It is from locations such as these that two other equally important Mesolithic assemblages have come. At Oversley Farm during excavations in advance of the second runway at Manchester Airport, a large collection of blades, scrapers and waste flakes was found close to a stream. At Bache, 1.5 kilometres to the north of Chester, near the modern zoo, workmen uncovered other small flints in the 19th century whilst draining a pool. It is believed that similar discoveries may eventually be found at other stream and riverside locations in the Cheshire area.

During the course of fieldwalking in the county, a number of isolated finds have been discovered in the areas surrounding the peat bogs and mires, which were probably areas of forest during the Mesolithic. In the 1990s a systematic survey of all the wetlands in Cheshire was carried out by the University of Lancaster as part of the North West Wetlands Survey, revealing a number of interesting finds. In the north of the county on a low, sandy ridge on the fringes of Woolston Moss near the Mersey several artefacts of imported high quality black flint, dating to between 6700BC and 3200BC, were recovered from an area on a crest no larger than ten metres in diameter. In mid-Cheshire, at Abbots Moss near Delamere, a microlith of Late Mesolithic date was found in the forest nursery. In the south, on land belonging to the estate of Crewe Hall, two black chert trimming flakes were recovered from the slopes of a subsidiary valley of the Englesea Brook, while a small blade of black chert was found by chance in a small arable field on the northern flanks of Wynbury Moss.

During the last few years excavations at the Old Vicarage in Mellor have revealed the site of another temporary camp. Here a number of worked flints, made from materials possibly derived from Lincolnshire and the East Yorkshire Wolds or the Trent Valley, were discovered along with flaking waste and discarded blade cores. Of particular interest was a line of flat

stones set upright in the ground; these are believed to represent the footings of a windbreak or temporary shelter which would have been made from branches and covered with skins.

At Walker's Heath in Gawsworth near Macclesfield environmental evidence from the peat bog indicates there was a reduction in birch pollen, accompanied by an increase in grasses and herbs in the Early Mesolithic. The presence of carbonised wood, dating to the same period, indicates that humans may have been responsible for burning woodland as early as the 9th millennium BC, much earlier than has generally been reported. Of course it could have been an accidental fire.

In the light of all this evidence, it would appear that Mesolithic people roamed far and wide across the county, if only visiting areas fleetingly in their search for food. They seem to have followed the movements of the animal herds, perhaps stopping off at familiar locations such as rock shelters and riverbanks year after year, and returning to a base on the Wirral during the colder months to meet up with their kin. Eventually, as they continued to tread these traditional routes, trackways would have been worn, paving the way for the long distance trade networks of the New Stone Age, to which we shall now turn our attention.

The area of excavation at Mellor hillfort where archaeologists have discovered Mesolithic flints and a possible temporary shelter (September 2003).

4 The Neolithic

(circa 4500BC to 2300BC)

At the beginning of the Neolithic period, some six and a half thousand years ago, the majority of Cheshire was still covered with forest. On the wetter, heavier soils this was very dense and difficult to penetrate but at higher altitudes where the soil was lighter and sandier, a larger proportion of birch, ash, alder, oak, lime and elm trees created a more open and accessible woodland. It was in these areas, namely the mid-Cheshire Ridge, the eastern foothills of the Pennines and the sandstone outcrops of North Wirral, that the Mesolithic hunter-gatherers slowly transformed into Neolithic farmers, and the first real physical impact was made on the landscape sometime between 4500BC and 2500BC.

During this time a social transformation took place across the British Isles. With it came new beliefs, long distance trading and the birth of architecture as well as agriculture. In Cheshire, as elsewhere, Neolithic people, possibly numbering only a few thousand in the county as a whole, began to exploit and change the countryside. They started by clearing the forest for grazing and cultivation in the areas where it was less dense. For the first time in history humans began to grow their own crops and breed their own livestock, on a small scale at first, but nevertheless reshaping the landscape as they did so. Environmental evidence from the peat deposits at Lindow Moss near Wilmslow, White Moss between Crewe and Alsager, Cocks Moss near Marton, and Danes Moss in Macclesfield indicates that forests were being cleared by burning in the 5th and 4th millennia BC.

One of the most interesting discoveries, however, comes from Bidston Moss in the North Wirral, now occupied by the Birkenhead Docks Complex. Here pollen analysis has revealed the earliest evidence for the adoption of cereal farming in the region with radiocarbon dates of circa 4900BC to 4530BC, between 500 and 1,000 years earlier than in other areas. This further supports the theory that the Mesolithic hunter-gatherers were using the Wirral as a semi-permanent base. What better place to begin experimenting with new techniques than in an area rich in other sources of food almost all the year round?

In east Cheshire, settlement first occurred on the sandy soils and well-drained gravels beside the main river valleys. In mid-Cheshire it was concentrated in the area around Delamere. Occupation was probably quite widespread, but because most of the buildings were made of wood, which has long since rotted away, it is often very hard to detect. Although the early farmers first settled in the sheltered river valleys, they almost certainly used the upland areas, such as the Pennine slopes, for seasonal grazing but there is no evidence to suggest permanent settlement there. They perhaps visited pastures on higher ground in the warmer months, but returned to a lowland base during the colder seasons, thus remaining mobile to a certain degree.

With farming came the accumulation of 'wealth' and resources, and a population that looked beyond one human lifespan. Neolithic people now had stability and time on their hands, and with the advent of farming came a more densely populated landscape, with communities living alongside each other. Our Neolithic ancestors were able to work in unison with their fellow farmers to create large-scale ritual monuments such as causewayed enclosures, long barrows, chambered cairns and henges, the likes of which had never been seen before. Constructed as investments for the future, these sites developed as a territorial focus, designed to impress. There must have been a great deal of inter-tribal contact, as the monuments were built in a tradition spanning from Cornwall in the south-west of England right up to the Outer Hebrides in the far north-west of Scotland.

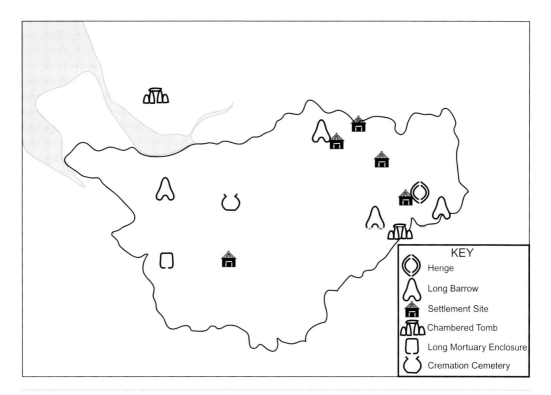

KEY
- Henge
- Long Barrow
- Settlement Site
- Chambered Tomb
- Long Mortuary Enclosure
- Cremation Cemetery

Figure 4 - Distribution Map of current known Neolithic sites in Cheshire.

As previously mentioned, such monuments are scarce in Cheshire with The Bridestones being the only authenticated surviving Neolithic structure. Three other possible long barrows are located in the east of the county at Bartomley Farm in Swythamley, Loachbrook Farm in Somerford near Congleton and in Tatton Park near Knutsford, but unfortunately no investigations have been carried out on these so it is impossible to say at the present time whether these mounds are man-made or natural. There is also evidence of a long mortuary enclosure at Churton in the west and a possible area of Neolithic activity at Eddisbury on the mid-Cheshire Ridge. Also of interest is a collection of highly decorated stones known as The Calderstones, which reside in a greenhouse over the border in Merseyside. Although not strictly within the bounds of old or modern Cheshire, because of their significant affinities and location across a short stretch of the Mersey Estuary, they cannot be ignored. All of these will be discussed subsequently in more detail.

So the question is 'why does Cheshire have so few Neolithic monuments?' Perhaps it is because the population was scattered in small groups here at that time, or maybe there were other similar monuments that have long since been destroyed. As in other areas sparse with ritual monuments made of stone, alternative materials would have been used. One example of this is the construction of timber circles with the local forests providing an easily accessible source of building material. Again these would only show up in the archaeological record as postholes, apart from in waterlogged areas conducive to the preservation of timber, as was the case with the famous circle of Seahenge discovered in the wet sands of a Norfolk beach in the summer of 1998.

Dr Nick Higham of Manchester University has suggested one plausible reason for this lack of Neolithic structures; it could be that the people, who lived in what we know as Cheshire today, were part of a regional community centred outside of the county. In the case of west Cheshire the population would have been part of the farming communities of north-east Wales

25

who built monuments such as the Ysceifiog henge in Flintshire and the chambered tombs of Branas Uchaf and Tyn-y-Coed in Denbighshire. In the east of the county the nearest neighbours were the residents of the Peak District. In order to understand more about the early Cheshire inhabitants, we will first take a look over the modern border into Derbyshire. There many more ritual monuments survive, and a great deal of research has been done by archaeologists such as John Barnatt and Keith Smith of the Peak District National Park Authority.

Neolithic Communities of the Peak District

In some respects the landscape of Neolithic Derbyshire was very similar to that of Cheshire. The most fertile areas of the Peak District were the shelves on either side of the river valleys (between the limestone plateau and the gritstone uplands), and it was here that semi-permanent occupation initially occurred. All of the early Peak monuments are located on the limestone plateau and, although the early farmers first settled in the sheltered river valleys, they almost certainly used both the plateau and upland areas for seasonal grazing.

In general, both in the Peak District and the UK as a whole, huge Neolithic monuments, such as henges, were created near the best grazing areas where the mobile farming groups were most likely to meet at certain times of year, perhaps reinforcing traditional claims to the pasture. Others, such as burial chambers and barrows, were placed close to the well-used pathways between the various regions. In Cheshire, the one surviving Neolithic monument fits in well with this pattern; this enormous chambered tomb called The Bridestones, with its commanding views across the Cheshire Plain, was possibly built by communities exploiting the Dane and Churnet valleys, providing a convenient boundary marker on the watershed of these water-ways. The Cheshire/Staffordshire border still runs along the site of the cairn today. The Bridestones is strategically located on the edge of the uplands, in one of the major passes from the Peaks to the Plain, and may have played a key role during seasonal movements between the two. It is often referred to as 'an outlier of the monuments of the White Peak', but interestingly

The chambered tomb of Five Wells at Chelmorton, near Buxton in the Peak District.

it is placed not to look towards the Pennines, but out across the Cheshire Plain. The significance of this will be discussed later in The Bridestones section.

During the Neolithic, for the first time in the history of mankind, permanent man-made features were erected which would far outlast the people who created them. The most impressive sites were the henges with their imposing banks and carefully quarried ditches of which Derbyshire possesses two – Arbor Low on Middleton Common just off the Buxton to Ashbourne road, and The Bullring at Dove Holes between Buxton and Chapel-en-le-Frith. Placed on either side of the natural boundary of the Wye gorge, it is believed they would have been adequate meeting places for the Neolithic tribes of the north and south Peak respectively. There may originally also have been many smaller ritual monuments on the limestone plateau, but these have disappeared over the millennia as the pressures of agriculture in these fertile areas led to increased demands on the land. One possible henge (now largely destroyed) was discovered in Cheshire, just off the Leek Old Road near Macclesfield, in the 1980s.

As for other Neolithic monuments, the Peak District is fortunate in having a number of chambered cairns similar to The Bridestones, all again located on the limestone plateau. These include Five Wells on Taddington Moor; Minning Low between Parwich and Elton; Green Low at Aldwark; Ringham Low near Monyash; Bole Hill on Bakewell Moor; Harborough Rocks near Brassington; Stoney Low near Aldwark and Long Low near Wetton.

Life and Settlement

Daily life in the Neolithic would have been hard, yet it is very difficult to estimate what the average human life span would have been at this time. Relatively few skeletons have survived to be examined, but of those that have, many did not survive beyond the age of twenty-five or thirty. Diseases such as tooth decay and osteoarthritis appear to have been quite prevalent. Society was certainly becoming more settled, however people would still have been reliant on hunting and gathering to a certain degree, particularly if the weather was bad and the crops failed. It was a dangerous place too with bears, wolves and wild boars roaming the countryside.

To begin with, the clearance of woodland for cultivation would have been on a relatively small scale, with areas used only temporarily by the farmers before they moved, allowing forest rejuvenation. Once they had removed an area of trees by cutting with stone axes (hafted into wood or antler) or by burning, they then used ploughs to break up the soil for planting. In the early stages these primitive ploughs were probably dragged by hand. Analysis of the pollen record has revealed that wheat and barley were being grown at this time. Once ripe the crop was harvested using flint-reaping knives. Often seeds from weeds, growing in amongst the crops, were also incorporated into the harvest and then into the diet. After reaping the grain was threshed, possibly in stone-lined pits, and ground into flour using grain rubbers comprising a saucer-shaped lower stone and a bun shaped upper stone.

In addition to growing cereal crops the Neolithic farmers also began to domesticate animals for the first time, mainly cattle but also sheep, goats and pigs. A study of Neolithic animal bones has shown that these must all have been imported originally from the Continent. Other food was provided by hunting and fishing. A number of early worked flint arrowheads have been found in Cheshire incorporated into later Bronze Age mounds such as at Woodhouse End in Gawsworth and Bearhurst Farm in Henbury. These may have been lost while hunting at an earlier period and accidentally included in the barrow material when the surrounding soil was scraped up to form the mound. As to the bows that fired the arrows, having been composed of wood they have rarely survived except in waterlogged deposits. None have been found in Cheshire, but in Somerset, a yew bow found at Mere Heath has given archaeologists an insight into the power of such items, even at this early period. The bow was 1.9 metres long, the same length as a medieval long bow, and was capable of firing an arrow a distance of over a hundred metres!

Food was usually cooked over an open fire or stewed using stones warmed in the fire (potboilers) to heat the water. Discarded potboilers, which often cracked in the flames, are a common find on excavation sites throughout the prehistoric period. Fires were lit by striking flint against certain types of stone. Evidence for such fire-making activities comes from a site at Castle Rock on Alderley Edge. There pieces of charcoal were found in association with a lump of cone-shaped haematite believed to be a striking stone.

Clothing was fashioned from leather or fur and fastened with bone and antler pins. Unfortunately being composed of organic materials again this has rarely survived apart from in areas such as peat bogs, but household tools like combs for dehairing leather, and awls for piercing are occasionally found during excavations.

Stone and Flint Tools

One of the main consequences of farming was that more sophisticated tools were required to clear the land and construct dwellings and ritual monuments. Living in a time before metals were discovered, the early settlers used flint tools such as knives, scrapers, borers and flint arrowheads, a variety of which have been discovered in Cheshire. As Francis Pryor commented recently in his in-depth study of British prehistory, *Britain BC*, 'Flint was the steel of the Stone Age in Britain. It felled trees, killed prey, built houses, butchered meat and fashioned clothes. Without it almost every daily task would have been harder work.' Recent research has shown that a polished axe in the right hands could cut down the average tree in approximately thirty minutes.

For over 2,000 years stone was the primary raw material. This in turn led to the large-scale mining of flint and quarrying of stone. Flint is second only to diamond in durability and hardness, and because of its excellent flaking qualities, it can easily be worked into a variety of shapes. Cheshire does not have a readily available source of flint, but early people exploited the pebbles of lower quality chert (a quartz-based stone resembling flint) found in the local boulder clay and river gravels. Later, once long-distance trading links had been established, good quality flint was imported from the chalk-rich areas of southern and eastern Britain, probably as prepared cores or blanks rather than as nodules. The closest known sources to Cheshire are the Lincolnshire and East Yorkshire Wolds and the Trent Valley. A study of flint mines has revealed that there were approximately twenty sites being mined on a large scale in the UK during the Neolithic. All of these were located either in Norfolk, West Sussex, Wiltshire or the eastern Highlands of Scotland, so from whichever source the high quality flint came to Cheshire, it had almost certainly travelled a great distance.

During the Neolithic period stone axe production was at its peak, with the main 'factories' located in the Lakes at Great Langdale and Scafell Pike; in North Wales at Graig Lwyd above Penmaenmawr and on the Lleyn Peninsula; at Mounts bay in Cornwall and in Northern Ireland at Tievebulliagh in County Antrim. Particularly prized were highly polished axes made from special hard stone which took hours, if not days, of grinding to produce. Such axes, however, appear to have been revered for their mystical properties rather than used for practical everyday application. The ritual significance of the axe is particularly evident at Stonehenge where several of the stones are incised with axes and daggers. As well as those visible to the naked eye, many more have been discovered by laser scanning techniques in 2003.

The trade of such prestigious items accelerated during the later Neolithic period and, by circa 2500BC, simple exchange had given way to major complex trading networks. Research in the British Isles has shown that items such as axes were transported along well-established trade routes and exchanged at certain 'safe' peripheral locations or staging posts. This increase in trade coincides almost exactly with the construction of the henge monuments. Axes from North Wales have been found in both Cheshire and Derbyshire, so traders must have been crossing the county.

Over the years many of the numerous axes discovered in Cheshire have had their petrological origins traced. Whilst some had originated in North Wales (from Graig Lwyd and the Lleyn Peninsula), others had emanated from the axe factories of the Lake District at Scafell Pike and

Great Langdale. Some had even been transported all the way from Cornwall together with samples from the Bluestone outcrops of the Preseli Mountains in Pembrokeshire. However, the most interesting axes, i.e. one from Chester and one from Lyme Handley, were fashioned from jadeite which was almost certainly imported from the Continent, perhaps from Switzerland or the Italian Alps.

A broken piece of a polished stone axe discovered by local metal detectorist, David Bailey, in Adlington near Macclesfield.

Apart from the jadeite example found in Chester, other polished axes found in the county include one from Astbury near Congleton (made from stone found in Bridlington, Yorkshire); a finely polished axe of grey flint from Gawsworth (Southern Britain); a polished axe found at Church Lawton (possibly from Cornwall and now in the Stoke-on-Trent Museum); two axes from Lyme Handley, one of brown flint and the one of jadeite already mentioned; a polished Neolithic axe from Great Budworth; and two axes from Macclesfield Forest. In the Wirral a number of axes have been found around the wetlands of Bidston Moss including a fine, unused basalt axe from North Wales.

A report in the *Transactions of the Lancashire and Cheshire Archaeological Society Journal* reports the discovery of one such axe in its Proceedings for the 12th January 1923: 'The Rev. Henry A. Hudson exhibited on behalf of Mr J.E. Bowers, of Old Trafford, a Neolithic Stone axe found in the year 1888 by Mr Richard Dunn, formerly of Macclesfield, in a small sandhole on the right-hand side of the road from Macclesfield to Macclesfield Forest. This site is situated some 300 yards above the reservoir and is about three miles from the town.'

In July 2000 a new axe was discovered close to Macclesfield Forest near a footbridge over the river Bollin in the village of Langley by Jack Mitchell, a boy from Macclesfield. The axe, considered to be ceremonial, is very large (207mm long by 125mm wide) and polished. It is very unusual in that it is Paleolithic (Old Stone Age) in shape, but manufactured from Neolithic material. Having been assessed by various experts at Manchester Museum, Liverpool University and The British Museum in London, it has been verified as dating to the Neolithic. The axe, which has since come to be known as 'Jack's axe', is made from Eskdale granite found in the Lake District. It was quite badly eroded on the surface suggesting it must have been in the river for a great length of time.

Another notable find came recently from excavations at the Mellor hillfort near Stockport, when a large polished flint chisel dating to the Late Neolithic period was unearthed. The tool is 70mm long by 20mm thick and may originally have been hafted in the centre to a wood or bone handle, and bound using wet sinew.

Pottery

The Neolithic also saw the introduction of the first pottery into Britain. For the mobile hunter-gatherer societies of the Mesolithic, fragile pots would have been cumbersome and impractical, but as they settled down into a more sedentary lifestyle, ceramics soon became a part of both domestic and funerary activities.

The earliest type of Neolithic pottery to be found in Cheshire, and in the British Isles in general, is known as Grimston ware. These simple, shallow bowls, fashioned from fine, hard fabrics were often burnished or tempered with grit, and appear in both ritual and domestic

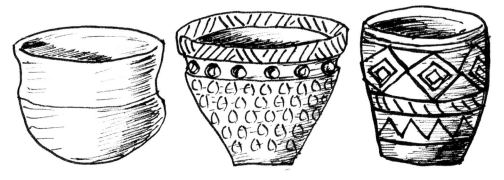

Neolithic Pottery - Grimston ware (left), Peterborough ware (centre) and Grooved ware (right)

contexts for almost a thousand years from the middle of the 4th millennium BC onwards. Several sherds of Grimston ware were found in a sand filled pit and surrounding plough soil during excavations of the medieval village at Norton in Cheshire in the 1970s, and also within Roman contexts at Abbey Green in Chester. Most interesting, however, is their inclusion within 'occupation debris' from around the Outer Gateway at Beeston Castle, which is discussed in further detail later in the chapter.

Following Grimston ware came Peterborough ware, named after the site in Cambridgeshire where it was first discovered. This coarse, thick, often round-bottomed pottery is also referred to as 'Impressed Ware' in the North, due to the fact that it is profusely decorated with a range of elaborate designs using stamps, combs, twisted cord, fingertips and bird bones. Some archaeologists believe that these intricate patterns may represent some kind of symbolism, the meaning of which has long since been lost. Interestingly the decoration on many pots is usually discontinued about two-thirds of the way down, suggesting that the bottom was not designed to be seen. The rounded bases may therefore have been placed in hollows in the floor for storage purposes or in the embers of an open fire for cooking. This is attested by the fact that some Peterborough ware has traces of carbonised material on it representing food residue. Examples from Cheshire include a huge collection from Gawsworth near Macclesfield and a single fragment decorated with whipped cord impressions which came from the shores around Meols in the Wirral. Not far from Meols a bone midden containing antlers and bones from deer and oxen, and radiocarbon dated to the Late Neolithic (circa 2800BC to 2300BC), was found in the silt on the foreshore at Leasowe in 1967.

From around 2700BC a new style of pottery was introduced throughout Britain. These barrel and bucket shaped vessels with thick walls and a flat base, highly decorated with geometric incised motifs and grooved lines, have come to be known by archaeologists as 'Grooved ware'. Some designs show affinities with the carved rock art motifs found on the megalithic tombs of the time, while others appear to mimic the patterns used in basket making. Grooved ware is essentially domestic pottery, but is often also found with ritual deposits in henge monuments. In Cheshire examples were discovered in association with burials at Eddisbury near Delamere.

Settlement Sites

Unlike the large ceremonial monuments of the period, Neolithic settlement sites are notoriously difficult to locate, primarily because any dwellings that were made from wood have long since rotted away, leaving only postholes and pits. It is therefore often the burial monuments or so-called 'houses of the dead', rather than the houses of the living, that receive most attention from archaeologists. Only a hundred or so New Stone Age domestic buildings are known throughout the British Isles, the most well-known being Skara Brae on Orkney, where dwellings built of stone were exposed from their covering of sand during a storm in 1850.

Elsewhere areas of habitation are often only discovered accidentally from related refuse deposits and fire pits, or because other domestic artefacts associated with them are discovered first.

In areas where structures have been found, it has been revealed that Early Neolithic people tended to construct square or rectangular buildings no more than twelve metres long, while in the Later Neolithic there is a propensity for round and oval dwellings, reflecting the architecture of the ceremonial monuments at the time. Houses were often very elementary with nothing more than a simple, open hearth inside. They generally occur in isolation and may only have been used on a seasonal basis for part of the year. In Cheshire evidence for structural activity comes from three sites at Beeston, Oversley Farm and Tatton Mere, but generally we only know that our Neolithic ancestors were active in other areas of the county by the distribution of flint and stone axes and small quantities of pottery. Discussed below are some of the more interesting finds.

Beeston Castle

Lying on a rocky summit close to the mid-Cheshire Ridge, 160m (500 ft) above the Cheshire Plain, Beeston Castle is well-known for its 13th century castle and Iron Age hillfort, but very few people realise that its origins lie thousands of years earlier and that it was actually one of the earliest known inhabited sites in the county. During excavations between 1968 and 1985 a number of Neolithic finds came to light near the Outer Gateway in a natural valley, where various features had been sealed beneath a deposit of soil washed down the hill in the Late Bronze Age. The hillside had been modified by a series of light circular terraces and hollows, represented by several postholes overlain with charcoal-rich 'occupation debris'. Close by lay the remains of a slight bank that may have formed part of an enclosure. This layer of debris yielded four leaf-shaped arrowheads, two Neolithic axes, several sherds of Grimston ware and charcoal, the latter radiocarbon dated to between circa 4340BC and 4003BC. Further possible Neolithic features were discovered on the plateau edge where pits had been cut into the bedrock. All the evidence points to some form of permanent occupation rather than a passing use.

Tatton Old Hall and Oversley Farm

Other Early Neolithic settlement sites have been discovered in the east of the county at Tatton and close to Manchester Airport. The former was discovered in the 1980s on the Tatton Hall estate, the ancient seat of the Egerton Family to the north of Knutsford, following the discovery of Mesolithic flints as part of the 'Tatton Park Project' mentioned in the previous chapter. Prior to this, the only artefact known to have come from the area, was a perforated stone adze or hammerhead found in the Mere in 1929 when the water level had dropped.

A remarkable discovery was made when excavations began on a medieval village site on a plateau in the park, lying above the west bank of the Tatton Mere brook. During investigations on the Old Hall site some postholes and flints dating to the Neolithic were unexpectedly uncovered. Four pits, one of which contained a flint flake and core, were located within the medieval long house itself and radiocarbon dated to between 3500BC and 2945BC. A further pit, incorporating samples of oak charcoal, fragments of charred bone, a small quantity of carbonised fruit together with cereal and weed seeds, all dating to between 3370BC and 2925BC, was also unearthed. Among the seeds were grains of hulled barley as well as sun spurge, bindweed and dock. These are weeds commonly associated with cultivation and may represent waste products resulting from the sorting and cleaning of the grain prior to storage. Discarded crop processing residue was often used for tinder and fuel. (Similar seeds were discovered in the stomach contents of the Later Iron Age or Early Romano-British body of Lindow Man, the remains of which were discovered near Wilmslow only 6 kilometres away).

Excavators concluded that this find may represent a rubbish pit which lay close to where cleaning and storage was taking place. An analysis of the pollen from the pit revealed a minute quantity of tree pollen interspersed with an abundance of grass, cereal and weeds, suggesting clearance and cultivation in the immediate vicinity. No pottery was found, but there were a number of tools made from a higher quality flint than those of the Mesolithic, suggesting that, by the Neolithic, farmers had developed long distance trade contacts. All the evidence points to the site being occupied only for a short time, perhaps as little as one season.

In 1982 another group of five postholes, arranged in an arc, was found approximately 35 metres north-north-west of the first group, with a sixth uncovered in 1983 providing a radiocarbon date of between 2195BC and 1690BC. These are believed to represent the footings of a timber-framed building.

The soils in the Tatton area are well-drained, light and sandy and would have been ideal for cultivation. According to excavator Nick Higham the land here 'was of exceptional quality by local standards' and lay close to a source of fresh running water. A second Neolithic habitation site was discovered in a similar location at Oversley Farm, during excavations in advance of Manchester Airport's second runway, carried out between 1997 and 1998. Occupying a terrace of sand and gravel close to a drove way and ford over the River Bollin, a rectangular structure was found aligned roughly north to south. Associated with this building were several pits containing pottery, stone tools, heat fractured stones (potboilers) and charred material including barley grains, confirming domestic occupation.

Excavations at Oversley Farm in advance of Manchester Airport's second runway, where evidence for Neolithic settlement was uncovered in the 1990s. (Courtesy of Dorothy Bentley Smith)

Gawsworth, near Macclesfield

Evidence indicating the presence of another possible Later Neolithic habitation site was unearthed at Woodhouse End in Gawsworth during the excavation of the Bronze Age Beaker barrow in the 1980s. In the mound material used to construct the barrow, over 160 sherds of Neolithic pottery, from approximately twenty-three different pots, were discovered. This was later identified as Peterborough ware, a type of pottery used in the 3rd millennium BC for both domestic tasks and ritual activities. It sometimes accompanied burials, but in this case it more than likely represents debris from domestic activities, as no associated Neolithic human remains were discovered during excavations. Unfortunately structural evidence in the form of postholes and pits was also lacking, but these could well have been destroyed during the construction of the later mound. In prehistoric times the site would have overlooked a wide shallow lake in the valley below, making it ideally suited for settlement.

The discovery of such a large quantity of Neolithic pottery is highly significant, particularly in light of the dearth of activity in the county generally at this period. Incredibly more

Peterborough ware was found here than at all the Peak District sites put together! A close examination of the decoration on the sherds by Terry G. Manby of Doncaster Museum revealed that they pre-dated the Beaker mound in which they were found by three or four centuries, placing them about the middle of the 3rd millennium BC, approximately the time when the huge chambered tomb of The Bridestones was built just a few kilometres away. In order to build a monument of such massive proportions requiring the investment of thousands of man-hours, there must have been quite a large community living somewhere in the vicinity. Owing to the richness of this find and the date, it is tempting to believe that these highly ornamented pots could have belonged to the builders of Cheshire's only known megalithic tomb.

Alderley Edge

In addition to the Bronze Age copper mines on the Edge, which will be discussed later, reference has also been made to what are believed to be several Neolithic settlement sites. Discussed by Roeder and Graves in the *Transactions of the Lancashire and Cheshire Antiquarian Society* there are three main areas i.e. Castle Rock, White Barn Farm and the Engine Vein where a number of worked Neolithic flints were discovered early in the 20th century. At Castle Hill implements were found on the margin of the field boundary and along the footpath to the east, and also what is referred to as 'an original Neolithic floor' consisting of 'friable brownish sandstone' and 'loose bleached sand'. With its caves and rock shelters and good supply of water, the Edge would undoubtedly have been an attractive site for Neolithic farmers.

Castle Rock at Alderley Edge, close to which the floor of a Neolithic settlement was discovered in the early 20th century.

Lindow Moss

During excavations funded by English Heritage in 1987 on Lindow Moss following the discovery of bog bodies, an environmental assessment of the area was carried out on the two sand islands in the Moss, with interesting results. The western sand island was shown to have been covered in woodland which had been burnt off by humans sometime around 3030BC in the Early Neolithic. The exploitation of the area cannot have lasted long, as burning led to rapid soil erosion and the redevelopment of woodland, later over layered by sphagnum peat. On the eastern sand island twenty-nine flint items were discovered, made from four different types of material which probably came from pebbles acquired in the local boulder clay or river gravels. Only three of the pieces, however, were not waste products – a single flake knife, a 'utilised flake' and a retouched lump. They lay in an undisturbed area suggesting the ground had not been cultivated since their deposition.

Neolithic Ritual Monuments

In addition to being changed by clearance and farming, the Neolithic landscape also witnessed the first man-made architecture on a grand scale as already mentioned. The sheer size of monuments such as henges, enclosures, long barrows, and chambered tombs proves that there must have been an organised society, with people working closely together to create 'sacred landscapes'. Recent research has shown just how much effort was involved in the construction of such sites. It has been estimated that it would have taken 10,000 working man-hours to erect a long barrow and a million man-hours to create a henge. All this would have been achieved using primitive tools such as ox shoulder-blade shovels, antler picks and rakes, bone wedges and flint and stone chisels, axes and adzes. The sheer quantity of red deer antlers used in such construction, as well as in the mining of stone and flint for the tools, seems to suggest that Neolithic man must have been breeding and managing his own animals.

Undoubtedly a large communal effort would have been required to first prepare the land, construct banks and ditches, quarry and transport stones and then dress and erect them. Even with today's technological advances it is still a skilled process to shape and erect stones of such large proportions. When considering that the only technology available to our Stone Age ancestors was wood, rope and human/animal power, (present evidence suggests that the wheel did not arrive until the middle of the 2nd millennium BC) it is a miracle that they were ever erected at all, as recent attempts by modern scientists have often proved.

Monuments of the Living – Henges and Causewayed Enclosures

The monuments referred to as henges are unique to the British Isles. Located mainly in areas that were reasonably well populated in prehistory, there are at least 300 scattered throughout Britain and Ireland ranging in size from as little as 9 metres in diameter to an incredible 450 metres. A henge is traditionally defined by archaeologists as 'a roughly circular earthen banked enclosure, usually with an internal ditch and one or more entrances, which may or may not have inner settings of timber or stone'. Very few sites, known as 'circle-henges', actually have or have had settings of stone within them, but excavations at many others have revealed that a large proportion did contain circular features of timber.

The Bullring at Dove Holes in Derbyshire, the closest surviving henge to the Neolithic communities of east Cheshire.

Causewayed enclosures, usually constructed between 3000BC and 2500BC, are similar to henges, but usually consist of one or more concentric rings of ditches broken into numerous segments by causeways, with the ditch material heaped up to create a low bank. Described by Mercer as 'probably among the least spectacular ancient monuments known today within the British landscape' and by Francis Pryor as 'among the most remarkable and enigmatic places in prehistory', there are about sixty known examples, the most notable closest to Cheshire being Gardoms Edge in the Peak District. They usually lie in lowland areas with earthworks placed on the slope of a hill, allowing the interior to be viewed from some distance away.

Henges and causewayed enclosures were essentially 'neutral' places where Neolithic people met to exchange items such as highly prized stone axes or special places where whole tribal groups could meet for ritual purposes. Some archaeologists have suggested that they may have been used as astronomical observatories, but with such a large bank the people within the monument would not have been able to see out to distant horizons, apart from at the entrances. Another explanation is that they were connected with the rituals of death. As Aubrey Burl points out 'In the new stone age, death and the dead obsessed the living'. In addition to the obvious funerary sites such as the chambered tombs and barrows, the statement appears true also for henges, enclosures and the later Bronze Age stone circles. Many have human remains buried somewhere within them. These may just be votive offerings, however, rather than graves in the sense we know them today. Enclosures may also have been used to expose the dead for de-fleshing before burial.

Leek Old Road Henge, Gawsworth

Up until the 1980s the earthworks of a possible henge monument lay in a field at Oakgrove alongside the Leek Old Road (the old turnpike road between Macclesfield and Leek) just behind the Fool's Nook public house in Gawsworth. The earthworks were roughly oval in shape with two entrances just slightly off a north-south axis. There was an inner bank of approximately three to four metres in height and an outer bank less than one metre, but no ditch. According to Gordon Rowley, 'in form it greatly resembles the 'henge' type of monument of the Late Neolithic era'. It is unusual for a henge not to have a ditch, but this could have easily silted up over the millennia. Sadly the earthworks were largely destroyed in 1986 'for agricultural reasons'. The 1909 Ordnance

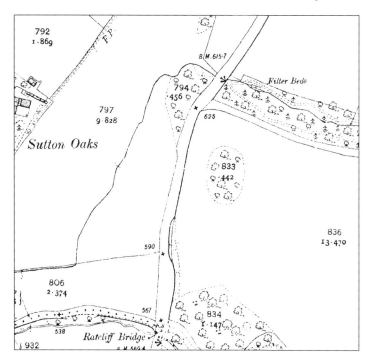

Survey map shows a roughly oval plantation of trees in this area and faint traces can still be seen on the ground, but without excavation not enough to discern whether or not it could have been a henge. There are several indicative pieces of evidence, however, which suggest it may have been.

An old map showing the oval of trees in the precise location of the possible henge, adjacent to the Leek Old road in Gawsworth. (Reproduced from the 1909 Ordnance Survey Map Cheshire sheet 43.4, scale 25 inches to 1 mile).

Firstly there is proof of Neolithic activity in the immediate and slightly wider locality. As previously mentioned on the opposite side of the modern Macclesfield to Leek road (A523), excavations at the Woodhouse End Beaker barrow produced an unusually large amount of Neolithic pottery, suggesting there must have been a settlement of some size in the vicinity at that period. In addition, the huge chambered tomb of The Bridestones, which would have required a large communal effort to construct, lies only 7.5 kilometres away to the south-south-west.

Secondly, the site is ringed by a number of Bronze Age round barrows including an example at Broad Oak Farm to the north and the Beaker barrow itself to the west. Round barrows were often

The round barrow on Broad Oak Farm, now home to a magnificent oak tree.

clustered around the earlier henge monuments, sometimes even placed within them. At Stonehenge numerous mounds such as the Great Cursus barrows and Old King Barrows, dot the landscape for miles around. At Arbor Low in the Peak District, a barrow was built into the henge bank itself and several, such as Gib Hill, were placed in close proximity to it; almost every surrounding hill is capped by a mound. Most interesting is the proximity to the nearby Beaker burial. In Wiltshire fragments of Beaker pottery have been found in association with the henges at Stonehenge, Woodhenge, Coneybury and Durrington Walls, whilst in the Peak District one of the two main clusters of Beaker barrows lies just to the south-east of the Arbor Low henge.

Thirdly, the orientation of the entrances roughly north-south fits in well with the alignments of other henges in the area. At Arbor Low they run north-west and south-south-east while at The Bullring, in the Derbyshire village of Dove Holes, they are again placed almost exactly north-south. Both the Peak henges share alignments with the axes of nearby Roman roads, almost certainly built along the line of former prehistoric trackways. It would make perfect sense for the henges to be placed close to tracks if they were used for trading and gathering

purposes. In Gawsworth the earthworks of the henge lie within metres of the old turnpike route from Macclesfield to Leek, which undoubtedly had its origins much earlier, perhaps even in prehistoric times. Here again the entrances more or less mirrored the line of the road.

The faint traces of what may have been a henge, in a field adjacent to the Leek Old Road in Gawsworth.

The remains of what is said to be a ceremonial avenue on the opposite side of the road to the Gawsworth henge.

Finally there has been much speculation about a 'ceremonial avenue' leading up to the Gawsworth henge, the supposed remains of which can be seen in the field on the opposite side of the old turnpike road. Ceremonial avenues appear at a number of other henges and later stone circles in Britain. At Stonehenge the faint earthworks of an avenue have been found running a mile and a half from the Wiltshire River Avon up to the entrance of the monument, while in Avebury two double lines of stones, known as the West Kennet Avenue and the Beckhampton Avenue, once lined the route to its twin entrances. It is entirely possible, therefore, that the earthworks still visible in Gawsworth today are part of such an avenue.

Evidence suggests that many henge monuments were deliberately constructed to enhance the visual impact they had on visitors. People were often led up to them along specific routes such as these 'processional avenues', which highlighted certain aspects of the surrounding landscape and made features of the henges themselves, as well as other monuments such as the outlying barrows. For the ordinary farmer in a world largely devoid of man-made constructions, seeing a henge for the first time must have been an awesome experience in itself, but to be ritually led up to it along a specific course must have made it all the more breathtaking.

The Bullring is the nearest known surviving henge to these east Cheshire communities and it is possible that if they were part of the Peak District tribe then they may have used this henge for larger tribal gatherings and trade. However on a day-to-day basis it would have made sense for them to use a smaller, local site such as here in Gawsworth. In the west of the county possible henge monuments have been reported close to the early Neolithic mortuary enclosure at Churton, near Farndon and also at Sutton Weaver and Winwick in recent years, but very little research has been carried out on these.

Monuments of the Dead – Long Barrows, Mortuary Enclosures and Chambered Tombs

From circa 3500BC, mounded structures began to appear in the Neolithic landscape of the British Isles. Essentially there were two main types – chambered tombs and long barrows. The earliest type were those with chambers, chambered cairns and chambered barrows. These monuments usually had one or more burial compartments and were constructed from large stone slabs and dry-stone walling, with one or more large capstones forming the roof. A mound of earth or stones originally covered the chambers, but at the majority of sites this has been removed or eroded away leaving only bare stones, as at The Bridestones. Some long barrows and chambered tombs also had elaborate forecourts where various rites were performed and feasting took place, making them just as much a part of the living as the dead. They should be seen therefore as places of worship rather than graves, similar to our churches today where influential local families have their vaults, and people have in the past been buried in and around the church.

The chambered long barrow of West Kennet in Wiltshire, said to be the largest of its kind in Europe.

The second type of Later Neolithic monument was the unchambered long barrow of which Loachbrook Farm at Somerford near Congleton, Bartomley Farm in Wincle and Tatton Park near Knutsford are possible examples. Consisting of a rectangular or trapezoidal mound, ranging between 20 and a 120 metres long, and between one and seven metres high, long barrows were normally orientated east to west. In the south of England, in areas generally lacking in stone, they were mostly made from earth, whereas in the north they were often constructed from stone and so, strictly speaking, should be called long cairns. The bones of the dead, both jointed (articulated) and disjointed (disarticulated), were usually placed on the floor of these structures but rarely had grave goods associated with them.

Excavations have revealed that many of the barrow mounds originally covered timber structures known as mortuary houses. Consisting of a rectangular box of wooden planks with a post at each end and a roof, they are often referred to by archaeologists as 'houses of the dead'. Some also had posts creating an elaborate façade and entrance, providing a ritual area where the sacred rites were carried out for the dead. Once they had served their purpose, most were eventually deliberately destroyed by burning and covered with a mound of turf or stones.

A long mortuary enclosure was discovered in west Cheshire at Churton, overlooking the floodplain of the River Dee. A cropmark revealed a rectangular ditch approximately thirty-three metres by eighteen metres with rounded corners. It was aligned roughly north-south and appeared to have had a large gap at one end. Long mortuary enclosures provided a similar function to mortuary houses, but were generally much larger. They were also composed of timber and often covered with a mound at a later date, and sometimes remained as free-standing monuments.

Long barrows and chambered tombs were almost certainly used to store specific bones for ritual purposes (usually the long bones and skull), rather than for the interment of whole bodies. Only rarely do excavations reveal entire skeletons. More often than not archaeologists are presented with a jumble of bones showing characteristic signs of weathering, indicating that the bodies of many individuals were first exposed to the elements until the flesh decomposed, perhaps in a mortuary house or on an excarnation platform. The condition of the bones varies from badly eroded to a relatively good condition, suggesting that the monuments may have been used by several generations of people. As to who was chosen to receive such a burial, we can only hazard a guess. Sometimes bones relating to only a few individuals are discovered, suggesting perhaps only the élite members of a society were selected, whilst others have been known to contain hundreds of bones, strongly suggesting communal burial vaults.

An old photograph showing a fragment of one of the Grooved ware vessels found at Eddisbury in the 19th century (Shone).

Individuals buried in Neolithic tombs were sometimes accompanied to the next world by a range of personal effects. These may have belonged to them during their lifetime or may, perhaps, have been gifts to the deceased from the mourners to assist them in the afterlife, thus preventing the dead from haunting the living. Some items found show signs of wear and were obviously used in life, while others appear to have been specifically made for burial. Occasionally the grave goods were deliberately ritually smashed before burial, leaving only flint flakes and shards of pottery, perhaps so the 'spirit' of the object might also go to the next world. The most common type of grave goods found in association with Neolithic burials are animal bones; flint and stone tools including axes, leaf-shaped and barbed and tanged arrowheads, scrapers, knives and stone wristguards worn by archers to protect their arms. Pots and bowls are also common.

As to those not buried in chambered tombs and long barrows, we rarely get to glimpse their final resting place. The majority of bodies may simply have been left to decompose in the open air, slowly eliminated by the elements and the native wildlife. Alternatively they may have been cremated, with their ashes scattered or simply buried in the ground. In Cheshire an interesting clue comes from Eddisbury Hill, well-known for the Iron Age hillfort of Castle Ditch, near Delamere. During quarrying activities in the spring of 1851 workmen apparently uncovered evidence of a Neolithic cemetery. In a quarry in Sandhole Field to the east of the hillfort a number of urns containing calcinated human bone were found. Unfortunately only a few fragments from one of these vessels have survived, but it is possible to tell from the sherds that the urn was one of the Later Neolithic Grooved ware type. The surface of the pot had been decorated with horizontal rows of impressed whipped cord and 'maggot' impressed zigzags and triangles.

This find is highly unusual, because the workmen reported that when they found the urns they were 'full of bones'. Although Grooved ware is often found in association with Neolithic burials and cremations, it is not directly used to contain them. Instead multiple pots accompany multiple burials in chambered tombs, and fragments, associated with cremations, have been placed in the ditches and around the banks of monuments such as henges, as is the case in areas such as Wessex. Further evidence for Neolithic activity in the Eddisbury area came in 1896 when five stone axes were found at the foot of the hill. Later hillforts were often built on sites already occupied by ritual monuments such as henges, causewayed enclosures, long barrows and round barrows. All this evidence points to the likelihood of Eddisbury being an early ritual focus for the communities in the mid-Cheshire area.

Long Barrows

As previously mentioned, there are three potential long barrows in east Cheshire, none of which have been subjected to archaeological excavation. The Chester City Council website refers to a fourth possible long barrow in the west of the county at Wervin to the north-west of Chester, but it has not been possible to find any further reference to this at the present time.

The first example, known as Loachbrook Farm or Somerford long barrow, is located close to the Loach Brook, 3 kilometres to the west of Congleton on boggy ground close to a stream. Composed of an earthen mound approximately 107 metres long, 25 metres wide and 2 metres high with a slight berm on the western side, the feature is orientated north-west to south-east. It was discovered in 1973 and scheduled in 1975. The mound is under grass and covered with trees so its identification has proved difficult, resulting in a great deal of speculation surrounding its origins.

The mound on Loachbrook Farm in Somerford near Congleton, believed to be a long barrow.

In a recent article in the *Transactions of the Lancashire and Cheshire Antiquarian Society*, David Mullin more or less dismisses the possibility of the site being a long barrow, stating that it is highly unlikely because, at over 100 metres, it is extremely long for a barrow. He suggests instead that the mound could be a mass grave for cattle which died during an outbreak of cattle plague in the 18th century. This statement cannot be denied, it is 'very long' for a barrow, but as can be seen when later discussing the huge chambered tomb of The Bridestones (which lies approximately 8 kilometres to the east), the Neolithic population in this area were not averse to building their monuments on a grand scale. Large mounds are also known from the Peak District, for example at Long Low near Wetton there are two smaller mounds linked by a massive bank, orientated north-north-east by south-south-west, with a total length of 210 metres – this is 'very long'. Also, surely if the Loachbrook Farm mound were simply a grave for dead carcasses, it would not have been so carefully landscaped and sculptured. Another possible explanation is that it is an entirely natural feature created by retreating ice at the end of the last Ice Age.

The second candidate lies on land belonging to Bartomley Farm near Wincle. According to Gordon Rowley, this mound on high ground could be the remains of a possible long barrow. A natural spur of rock forms part of the hillock, but the area around it has been adapted with an artificial covering of stone. Again the site has never been scientifically excavated, but a flint blade core was found half a metre down in its eastern side some years ago, suggesting it could be authentic.

The possible long barrow at Bartomley Farm near Wincle, where a flint blade core was unearthed some years ago.

A third prominent mound, lying in Tatton Park, has recently been identified as another possible instance of a long barrow. The mound made of sand has been investigated by a resistivity survey and, as at Loachbrook Farm, may also be of a fluvio-glacial nature. In its favour, it does lie in close proximity to the Neolithic settlement discussed previously. As with the other two sites only an excavation will hopefully satisfy many of the queries.

The Bridestones Chambered Cairn

Often described as an 'outlier of the Neolithic monuments of the White Peak', The Bridestones, lying along the line of the Cheshire/Staffordshire border is undoubtedly Cheshire's most impressive and well-known ancient monument. The remains of this once-great chambered tomb lie between the hillside of Bosley Cloud and Wolfe Lowe, close to the east Cheshire town of Congleton. Located at 250m (820ft) above sea level, the monument lies on the western crest of a pass running in a north-south line at the foot of the Pennines and has spectacular views across the Cheshire Plain.

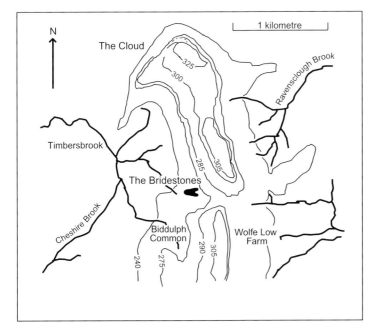

Figure 5 – The location of The Bridestones. Reproduced by kind permission of Ordnance Survey.© Crown Copyright NC/04/26823.

There are several legends concerning The Bridestones' name, and unsurprisingly most are connected with the theme of marriage. In the 19th century, local landowner Sir Philip Brocklehurst stated 'The peasants of the neighbourhood have a curious legend respecting the origin of "The Bridestones". "When the Danes invaded England," say they, "a Danish youth became enamoured of a Saxon lady, and in the end the two were married at Biddulph Church (about a mile and a half distant); but on returning from the wedding, they were here met and murdered, and after their interment had taken place in the spot where they fell, these stones were laid around their grave, and the name Bridestones given to it from that circumstance." So much for public opinion.'

Bride may also be a derivation of Brigid, Brigit or Bridget, a name common in Celtic folklore. Brigid whose festival day is the 1st February (Imbolc) may also be associated with the goddess Brigantia, worshipped by the pre-Christian Brigantes tribe of Northern Britain who may have inhabited this part of Cheshire in the late prehistoric and early Romano-British period. Other similarly named sites can be found in North Yorkshire with The Bridestones, High Bridestones and Low Bridestones stone circles.

A further theory has been advanced by local historian Dorothy Bentley Smith. In the language of Old English (Anglo-Saxon) 'brid' was bird, and 'briddes', birds. As the name also appears in North Yorkshire, the meaning seems to be of a more general nature rather than reliant on local folklore. Cheshire was well endowed with meres and fish and, therefore, birds and wading birds would be plentiful. An interesting fact is that the North American Indians used the term 'bird-stone' for prehistoric stone objects for which there was no obvious purpose. These stones usually resembled or even remotely suggested the shape of a bird. Perhaps the early Anglo-Saxon settlers in the area of the Bridestones also saw a similar likeness, and adopted the name 'Briddes stones' which was later corrupted to 'Bridestones'. Intriguingly, birds are also associated with Brigid whose symbol was the white swan.

The remaining stones of the once great chambered tomb of The Bridestones near Congleton.

Over the years The Bridestones has appeared in literature on several occasions, but three sources are of particular interest. The earliest description of the monument comes from the Reverend Thomas Malbon, a parson from Congleton, who visited the site in the 18th century. Luckily in Henry Rowlands' *Mona Antiqua Restaurata* in 1766, he described the various elements of the site prior to large scale ransacking by workmen building the nearby turnpike road. For ease Malbon's description has been broken down into the various features discussed:

The forecourt and façade: 'There are six upright free stones, from three to six feet broad, of various heights and shapes, fixed about six feet from each other in a semicircular form, and two within, where the earth is very black, mixed with ashes and oak-charcoal. It is apprehended the circle was originally complete, and twenty-seven feet in diameter; for there is the appearance of holes where stones have been, and also of two single stones, one standing east of the circle, at about five or six yards distance, and the other at the same distance from that.'

The main chamber: 'A little west of the above stones are two rough, square tapering stones 4ft. 3in. broad and 2ft. thick, standing at the north and south angles of a kind of artificial stone cave or chest. This is paved with broken pieces of stones about 2½ inches thick, overlaying some pounded whitestone about six inches deep; two inches of the upper part of which are tinged with black, supposed from ashes falling through the pavement which was covered with them and oak-charcoal about two inches thick, along with several pieces of burnt bones. The sides of the cave, if I may so call it, were composed of two unhewn stones about 18 feet in length, six in height and fourteen inches thick at a medium. Each of them is now broken in two.'

The holed stone: 'There is a partition stone across the place, about five feet and a half high, and six inches thick. A circular hole is cut through this stone, about nineteen inches and a half in diameter'.

Thomas Malbon's 1766 diagram of the remaining stones at The Bridestones (*Mona Antiqua Restaurata*).

A sketch from Dr J.D. Sainter's *Scientific Rambles Round Macclesfield* showing the holed stone in the 19th century.

The subsidiary chambers: 'There remains another place of the same construction but smaller and without any inward partition, about 55 yards distance from this. It is 2½ yards long, 2½ feet broad and 3ft. 2in. high. There is also part of another.'

The cairn: 'There was a large heap of stones that covered the whole, 120 yards long and 12 yards broad. These stones have been taken away from time to time by masons and other people for various purposes. And in the year 1764 several hundred loads were carried away for making a turnpike road about 60 yards from this place, which laid it open for examination.'

The site was later revisited and sketched in the 19th century by local amateur archaeologist, naturalist and geologist Dr J.D. Sainter. A full account of Malbon's description as well as illustrations of the stone circle and holed stone can also be found in Sainter's book *Scientific Rambles Round Macclesfield*, published in 1878.

In the years following, the stones were further plundered and ravaged, so much so that by the 1930s The Bridestones was in such a poor condition that the Ancient Monuments Board (who were superseded by English Heritage but still have a sign on site today) commissioned Margaret Dunlop to undertake excavations and to restore the site as part of the scheduling and protection process. The excavations were undertaken by Professor Fleur of Manchester University in 1936 and 1937 and a preliminary report on the project was published in 1938 in the *Transactions of the Lancashire and Cheshire Antiquarian Society*. A comprehensive excavation, which aimed to restore the site 'as far as possible to its former state', was undertaken. The results confirmed the antiquarian descriptions to be correct.

So what was The Bridestones?

Evidence from all these sources indicates that The Bridestones was a Later Neolithic chambered tomb of massive proportions, with a paved crescentic forecourt and a portholed stone dividing the main chamber. Two subsidiary chambers lay some distance away from the main one. If Malbon is to be believed, the complex was supposedly 110 metres in length, with the horned cairn being 11 metres wide. To put this in perspective, the chambered tomb of West Kennet in Wiltshire often described as 'the largest monument of its kind in Europe' is actually about 10 metres shorter, being approximately 100 metres in length.

Some historians have disputed the fact that the cairn was so big, implying that Malbon had a tendency to over exaggerate. This is based on a quote cited by Sainter (supposedly from the 1766 description) which states that the holed stone stood 'eight feet across' the chamber. Upon returning to the original source of *Mona Antiqua Restaurata*, however, there is no mention at all of the stone being 8 feet across, only that it is '5½ feet high and 6 inches in depth'. It must therefore be presumed that this extra measurement was either misquoted from elsewhere or added in by Sainter at a later date. As all the other dimensions given by Malbon fit with the surviving stones today, there is little reason to doubt that the measurements of the elements, which have long since disappeared, are not also correct.

Chambered tombs with crescentic forecourts are normally found in the Clyde region of Scotland (Clyde Cairns) such as at Cairnholy and Carn Ban, with concentrations in Arran, Kintyre and outliers in Galloway and the Outer Hebrides. They were developed in a topological sequence with the later stages borrowing features from adjacent areas such as Northern Ireland, where chambered tombs known as Court Cairns had forecourts ranging from slight crescents to half circles, and ultimately ones which were completely enclosed.

No other tombs with crescentic forecourts are known from England, the closest being Casthal-yn-Ard and King Orry's Grave on the Isle of Man. According to the stone circle expert, Dr Aubrey Burl, such 'crescentic forecourts, some as deep as semicircles' were the forerunners of true stone circles. They appear at the later Clyde tombs in south-western Scotland and in the Court Cairns of northern Ireland where over 400 examples are known. By building these forecourts it would have enabled more people to join in with whatever rites were taking place at the burial chambers. As Burl says 'What had been undertaken by a few in the dimness of a claustrophobic chamber could now be shared by the community in the light of the open air'.

The chambered cairn of Cairnholy in Dumfries and Galloway, a typical example of a Clyde Cairn showing the stones of the crescentic forecourt.

The chambered tomb of Casthal-yn-Ard on the Isle of Man, the closest known example with a crescentic forecourt to The Bridestones (courtesy of Peter Herring).

Burl continues 'Such outstanding forecourts are known to be ultimate developments in the typology of chambered tombs'. Taking south-western Scotland as an example, it appears that the earliest cairns were built on land below 46m (150ft) where settlement first occurred. These were followed by those built at greater heights 'on soils less easy to till' indicating expansion on to higher ground, while the final phase of tombs with roomy and airy forecourts took place on even higher ground, as at Carn Ban on Arran at 274m (900ft).

This final phase of development fits perfectly with the description of The Bridestones, which stands at 250m (820ft) above sea level, and would therefore suggest that it was constructed sometime around the middle of the 3rd millennium BC. In order to carry out such a massive undertaking there must have been a large population living locally. The huge quantity of Peterborough ware pottery found at Woodhouse End in Gawsworth, 7.5 kilometres to the north-north-east of The Bridestones, was also dated to circa 2400BC. This certainly suggests more than just coincidence.

In addition to its paved forecourt, The Bridestones also has another interesting feature in the portholed stone, a characteristic usually associated with chambered tombs from the Cotswold-Severn region. Unfortunately only the base of this stone survives today, but a holed stone of almost identical proportions can be found at Mucklestone in Staffordshire – The Devil's Ring and Finger – which is also believed to have once been part of a Neolithic burial chamber.

Stones with holes in have long been of interest to antiquarians, archaeologists and people seeking blessings and cures. Such holed stones have been surrounded by myth and folklore for hundreds of years, with people believing that by passing through the hole they could cure diseases. As early as the 1700s the famous holed stone at the Men-an-Tol in Cornwall was

A reconstruction of how The Bridestones may have looked originally.

renowned for curing back pains. Naked children could be protected against dreadful diseases if passed through the hole three times and dragged anticlockwise around it. Interestingly holed stones were also often used for ratifying marriages, with couples clasping hands through the hole whilst making their vows. This could be another explanation as to how The Bridestones got its name.

Most of these stones however are in the open air, either forming part of a stone circle or as standing stones, but in the case of The Bridestones the 'holed stone' divided the two compartments of the main chamber. The question is what purpose did it serve? Some believe it was for ritual purposes – to allow food to be passed to the deceased or to allow the spirits to move between the chambers. On the other hand it could have been purely for practical reasons. Once the monument was covered by the mound, there would only have been one entrance into the first part of chamber from the forecourt. Therefore the only way of gaining access to the rear half of the chamber would have been through this hole – at 50 centimetres, it would have been large enough for a person to crawl through.

The holed stone at the Devil's Ring and Finger, almost identical in size to the one which once divided the chamber at The Bridestones, and large enough for a small person to crawl through.

In recent years there has been a long running debate as to which way the cairn at The Bridestones extended. A myth, that it ran east of the chamber into the grounds of the neighbouring Bridestones House rather than west down the slope, was started by Mr Bertram B. Simms (MBSS, MERS) in an article in the *Congleton Chronicle* in 1936. Simms took the early references and re-interpreted the monument:

'The Bridestones chamber was originally capped with a huge slab. The one monolith (there was another 25 years ago) is all that remains of a pear shaped arrangement of similar pillars, some 12ft. high, which, interspaced with stones as walls and capped with slabs formed another chamber, hall or chapel, approximately 30ft x 45ft, where fire ritual ceremonies were performed to sever the spirit of the dead chief from earthly things.'

An accompanying plan shows a long, thin, leaf-shaped cairn enclosing the stones of the forecourt and the outlying standing stones to the east. This interpretation is complete nonsense as the forecourt was designed to be used as an open ritual area. It may eventually have been blocked and sealed up at the end of use, but there is no evidence from any other site that the forecourt was covered by a roof and cairn. In all other contemporary monuments the cairn runs away from the forecourt and chamber, which at The Bridestones would mean it went west.

Destruction of the Monument

After reading various accounts of The Bridestones a sad tale of vandalism and destruction unfolds. The main period of ransacking occurred in the 18th century when hundreds of tons of stone were taken from the cairn by the builders of the nearby turnpike road in 1764. Other stones were used to build the adjacent house and farm (many can still be seen in the rockeries of nearby Bridestones House), while yet more were recycled into an ornamental garden in Tunstall Park. The two small subsidiary chambers must also have been removed at this time as subsequent accounts do not mention them on site.

Sometime between 1766 and 1854 the holed stone was broken off, for by 1854 it was in a similar condition as today 'standing only a few inches above the ground', but according to Sainter it had not been completely destroyed as 'the broken off part was found and replaced in 1877'. This reconstruction did not last however, as at the time of the 1935 excavations the porthole was again incomplete.

The main chamber showing the broken holed stone dividing the two compartments.

The sides of the main chamber were originally built from one large stone, but an account by Ward in 1843 records how a picnicker's bonfire split it. 'The whole of the southern side was formerly composed of an entire stone, measuring 18 feet in length, which must have been of at least ten tons; but a large fracture in the middle was produced by a bonfire, made in the cavity about 20 years ago, and it has fallen from its perpendicular.'

As for the portal stones either side of the entrance to the chamber, they have also suffered in recent years. Only two now remain to the south, one of which was cemented back together during excavations in the 1930s (although on close inspection these two pieces do not seem to fit correctly together). According to a newspaper report which appeared in the *Congleton Chronicle* in 1936 'many years ago an engineer engaged in the cutting of the Manchester Ship Canal, visiting the spot, actually used one of the biggest monoliths for the purpose of carrying out a demonstration with a detonator, as a result of which the great stone was broken off close to the ground.'

The stone circle delineating the forecourt also suffered attack during the first half of the 19th century. Of the eight remaining stones, six forming part of the circle and also two within the forecourt, all were still in position in 1832, but by 1854 further damage meant that 'of the semicircle of six stones standing immediately east of the cistaven none remain; but one is thrown down.'

Above: Sainter's 1878 picture showing the chamber and circle of forecourt stones.

Left: The few remaining stumps and one standing stone of the forecourt today.

In just over 200 years The Bridestones has gone from being possibly one of the UK's most impressive burial chambers to little more than a few stones on the edge of a plantation. There can be no doubt, in the light of all this evidence, that it is of great significance, not only within Cheshire, but within the UK landscape as a whole. Several questions remain unanswered – why does a chambered tomb in Cheshire share so many characteristics with sites at considerable distances to the north and west, and why is it the only one of its type in the area? Not even the nearby Neolithic-rich Peak District has anything comparable to offer. We can only speculate as to the possible relationships with the megalith builders both to the north and west (as well as to the south where the Cotswold-Severn tombs were being constructed), but one tantalizing thought is that The Bridestones may not be the only prehistoric site in Cheshire sharing affinities with monuments in the Clyde region of Scotland.

As can be seen in the next chapter, around eight kilometres to the north-east of The Bridestones is another scheduled ancient monument known as The Bullstones. This is a Bronze Age site classified as the 'site of a Bronze Age cremation burial' in the *Cheshire County Sites and Monuments Record.* However, a recent survey by John Barnatt of the Peak District National Park Authority has revealed that it may well be a centre-stone circle consisting of a large central stone surrounded by a tight water-worn ring of smaller cobbles. It is uncannily similar to the Scottish stone circle of Glenquickan (NGR: NX508583) which, incidentally, lies within a few kilometres of the Clyde Cairns of Cairnholy.

Other intriguing questions beg answers: Why is The Bridestones situated where it is? Why, if its builders were part of a Neolithic community in the Peak District, as others have suggested, did they place it to look out across the Cheshire Plain rather than up towards the hills? One suggestion is that as many of the entrances to this type of tomb seem to favour the east, The Bridestones included, they may have been designed as a ritual focus for the rising sun. An in-depth study on possible alignments is currently being carried out by local astronomer Kevin Kilburn for a forthcoming publication. Of particular interest are his calculations which show that on midwinter's day the sun would have set on or very close to the summit of Mow Cop hill when viewed from the forecourt of The Bridestones. He has also proved that in order to view both summer and winter solstice sunsets the monument could not have been placed anywhere else on the slope on which it sits without blocking the sight line of one or the other. In short, The Bridestones appears to have been deliberately positioned to view not the sunrises

The Bridestones as the sun sets over the Cheshire Plain beyond.

to the east but the sunsets to the west, from midwinter to midsummer and back again, and is aligned very precisely towards the equinoctial sunset.

However, research carried out on The Bridestones' Scottish and Irish counterparts may provide another explanation. Some consider that Neolithic people believed the chambered tomb was the means by which the dead returned to join their ancestors, and that the tail of the cairn might point in the direction from which those ancestors came. By carrying the body through the entrance into the burial chamber the spirit could start its journey in the direction of the land of the ancestors. *Megalithic Enquiries in the West of Britain* reveals the results of an experiment where orientations were plotted for ten of the Clyde Cairns in Kintyre. Some pointed east, others south, but the ones with the concave forecourts pointed in a westerly direction towards Ireland. This is very interesting in light of the fact that the concave façades in the Clyde region are believed to be of Irish inspiration. Could the builders of The Bridestones have had something similar in mind, looking west over the Cheshire Plain towards the communities across the Irish Sea whose megalithic architecture found its way into this one unique monument in England?

The Calderstones

In light of the evidence linking The Bridestones to the architecture of Ireland, it is important to mention another collection of Neolithic stones in the region, which share similar affinities. Although never located within the boundaries of Cheshire, either ancient or modern, they are close enough (over a short stretch of the Mersey Estuary) to warrant inclusion. These stones once formed part of a chambered tomb in what is now the area of Allerton, six kilometres to the south-east of Liverpool. They lay on an elevated plateau of sandstone, on light, well-drained soils at the head of a small valley, but all that remains of this tomb today are six highly ornamented stones known as The Calderstones (a name said to derive from Anglo-Saxon translating as 'Enchanters Stones'). They are now housed in the Harthill Greenhouses in Calderstones Park having been moved from their previous location in an enclosure just outside the park gates in 1954 to protect them from further decay in the elements.

The Calderstones today, located in a greenhouse in Calderstones Park in Allerton near Liverpool.

The first reference to The Calderstones comes from a boundary dispute between Allerton and Wavertree in 1568 when they were referred to as 'the dojer, rojer or Caldwaye stones'. A map of the time shows three stones within an oval mound, but a certain Robert Mercer who was a witness in the dispute recalls that a fourth had been removed some 18 years previously (the rest of the stones were presumably still buried within the mound). The Calderstones were not mentioned again until 1825 when it was reported by Baines in his *History, Directory, and Gazetteer of the County Palatine of Lancaster* that during disturbance of the stones '...in digging about them, urns made of the coarsest clay, containing human dust and bones, have been discovered, there is reason to believe that they indicate an ancient burying-place...Some of these urns were dug up about sixty years ago, and were in the possession of Mr. Mercer of Allerton'. These probably represent secondary Bronze Age burials interred in the mound at a later date.

Towards the end of the 19th century the cause of The Calderstones was taken up by William Herdman, Professor of Natural History at Liverpool University, and local antiquarian, Edward Cox, when a series of letters appeared in *The Daily Post* newspaper. Mr Cox's gardener, John Peers, had worked on Calderstones Farm as a boy and recalled the workmen spending many an afternoon lying on the mound in the sun after work. At that time 'only a few of the larger stones could be seen lying flat near the top, partly buried in the earth, and a few of the points of the other stones'.

As at The Bridestones a catalogue of pillaging has left the stones in the condition in which we find them today. The destruction first began in the late 18th or early 19th century when the mound was largely removed to provide sand for making mortar for a Mr Bragg's House on Woolton Road. It was at this time that a 'fine sepulchral urn rudely ornamented outside' was found inside. The entire monument was finally destroyed around 1833 when the road was widened. Mr Cox recalls his gardener's observations on their removal in a letter which appeared in *The Daily Post* in 1896:

'When the stones were dug down to, they seemed rather tumbled about in the mound. They looked as if they had been a little hut or cellar. Below the stones was found a large quantity of burnt bones, white and in small pieces. He thought there must have been a cart-load or two. He helped to wheel them out and spread them on the field. He saw no metal of any sort nor any flint implements, nor any pottery, either whole or broken; nor did he hear of any. He was quite sure the bones were in large quantity, but he saw no urn with them. Possibly the quantity was enhanced by mixture with the soil. No one made much of old things of that sort in his time, nor cared to keep them up...'.

Robin Hood's Stone in Allerton, perhaps originally one of The Calderstones.

The stones were placed on a local farm and eventually six of them were set up in a circle and enclosed in iron railings in 1845 close to their original position near the entrance to the park. Another was removed by a certain Mr Booker and set up as a rubbing stone for his cattle. A further standing stone, known as Robin Hood's Stone, which is still located on the junction of Booker Avenue and Archerfield Road in Allerton, may have received a similar fate. This stone has a number of grooves on it similar to The Calderstones, and an old photograph shows cupmarks on the end now buried. The circle of six Calderstones remained in their enclosure until the 2nd September 1954 when they were removed to the City Museum in Liverpool and placed under the care of James Forde-Johnston. Unfortunately in the years since they had been uncovered, many of the markings had been defaced, covered in a black patina and become overgrown with lichen. Forde-Johnston set about examining the stones and made a full record of their decoration using photographs, line drawings and latex moulds.

From the description it appears that The Calderstones may once have formed part of a chambered tomb known as a passage grave. Passage graves utilised the same construction material as other chambered tombs, but instead of having a main chamber directly behind the entrance, they usually had a passage, about one metre wide and less than one metre high, leading to a central main chamber. This could be square, rectangular, circular or polygonal and was usually covered by a circular mound of earth or cairn of stones.

The most interesting aspect of The Calderstones is their decoration comprising highly ornamented, carved motifs or 'rock art' including spirals, concentric circles, arcs, cupmarks, cup and ring marks and footprints. Before discussing the designs in detail, it is important to consider prehistoric rock art in general, in order to put the carvings into perspective.

Prehistoric Rock Art

Prehistoric art is common throughout the world. Images of cave paintings, such as those found in Lascaux in the Dordogne region of France, depicting animals and men hunting and gathering, adorn a variety of modern merchandise ranging from books to T-shirts. Until recently it was thought that the ancient Britons did not decorate their caves, but the recent discovery of incredibly rare paintings at Creswell Crags on the Derbyshire/Nottinghamshire border means that the history books will need to be re-written. In general, however, the majority of surviving prehistoric rock art in Britain was carved on outcrops, crags, stone circles and cairns, across the north of the country. Here ancient man laboriously etched abstract patterns, perhaps using a hard stone tool and a mallet. Motifs include rings, hollows (cupmarks), zigzags, spirals, and arcs. Over 2,500 sites are currently known, with the most southerly concentration located in Derbyshire.

Rock art is very difficult to date, but as it sometimes appears in association with prehistoric monuments, it is generally considered to have been common for over 1,000 years in the Late Neolithic and Early Bronze Age. Some of Britain's most famous examples include the standing stone of Long Meg near to a massive stone circle in Cumbria, and Little Meg close by, both of which are covered in a series of spiral patterns and lines. The rock art at The Calderstones most closely resembles that on the passage tombs of the Boyne Valley in County Meath in Ireland, the most famous of which is Newgrange. Here on the morning of the mid-winter solstice the rising sun shines through a specially created box illuminating the normally dark 24 metre long passage. Interestingly though recent research has shown that the carvings appear to have been placed in areas which remained in darkness, where the sunlight did not penetrate. The Irish passage tombs date to around 2500BC and are therefore roughly contemporary with The Bridestones. Other examples lie in North Wales with Barclodiad-y-Gawres and Bryn Celli Ddu on Anglesey and these are the nearest to Liverpool yet found.

Many rock art motifs are based upon the circle, one of the strongest symbols in prehistoric society. The simplest and most common design is the cupmark – a circular indentation chipped into the rock. Cupmarks are found singly, in addition to being randomly scattered over the rocks and incorporated into larger, more complex designs. Others have 'rings' surrounding them, reminding one of the bank and ditch of a henge, or the eyes of some strange creature. Cup and ring marks appear in over 70% of British designs. Some patterns have 'grooves' taking the form of lines, chevrons, and even serpent-like trails. Spirals also occur, but these are quite rare in comparison to other designs.

Rock art motifs are also occasionally found on stones in Bronze Age cairns. Some are eroded and appear to be broken off larger surfaces, suggesting they were previously decorated and reused, while others seem to have been produced specifically for certain monuments. A number of cairns contain stones with freshly decorated cup and ring marks, mostly placed face down, and may have been gifts for the dead. At the site of the second runway at Manchester Airport on Oversley Farm in Cheshire, a cupmarked stone had been deliberately buried face down in the bottom of a Bronze Age hearth, perhaps as a ritual offering to invoke protection. Occasionally rock art is also found on Iron Age sites such as the hillforts of Ball Cross and Burr Tor in the Peak District, but it is likely that these stones were reused and incorporated into later structures.

Patterns may also have been painted or carved on wood, woven into materials and even tattooed on the skin. In 1991 a well-preserved, 5,200-year-old body was discovered in a glacier in the Alps. A close inspection of Ötzi the Iceman, as he came to be known, revealed a number of interesting tattoos on his arms, legs and spine. Forensic evidence demonstrated that these had been created by rubbing a blue-tinted paste, made from charcoal, into a pattern which was pricked into the skin using a sharp instrument.

Whatever the symbols actually represented, or meant to prehistoric man, we will probably never know. Over the years there have been hundreds of suggestions ranging from fertility symbols, copies of tree rings and ripples, to mixing vessels, boundary or route markers, a kind of shorthand, perhaps logos similar to washing instructions and road signs today or even a tattooists shop window. Some believe that the simple shapes, such as cupmarks, were designed to hold water and may have represented the moon, sun and stars, as most of the art on natural outcrops is found on the horizontal surfaces of earthfast boulders facing skywards. Zigzags and chevrons, on the other hand, may symbolise the human trance.

The Calderstones can now be considered in comparison to other sites. They consist of six blocks of locally acquired sandstone which have been ornately decorated with a range of complex motifs. Unfortunately the designs are badly weathered, making many of the carvings almost impossible to see, but latex moulds have been made for future examination. The first stone, which is just two and a half metres tall and one metre wide, is decorated front and rear with a complex pattern of concentric circles, parallel lines, spirals and two footmarks, the square cut heel of one of which is clearly defined. The second stone, about the same width but slightly shorter than the first, has markings only on one face but also on two of the edges. In addition to a number of abstract circles, spirals, cupmarks and arced lines, there are three footprints (one with six toes), and a Bronze Age axe head (halberd) complete with haft.

The third and largest stone is covered on both faces with numerous cupmarks interspersed

with a group of four concentric circles on one side and several spirals on the other. The fourth, which is approximately five metres long and one metre wide, is decorated on the front face by three cup and ring marks, and on the reverse by seven boot imprints created by workmen in the 19th century. Mr Cox's gardener admitted to cutting one of these himself. The fifth stone is ornamented on the front face with various single and conjoined spirals, one of which resembles a figure of eight. On the rear are four footprints (one with only four toes) and a Maltese Cross believed to be from the medieval period. The sixth and smallest stone, at only one metre long and 0.75 metres wide, is decorated with a solitary wheel or sun motif.

Features such as conjoined spirals, concentric circles and sun or wheel motifs are common in Irish Neolithic art but rarely found in England suggesting that, as at The Bridestones, the tomb builders in the region were influenced by the communities across the waters of the Irish Sea. In an article of 1954, James Forde-Johnson concludes 'The location of the tomb, two miles from the coast, suggests that the Mersey estuary and coasts of North Wales may have had greater significance than has generally been recognized as a maritime route, providing a link between the Peak limestone and the west'.

One of The Calderstones decorated with a beautiful spiral motif.

With regard to the other motifs such as the footprints, cup and ring marks and the carving of the axe, these may have been slightly later additions. Carved footprints are found widely across Scandinavia and Brittany and at a few other sites in the UK but, apart from at a couple of locations, they are not usually associated with megalithic tombs, only with monuments dating to the Bronze Age. The rare exceptions include two footprints (of a left and right foot) found on the wall of the Dolmen du Petit in Brittany, and a footprint discovered in 1831 on the underside of a boulder next to a cist, when the Fairy Knowe barrow in Carnyllie near Forfar was being removed. The only other known examples from England are a single footprint discovered on the side of a cist at Harbottle Peels in Coquetdale, Northumberland (now in The British Museum) and six foot-prints found on a stone cist at Pool Farm in Somerset in 1930 (now in Bristol City Museum). The carving of the Bronze Age halberd is equally rare in Britain and may possibly be the country's only example. Contemporary axes and daggers have been found carved into several of the stones at Stonehenge, on the Ri Cruin burial cist and Nether Largie cairn in the Kilmartin Valley, Argyll, and at Badbury barrow in Dorset, but no hal-berds, which were a combination between a spear and a battleaxe.

Above: A close up of some of the incredibly rare prehistoric footprints carved into The Calderstones.

Left: The Bronze Age halberd on one of The Calderstones, a carving so far unique in the British Isles.

5 The Bronze Age
(circa 2300BC to 800BC)

Sometime around 2300BC there was a major transformation in the society of Britain. The large ritual monuments of the Neolithic, such as the henges, were no longer constructed, and the chambered tombs, which had been in use for thousands of years, were sealed up and abandoned. The focus shifted from these large communal monuments to smaller, localised stone circles and round barrows, with groups of extended family living together on small farming settlements. The 'spirits of the ancestors' were deserted and forgotten, but why?

The answer may lie in the natural world. Environmental evidence from tree rings, peat bogs and ice cores in Greenland, indicates that a major natural disaster occurred between 2354BC and 2345BC causing widespread disruption across the world. Trees in both Ireland and Lancashire show a reduction in ring growth at this period indicating that Britain too was affected. Some scientists believe this was perhaps due to an eruption of the volcano Hekla 4 in Iceland, while others put it down to an asteroid or a comet either passing close to the earth's atmosphere or perhaps even impacting with the planet itself. Whatever the cause, this disaster seems to coincide almost exactly with lifestyle changes in prehistoric communities throughout the world. In Britain the old ways and the long-standing beliefs of the Neolithic were abandoned in favour of a new religion, which appears to have centred on the sky and the natural world, rather than the bones of the ancestors.

By the Early Bronze Age, populations in the British Isles were becoming more organised and joining together to form large tribal groupings. With the emergence of strong political leaders, came increased trade links resulting in exotic goods, such as the finely decorated pottery vessels known as 'Beakers', being imported from the Continent. But the most important breakthrough at this time was the importation of new metal technologies. The first copper and gold objects soon arrived in Britain, closely followed by those who knew where and how to find the ore.

Although metals were now available, it would not really have affected the average person in the fields. Metal tools, like the polished stone axes before them, were seen as prestigious goods and appear largely in the burial deposits and round barrows of the élite. Farmers would have continued to use stone and flint on a day-to-day basis for some time. During this metal revolution, Britain held a very strong position, in that it was one of the very few places in Europe where tin (combined with copper to make bronze) was readily available. Cheshire was to play a significant role in this development with the exploitation of England's largest known surviving prehistoric copper mine at Alderley Edge.

After about 1700BC, the British population had undergone a massive expansion. Within the settled farming communities wealth was becoming more widely distributed and bronze tools were reaching places far and wide. The extent of farming was so considerable that it encompassed massive tracts of land on a scale that has hardly been witnessed since.

Life and Settlement

With a more settled economy came a more settled society. By the Bronze Age, people had begun to live in small permanent communities, suggesting groups of extended families. Each kin group had its own houses, field systems, crops and livestock, funerary monument (round barrow or cairn) and ritual focus, such as the stone or timber circle. Early settlements were often unenclosed, but by the Late Bronze Age they were becoming more defensive in nature and frequently surrounded by banks and ditches. The landscape was carefully laid out, with animals penned in using fences, ditches and hedges. Drove ways or hollow ways (essentially sunken lanes) enabled livestock to be easily led to water.

As in the Neolithic, Bronze Age people practised mixed farming, managing cattle, sheep, goats, horses and pigs for meat, dairy products and wool, in addition to growing crops for bread, porridge and beer. Dogs were kept for guarding, hunting and herding. Cereals such as wheat and barley, were reaped using sickles with blades of flint or bronze and ground with grain rubbers and quernstones. Examples from Cheshire include a grain crusher from the grounds of a Nurses' Home in Delamere Forest, and a large hand grain rubber made of greenstone and weighing approximately 11kg from Macclesfield cemetery. Food was preserved in a number of ways. Fish and meat were dried, salted or smoked over an open fire, while dairy products were buried in cool, damp environments such as peat bogs. Fruit and nuts were dried or made into jam.

There is also evidence to suggest that farmers continued to hunt on a small scale, tracking animals such as deer, whose bones and antlers provided a good source of raw material for tools and handles as well as combs, buttons, beads, belt rings and pins. A collection of bone pins was unearthed on Foregate Street in Chester during construction of a Co-operative store early last century, whilst an axe hammer with a handle of red deer antler came from the site of the gasworks on the Roodee in 1885. In Lymm an implement of red deer antler was found during the cutting of the Manchester Ship Canal.

Above: The hand grain rubber found in Macclesfield cemetery in the 19th century (Sainter).

Fishing with nets, traps and spears was also practised both on the coast and in inland rivers and lakes. A number of bronze fishhooks were uncovered many years ago along the shoreline of the North Wirral at Meols, whilst a net-sinker of baked boulder clay, now in The British Museum, was pulled out of the cemetery brook in Macclesfield in the 19th century.

Above: Bone pins found on Foregate Street in Chester early last century (Shone).

Left: The net-sinker discovered in the Macclesfield cemetery brook in the 19th century (Sainter).

The Bronze Age also saw the birth of widespread textile production. Postholes discovered within houses may represent the footings for corn drying racks or looms. Spindle whorls and loomweights made from baked clay, stone and bone have also been found, indicating that people were now beginning to weave their own fabrics and were not just wearing leather and fur as in the Neolithic. Remains of textiles, such as wool, linen, woven grasses and leather, are occasionally preserved in burials. In Cheshire two stone spindle

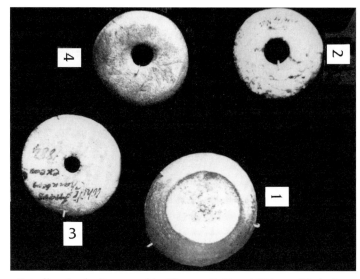

Spindle whorls discovered in Chester (2-3) and Bidston (4) during the 19th century (Shone).

whorls were uncovered in 1893 on the site of what is now the Grosvenor Museum in Chester, with a third unearthed in Bidston near Wallasey on the Wirral. Others have come to light during excavations in the Outer Gateway at Beeston Castle in recent years. As for woven material, fragments of some kind of coarse cloth, which 'fell to pieces upon being touched', were discovered in an urn burial in Wilmslow in 1857.

Other items, for example, bowls, spoons, ladders, boxes, spades, boats and trackways were fashioned from wood. Three ancient canoes or logboats have been found in the region, one in a peat bog near Cholmondley Castle, another in silt on the bank of the River Mersey in Warrington and a third in Baddilcy Mere near Nantwich. The first, reported in the *Chester Chronicle* in 1819, was described as being '11 feet in length' (3.4 metres) and '30 inches in breadth' (0.8 metres) and hollowed out of the trunk of a single tree. The second, found in Arpley Meadows close to the west end of Walton Lock in 1893, was according to Shone '12 feet, 4 inches long and 2 feet, 10 inches wide' (3.7 metres, 0.9 metres). Wooden pegs had been used to fasten the crescent-shaped stern pieces, the seat across the stern and other parts. The third was discovered in 1911 at Baddiley Mere in the south-west of the county, when the mere was being cleaned in order to improve the water supply to Nantwich. The boat was approximately six metres long and one metre wide. A fourth boat found at Ciss Green in Astbury in 1923, the star attraction in Congleton Museum, was until recently thought to be prehistoric but has now been dated to about 1000AD. At Tytherington Fields near Macclesfield a prehistoric oak paddle, 'perhaps of early coracle age' according to Sainter, was unearthed from a peat bog on the site of an ancient lake during the construction of the Marple railway line.

The logboat found in Walton Lock near Warrington on the right bank of the River Mersey in 1894 (Shone).

Cheshire has a wide variety of these boggy localities (see the final chapter on Lindow Moss). Raised trackways were often erected across areas of swamp from the Neolithic onwards, but were most prolific during the Late Bronze Age. One of the best-known ancient trackways, The Sweet Track uncovered in the Somerset Levels, is a testament to the tool manufacture of prehistoric people. There 400-year-old oak trees, over one metre in diameter, were felled using stone axes and painstakingly cut up into planks, rails, stakes and pegs. Excavations have revealed that the builders first laid a pole on the peat surface below the water and then hammered pairs of stakes over the top forming an 'x' shape. Split planks were then rested on this cradle to form a walkway. Evidence for prehistoric trackways in Cheshire comes from Lindow Moss in Wilmslow and from the boggy ground around the Marbury Meres near Great Budworth. At the latter, work on a sewerage trench in 1973 revealed a timber trackway overlain with brushwood and sealed with cobbles. Unfortunately it has not been dated.

The increased level of wealth in society in the Bronze Age was reflected in the emergence of luxury goods. Jewellery such as beads, pendants, rings and earrings made from perforated teeth, shale and jet made an appearance at that time. Examples from Cheshire are quite rare but two jet girdle rings dating to around 2000BC have been discovered in a barrow at Woodhouse End in Gawsworth near Macclesfield, and two shale bracelets of Bronze Age date came to light during excavations in the Outer Gateway at Beeston Castle. Other archaeological evidence reveals that our prehistoric ancestors even had musical instruments, many in the form of drums and whistles, with the latter fashioned from materials such as the perforated leg bones of a swan.

One of the most important developments of the period was undoubtedly the introduction of the wheel in the middle of the 2nd millennium BC. Considering the Bronze Age people's obsession with circles in their houses, burial monuments, art and ritual monuments, it is hard to believe that the wheel was so long in coming. Despite all these advances, life was still hard however. Infant mortality was high and life expectancy was quite low, with over half the population not even attaining the age of 30 years. Anyone reaching 50 would be considered of ripe old age.

Settlement Sites

As in the Neolithic, very little is known about the exact location of the majority of Bronze Age farming settlements in the county. This is due to several reasons. Firstly, dwellings largely composed of wood are notoriously difficult to locate, because they mainly survive as postholes and are usually only discovered by chance during construction work or on aerial photographs. The problem with Cheshire is that the soils on the Plain are largely composed of boulder clays which retain water well. In these conditions any buried archaeological features do not show up as parch or cropmarks on aerial photography. The county has also been intensively farmed over the last few millennia, and the area of potential for discovery becomes limited to the regions of sand and gravel and the upland fringes.

Nevertheless research into prehistoric dwellings has come a long way in the last half century. In 1934 J. Wilfrid Jackson, the president of the Lancashire and Cheshire Antiquarian Society, surmised that 'The inhabitants possibly lived in tents in the open country, like gypsies, and if so no remains would be preserved'. Evidence from Britain in general now indicates that most Bronze Age (and later Iron Age) dwellings were permanent and circular in shape with a roof of turf or thatch. Occasionally, in areas where stone was prevalent, for example in the Peak District, they may have had footings of stone which are sometimes mistaken for burial sites known as ringcairns. Currently only a few Bronze Age occupation sites are known in Cheshire with certainty, and most of these are located in lowland areas on well-drained sand and gravel deposits.

One such enclosure has been discovered at Arthill Heath Farm close to Rostherne Mere near Tatton. Here a series of enclosures and field boundaries were first identified by aerial photography and excavated between 1987 and 1988. The remains of a revetted timber bank, consisting of an enclosed ditch with two internal post trenches, were found surrounding four circular and two rectangular structures. Radiocarbon analysis from one of the circular structures gave a date of circa 2280BC to 2036BC in the Early Bronze Age. Another site at Beeston Castle on the mid-Cheshire Ridge (see the Iron Age chapter for further details) shows evidence for settlement activity in the 12th century BC, and bronze working there in the 9th and 8th centuries BC may also indicate occupation at that time.

A further prehistoric settlement site, with origins in the Late Bronze Age, has been uncovered recently during the construction of a gas pipeline by Transco from Birch Heath to Mickle Trafford in the west of the county, situated in the parish of Bruen Stapleford, near Brook House Farm. Excavations carried out by Network Archaeology and funded by Transco showed it to have been occupied for hundreds of years from the Middle Bronze Age to Late Iron Age. The earliest phase of activity was centred upon a roundhouse approximately eight metres in diameter. Finds included fire cracked stones (potboilers) and a large collection of pottery. Burnt food debris on this pottery was radiocarbon dated to between 1050BC and 800BC. Within the house archaeologists uncovered a hearth containing charcoal, coarse pottery, burnt bone and emmer/spelt grains. These provided a radiocarbon date contemporary with the food debris on the pottery. Excavations elsewhere revealed that the site was possibly enclosed by a large boundary ditch just over one metre deep and almost seven metres wide. A similar multi-phased site is also known from Irby on the Wirral. Both of these will be covered in more detail in the Iron Age section.

In addition to the settlement site at Irby, coastal erosion of the Red Rocks area around Hilbre Point near Hoylake has revealed indirect evidence for settlement elsewhere on the Wirral. Here several hundred flints appeared from the sands in association with pig, oxen, sheep and goat bones as well as shells. The flints, which consisted of a barbed arrowhead, scrapers and borers, are all of Early Bronze Age type. Several items of metalwork have also been found in the area, including a Middle Bronze Age dirk uncovered by a metal detectorist on a beach in Leasowe in 1982, and a socketed axe from Hilbre Island itself.

Oversley Farm

One of the most important pieces of evidence for settlement activity in the Cheshire area comes from excavations at Oversley Farm in advance of Manchester Airport's second runway in 1997 and 1998. The farm lay on free-draining, fertile soils on the edge of a natural escarpment overlooking the Bollin valley, on the boundary between the Cheshire Plain and the foothills of the Pennines. Approximately half a kilometre away is the Oversley Ford, which has been an important crossing point over the Bollin since prehistoric times. In order to accommodate the construction work, part of the river course had to be altered and in doing so a number of ancient features were revealed along with one or two modern artefacts.

The area of prehistoric settlement at Oversley Farm, excavated in advance of Manchester Airport's second runway between 1997 and 1998 (courtesy of Dorothy Bentley Smith).

The earliest archaeological evidence on the site was a track or hollow way running almost exactly north-south (parallel to the modern Altrincham Road) which may have served as a drove way to move livestock down to the ford. Within this track, which had a patchy metalled surface, several midden deposits were discovered within pits. The contents of these included pieces of pottery, flint and the charred remains of seeds and crops which were radiocarbon dated to around 1600BC. A radiocarbon analysis of the trackway itself produced slightly earlier dates of between 2330BC to 1935BC. However, as the hollow way was already well worn down by then (and as mentioned in the last chapter there was evidence for Neolithic settlement here also) it is likely to have originated much earlier.

Elsewhere on the Oversley site archaeologists uncovered a pit containing fire-cracked stones perhaps used as potboilers, sherds of Beaker pottery and more importantly, evidence for settlement. There had been several phases of occupation at the farm during the Bronze Age with structures moved around over time within the area defined by the sand and gravel terrace. The whole site was enclosed by a ditch with a wickerwork fence rising from its inner lip and a possible entrance to the south.

The first phase of building activity consisted of two oval structures 40 metres to the east of the hollow way and 40 metres apart. The smaller of the two (six metres long and four metres wide) had its long axis running north-south with an entrance gap to the east. Doorways in prehistoric buildings often faced east. This may have had some symbolic significance with orientation towards the rising sun. Alternatively, it could simply have been down to practicalities, positioned to make the best use of light or avoid the prevailing winds. The building was constructed from a continuous wall of upright slats set into a slot in the ground and associated with a number of nearby pits which appeared to have had differing functions. The first of these hollows was lined with some kind of organic material, such as leather or wood, and may have served as a container for holding rainwater. The second, with an inner lining of small pebbles, was possibly used for threshing cereals, while the third, which had been backfilled and contained 30 sherds of Beaker pottery, may have served as a storage pit. Archaeologists believe that this building was used as a workshop area where cooking and craft-type activities were carried out.

The second structure was slightly larger at seven metres by four metres, with its long axis running east/west, and an entrance again to the east. Postholes (dating to between 2135BC and 1745BC) demonstrated that the dwelling had been constructed from upright posts set into the ground and infilled with wattle and dawb panels. Two stakeholes in the interior suggest that it may have been partitioned with a possible hearth towards the eastern side, while a further two postholes outside may represent the footings of a porched entrance. One of the most

Artefacts found at Oversley Farm during excavations in the 1990s including the cupmarked stone (top left), a number of flints (centre) and a reconstructed Bronze Age urn (courtesy of Dorothy Bentley Smith).

interesting aspects of this building, which was almost certainly used for domestic occupation, was the discovery of three carefully chosen objects placed deliberately within the hearth and covered with a cap of clean yellow clay to form a false bottom. These consisted of a broken fragment of a saddle quern placed on end at the side of the pit, the flat blue-green volcanic stone originating in the Lake District (already mentioned), with two cupmarks pecked into its surface and placed face down to conceal the decoration in the bottom, and a decorated rim sherd of an unusual small cordoned cup. The cupmarked stone is a very rare find for this region and is, so far, Cheshire's only known example of prehistoric rock art (for more details on rock art see pages 53-55). One can only speculate as to why these objects had been so carefully placed and hidden here in the hearth. Perhaps they served as a blessing for the house or an offering to whatever gods they worshipped to protect their crops and their hearth. Fire would have been one of the most important assets for prehistoric people, burning day and night.

The second phase of building activity on the site was centred on the hollow way itself with four structures built immediately to the west. The first consisted of a roughly circular timber house (radiocarbon dated to between 1975BC and 1635BC). This dwelling had an internal floor of sand ten metres in diameter, the centre of which was defined by a large pit, possibly the remains of a hearth or a hole for a large post supporting the roof. A gap in the eastern wall may again have represented an entrance. Outside a shallow channel was located running away to the south, thought to be a gully to drain water away from the eaves drip. Five metres to the north of the house archaeologists discovered a 1.4 metre square post structure, perhaps the footings of a freestanding frame for drying hides or a loom for weaving fabrics. Sixty metres to the south of this lay an-

other slightly larger four post structure (2.2 metre square) which may have been used as a granary building with a raised floor to keep the grain well ventilated. This is further suggested by the discovery of a piece of quern within the fill, conceivably placed as a ritual deposit to safeguard the crop.

From within the trackway itself a fourth structure was uncovered comprising a rectangular wooden building five metres by six metres. This had been constructed using earthfast timber posts and had an internal floor of sand and

The granary at Castell Henllys in Pembrokeshire showing how the four post structure at Oversley Farm may have looked.

gravel covered with layers of occupation debris; this has been radiocarbon dated to between 1890BC and 1680BC. The main feature of the interior was a hollow, possibly representing a hearth or storage pit, which had been backfilled with domestic waste.

During this second phase a complex sequence of deposits were also placed within the hollow way. Close to the freestanding frame or loom a deposit of midden material was discovered containing Early Bronze Age pottery, flints and pollen from naked barley and emmer wheat together with ten varieties of weeds commonly associated with cultivation. Two radiocarbon dates (1965BC to 1630BC and 1985BC to 1660BC) were derived from this material. The variety of environmental evidence points to the surrounding landscape supporting both arable and pastoral farming at this period. On or near the floor of the circular timber house meadowsweet seeds were also found. During excavations in the 1970s at North Mains near Strathallan in Scotland, a Beaker containing the remains of a brewed drink, radiocarbon dated to circa 1540BC, was discovered in a Bronze Age cist. An analysis of the pollen revealed that meadowsweet had been used as a flavouring, in a cereal-based drink of ale or mead. Perhaps the meadowsweet here in Cheshire may have been used for a similar purpose.

During the later Bronze Age the structural evidence for settlement diminishes. We know that people were still using the area, however, because a great deal of time and effort was invested in metalling the hollow way. In addition four isolated pits were dug between 1420BC and 760BC, one of which contained a saddle quern and a grinding stone. Finally, on the dawn of the Iron Age, a possible roundhouse, represented by only four badly ploughed postholes, was constructed towards the northern end of the trackway.

Clulow Cross

There is a suggestion that a settlement in east Cheshire may have existed at Clulow Cross in Wincle, close to a stone circle known as The Bullstones, which will appear later in this chapter. In the adjoining field southwards local antiquarian, Dr J.D. Sainter, described 'some small stone circles and square enclosures six feet in diameter, of which, when dug into, the surface soil was black for 18 inches in depth, succeeded by red soil containing a few rough pieces of gritstone'. Gordon Rowley suggested that these may have been the remnants of huts with the 'black earth' being accumulated occupation debris. Until further archaeological investigations are carried out in the area it is impossible to verify this, but it is likely that the community who built the stone circle would have lived somewhere in the locality.

The Wider Environment

Apart from these few exceptions, there is a marked absence of direct prehistoric settlement evidence from much of Cheshire. We must therefore look to the neighbouring communities of the Peak District, where many sites remain in out of the way places, to give an insight into how Bronze Age people lived. Following considerable research in Derbyshire by John Barnatt and Ken Smith of the Peak District National Park Authority, it has now been established that by circa 2000BC agricultural communities of kin and family groups had begun to find permanent settlement on the limestone plateau in addition to the lower slopes of the fertile gritstone uplands.

Of particular interest are the Eastern Moors above the Derwent and Hope valleys which, although bleak expanses of uninhabited moorland today, were once thriving agricultural communities. During the Early Bronze Age the soil here was sandy and well drained, perfect for farming crops. In fact, it was only towards the end of the 2nd millennium BC that a rapidly deteriorating climate with increased rainfall caused peat and blanket bog to form on the higher ground, leaving it in its present state. It is thanks to this worsening climate, however, that the ancient monuments in the area are so well preserved. Unlike on the limestone plateau of Derbyshire and much of Cheshire, where over the millennia the pressures of intensive farming have led to the destruction of many ancient monuments, these upland areas have largely remained untouched. Stone circles, barrows and cairns abound and even dwellings are preserved to some extent.

Although there is a lack of physical evidence for prehistoric houses over a large part of Cheshire in the Bronze Age, nevertheless there are many other clues to indicate that there was quite a large farming community living here at that time. In addition to a distribution of flints and other stone tools, there are several surviving stone circles and standing stones, and particularly important, numerous barrows which, taking evidence from the Peak District, nearly always appear to have been constructed in the vicinity of contemporary settlements. A quick glance at the distribution map (see Figure 9) reveals that there were high concentrations on the fringe of the Pennines around Macclesfield and on the eastern slopes of the mid-

Cheshire Ridge close to Delamere. As far as Bronze Age activity goes, the area in the middle of the Plain is quite barren, apart from on the fringes of the main river valleys, indicating that it was still heavily forested at that time.

An examination of pollen specimens from a number of sites has revealed that during the Early Bronze Age (circa 2300BC to 1500BC) a warm dry climate led to the clearance of some areas of the forest and agricultural cultivation. Barrows abound in the areas of land between 60m and 120m above sea level where the free-draining sand and gravels would have been ideal for farming. Additionally there is also a significant number of burials on ground between 240m and 425m above sea level indicating settlement in areas which were to become marginal after the climate worsened towards the end of the 2nd millennium BC.

By about 1500BC the exploitation of Cheshire's ground for agricultural purposes was at its peak, but in the years that followed, perhaps because of soil erosion and the deteriorating climate, many of these once fertile areas were abandoned, reducing the amount of land available and forcing reorganisation. Evidence of this degeneration comes from the soils used to construct a round barrow at Old Withington near Holmes Chapel, where burials were radiocarbon dated to the latter half of the 2nd millennium BC. Pollen analysis suggested that the mound was formed at a time when the cultivated land was losing its fertility and slipping back into wilderness. This was further confirmed by samples taken from the turf where herbs, alder and hazel were so prevalent that archaeologists deduced the site must have reverted to woodland. During this period very few new barrows were erected, instead the dead were either interred in existing mounds or placed in flat cremation cemeteries. Increased pressure on the land, and a further down turn in the weather, eventually led to the onset of the Iron Age with its large defended hillforts and enclosures.

Tree rings from all over the world indicate that during the Late Bronze Age, in exactly 1159BC a major catastrophe affected the earth. The planet was shrouded in dust, possibly caused again by a comet or asteroid travelling near the earth's surface. The dust partially blotted out the sun causing the planet to cool. Trees did not grow for a whole year and crops failed. In areas such as Britain, farmland flooded, whilst further south on the planet this natural disaster may have caused widespread droughts leading to famine and the downfall of some of prehistory's greatest civilizations (for example The New Kingdom in Egypt and the Shang Dynasty in China). Evidence from tree rings in Ireland indicates that the immediate effects of this 'Near Earth Object' would continue to be felt for a further 18 years, followed by a more permanent downturn in the weather leading to a generally colder and wetter climate in the north, which continued for the next millennium. It comes as no surprise, therefore, that at this time communities began to abandon the old traditions of building barrows and turned instead to a new religion focusing on watery places. Just as the Bronze Age in Britain appears to have begun with a natural disaster, so it ended with one.

Prehistoric Copper Mining and Metalworking

Introduction by D. Bentley Smith

There is always a danger in categorizing things for inevitably exceptions will arise, and nowhere more so than in the historical and prehistorical period names. For convenience, of course, boundaries must be set within which subjects can be placed, but it is important to remember that these boundaries are simple guidelines which time and place can alter considerably. The more man digs and reveals the past, the more this concept is enforced; for what appears early in one continent, or region of the world, might take centuries to appear in another. This is certainly the case with one of the world's most versatile metals – copper.

Copper is 'malleable, ductile and very tenacious'; difficult to smelt because of the impurities with which it is often combined, but easier in its more pure forms. Due to its unfortunate ability to combine readily with oxygen, only in very rare instances does it occur as native or pure copper.

In its natural form the copper oxide is known as the red ore, cuprite (88.8% copper content) or tenorite (80% copper content) of a grey black colour, but even these have to be heated to temperatures in excess of 1000°C to drive out the oxygen; the copper itself melts at 1083°C a relatively high temperature for metals. The melting point of tin is only 327°C, and lead even lower at a fraction below 232°C.

Copper objects are also prone to oxidisation; the result, to use an everyday term, they become tarnished; this appears in the form of a green surface rust known as verdigris (copper oxide). Smelting copper, therefore, has nearly always caused problems, requiring great skill in judging at what point enough oxygen has been expelled from the smelt in order to prevent cracks developing in the cooling metal. As late as the 16th century AD smelters from the Germanic region of Augsburg knew how difficult the process was, claiming it was far easier to combine ores from two different mines for smelting purposes. They, of course, did not understand the chemical changes taking place, but had learnt from centuries of experience and experimentation the best methods to use. It is therefore incredible to understand how primitive man discovered the secret of copper smelting thousands of years ago, and his subsequent capability of combining it with other metals, as in the instance of lead or tin to produce ancient bronzes.

The First Steps

To date the story begins in the Near East, although China has yet to yield up many secrets. Archaeological discoveries, such as pins and simple instruments, have placed Anatolia (now part of Turkey) to the forefront of the transition from the Neolithic (Stone Age) to the Chalcolithic (Copper Age) – the precursor to the Bronze Age – at about 6500BC. Yet, whilst these finds are at present the earliest to be recorded, obviously mining and smelting were already known. The earliest date suggested for the beginning of the copper era is 10,000BC, but this does vary throughout the world.

The first complete smelting installations were discovered in the mid 1970s in the Timna Valley, Wadi Arabah, situated close to Eilat on the shores of the Gulf of Akabar in southern Israel. They have been dated to approximately 4000BC.

It is far more difficult to discover where and when the earliest copper mining took place, partly because the sheer magnitude of modern mining has eradicated the evidence on many sites, and also because the existing evidence, now beginning to appear, is in the most remote places. However, before the smelting could begin, it was the ability to recognise that particular rocks could be transformed, by heat, into something unique, which is the most surprising development.

Native or pure copper, as already mentioned, is extremely rare, and the two major sources are in the Near East; one, not surprisingly, in central Anatolia (originally part of Asia Minor), and the other in central Iran near Anarek. This pure copper ore is the colour of produced copper and often tarnished green where weathering has occurred. It has all the properties of produced copper and therefore can be pounded into various shapes, stretched to form wire and cut into slices. It would have been comparatively easy to work and therefore Anatolia is the obvious choice of area for the earliest use of copper by primitive peoples.

By the Late Chalcolithic the region was producing 'more sophisticated copper tools', which heralded the Early Bronze Age. This began at the end of the 4th millennium BC and lasted until the 2nd millennium BC, and had within its scope the several stages of the development and destruction of Troy. The very earliest finds from the first small settlement have proved that the addition of tin to copper, to produce a much tougher metal, was understood. Also the resulting metal, bronze, had a lower melting point and was therefore much easier to work and cast.

Tin, at that period, was probably coming from Caucasia in Asia Minor and also Persia. However the tin supplies were soon depleted, with bronze production severely curtailed for a time, until the Phoenicians and Early Greek traders found alternative sources in Europe, particularly in Cornwall, England.

Developments in Europe

The Chalcolithic period began in mainland Europe about 4500BC, some 2,000 years after the Near East, so inevitably the making of bronze was also delayed. The casting of bronze tools and weapons, understood so well in Mesopotamia by the mid 4th millennium BC, were soon becoming known along the vast trade routes, and by 3000BC had also begun to infiltrate the Neolithic cultures of Europe. It was not until circa 1000BC that the Bronze Age finally drew to a close with the proliferation of the ability to heat and forge iron.

Anatolia was at the crossroads of civilisation and was the nucleus for the trading routes crossing from Asia into Europe from the earliest times. At the end of the Early Bronze Age, circa 1950BC, the Hittites occupied the land, but ironically were totally defeated by Indo European tribes (probably Greeks) who possessed iron weapons; the Hittites were still using bronze weaponry. At this time the Bronze Age was just beginning in Britain, whereas Greece and China could claim an earlier start from at least 3000BC.

The Neolithic cultures north of the Alps were certainly in possession of highly sophisticated tools and weapons by 3000BC; some could have come along the migratory routes from Spain, but the discovery of the 5,200-year-old Ice Man, named Ötzi, on the Austro-Italian border in September 1991, and his axe with its superb copper blade, has left many questions unanswered. Meanwhile copper technology had finally reached the British Isles circa 2500BC.

Whilst in England no evidence of prehistoric smelting sites has so far been found, several large smelting sites have been identified in Scotland, many in Aberdeenshire. These were considered in the early 20th century, to date between 1800BC and 1500BC, due to the presence of stone moulds, mainly of sandstone, used for casting axes, rings and bars. A clay mould of Bronze Age date was also discovered in Bute for casting a bronze butt end of a spear. At Traprain Law in East Lothian a fascinating collection of moulds, dating to between 200AD to 400AD, for making dress fastenings, rings and pins, together with triangular-shaped fireclay crucibles with iron tongs for lifting purposes, demonstrates how advanced the metallurgy had become by then.

Along the south-western coastline of Scotland thin veins of copper ores are numerous and easily seen with their bright green colours. Therefore it seems probable that the copper being used was from the local areas. Although Scotland does not feature in the present scheme of things with regard to present day archaeological copper interests, neither does Sweden, yet both have the potential to be there. Sweden is an enigma. It is so renowned for its copper, bronze and later brass productions from the Viking era onwards, yet it is regarded as a non-starter in the prehistoric period. The vast treasures in its museums are accepted as being made from imported copper. If its mines had not then been developed where was the copper

The prehistoric copper mines on The Great Orme in Llandudno, worked for over 1,000 years in the Bronze Age.

imported from? Only analysis of the metals will give an adequate indication to a possible source.

The Scandinavian people soon acquired metallurgic skills to an exceptional degree. In 1943 at Vester Doense in Himmerland, Denmark, whilst peat digging was in progress, a large quantity of two-sided casting moulds of soapstone and clay were discovered in the peat bog, and dated to the Bronze Age.

Due to the weight of copper, whenever possible it was conveyed by water rather than overland. And if it is discovered that the Scandinavians were importing copper from the British Isles, perhaps in exchange they were conveying their secrets of smelting.

Whilst it is easier to understand how copper was first discovered and worked in Anatolia, it is far more difficult to judge how the European tribes succeeded in their endeavours, and particularly those of Britain.

Great discoveries during the mid 1980s onwards have now placed Ireland firmly on the map of prehistoric copper production, both with regard to mining and smelting sites, and small communities living close by. The largest concentration is on Mount Gabriel in the Mizen Peninsula, west of Cork, dating to between 1700BC and 1500BC. And prehistoric copper mining has now been discovered as early as 2400BC to 2000BC in County Kerry at Ross Island.

Wales also claims some exciting finds, particularly in the Great Orme Mines in North Wales, considered to be the largest of the copper mining sites in Bronze Age Britain. The old workings can still be seen, and the stone hammers, bone tools and charcoal from the debris have given a radiocarbon date of between 1300BC to 1020BC. Elsewhere in Wales finds on Parys Mountain, Anglesey and around Cwmystwyth (mid Wales) also point to prehistoric activity. In all 26 Welsh sites have yielded artefacts apparently relating to the Bronze Age, but so far only four have been confirmed by radiocarbon dating.

The evidence, apart from the tools etc. found on site (which I feel is not my remit to discuss, but will follow in the next section), is that of fire setting. Stone Age people had learnt that by setting a fire against a rock face, then pouring cold water on the hot rocks, fractures would occur which, when worked upon by primitive axes and picks, allowed the rocks to be more easily fragmented.

Many discoveries are by accident, and even this method could have arisen from the primitive method of cave dwelling where fires would have been lit, perhaps against the wall of a cave to allow the smoke to rise high into the roof. And it is not beyond the bounds of possibility that, perhaps during a storm, heavy rain caused a sudden surge of water from the roof which extinguished the fire and rapidly cooled the surrounding wall, causing fracturing of the rocks. Stone Age people would have utilised this method in their eagerness to find better pieces of stone with which to work, and the method would have rapidly spread from group to group.

In doing this, in some places they must have found the superbly coloured ores of copper. What delightful pieces to hang around the neck (they would soon discover that arsenite was not ideal but it could have helped with enemies). Many are bright green or blue, whilst others have red and yellow tones, and even a peacock ore exists, found in Cornwall although not until the 17th century onwards. Even today the lovely marble quality of the dark and light polished malachite is a great favourite for jewellery. Perhaps this very thing could account for bodies stained with copper, which have been cremated. Or perhaps the individuals had smeared their bodies with the bright blue or, more true to Alderley Edge, green ores. If the pyre was large enough the heat in the centre would be intense enough for the copper to melt, otherwise, in the smelting process, Bronze Age smelters had to use a form of bellows to raise the temperature of the charcoal fire, which was no easy task.

As the main focus of this book is prehistoric Cheshire I shall now leave the story in capable hands to be continued.

* * * * *

Prehistoric Mines in Cheshire

For Bronze Age people the most important factor in determining which copper mine was the most viable, was purely down to practicalities. Armed only with stone tools and fire, the copper ore had to be easily obtainable from the surface. The miners would first locate an exposed mineral vein and then work it down into the ground. Often the hard rock was weakened by burning fires against the surface. They would have been aware of the propensity of fire and cold water to fracture rock from the use of heated stones as potboilers, commonly found on archaeological sites throughout the prehistoric period. Once brittle it was more easily shattered with hammers to remove the ore. Picks made from antlers and carved hazel stems were used to prize out smaller fragments which were then collected using wood or ox shoulder-blade shovels. Spoil heaps and associated charcoal deposits are frequently found on sites along with hut shelters and cooking hearths.

Dr J.D. Sainter's sketch of stone hammers discovered at Alderley Edge, which would have been used for crushing the copper ore.

Archaeological evidence from these spoil heaps indicates that once the large pieces of ore had been brought to the surface they were then further crushed using large stone hammers so that the copper minerals could be carefully picked out. This method appears to have been highly successful as very few waste deposits contain traces of copper ore. What is interesting though, is that in places such as Cwmystwyth where lead was also present, the lead ore has been dumped showing that the prehistoric miners were only interested in the copper.

Unfortunately, after the mineral extraction process, the archaeological evidence comes to an end. On most sites there is little or no evidence of prehistoric furnaces or slagheaps showing smelting. This may have taken place in nearby settlements, but until one such site is discovered the debate will continue. No major settlement has yet been linked specifically to prehistoric mining activities in Britain. The general lack of evidence for smelting might just be down to the fact that the simple bowl-shaped furnaces used for extracting the copper leave little or no trace in the archaeological record.

Alderley Edge Copper Mines

In England a few artefacts have come to light in mines in the Peak District, such as at Ecton Hill as well as in Cornwall, but the best-known and most well preserved ancient site can be found at Alderley Edge in Cheshire. The sandstone escarpment lies at 120m (394ft) above sea level close to the east Cheshire town of Wilmslow. On a clear day visitors are presented with commanding views across the Cheshire Plain to the mountains of Wales in the west, Liverpool to the north-west, Manchester and beyond to the north, and east across to the Pennines. Evidence from flint scatters indicates that the Edge was settled from early times, as discussed in the first chapter. Copper, lead, cobalt, silver and iron have been found in the mines, but prehistoric activities were limited only to copper. These same ore-bearing rocks are also found a few kilometres to the north-east in Mottram St Andrew. The Edge would have been particularly attractive to Bronze Age miners because it was fortunate in having a prominent exposure of malachite. Walking close to the Engine Vein mine today it is still possible to see the ground flecked with traces of this green ore.

During more recent mining operations between 1855 and 1878AD a number of ancient mines were discovered both on the Edge itself and at nearby Mottram St Andrew. Approximately three-quarters of the surface workings on the Edge are accessible but in Mottram, unfortunately, the mines are largely flooded so little can be deduced. The first indication that the Alderley mines dated back as far as the Bronze Age came to light during operations at Brindlow in the 19th century. The following extract comes from the pages of local writer, Dr J.D. Sainter in 1878:

A reconstruction of a copper-smelting furnace at the Great Orme Mines.

The Engine Vein at Alderley Edge where prehistoric miners exploited the green malachite ore.

'A short time ago as some miners were at work on the Edge, they came upon a large collection of stone implements, consisting of celts, adzes, hammer heads or axes, mauls, &c. Some were lying upon the sand and gravel, from one to two feet below the surface, along with foreign boulders and pebbles belonging to the drift period; and others had been left in some old diggings of the copper ore, from three to four yards in depth, along with an oak shovel that had been very roughly used. Nearly the whole had been rudely made, and were more or less smashed; and they appeared to have been thrown aside, having become useless.'

He continues: 'They varied in size, and ran up to ten or twelve pounds in weight; and not one that I have noticed has been perforated for the insertion of a handle, but there was a groove formed around each, near the middle so that by bending a tough stick slightly along the groove, and securing it below with thongs, and then fastening the ends of the stick together these would form a handle.'

These tools, used for pounding and crushing the ore, had been made from glacial erratic boulders found in the immediate neighbourhood. Some appeared to be relatively new while others were well-worn indicating prolonged use. Two of the hammers had even been sharpened as if for cutting. Unusually all were found together side-by-side, as if dumped, suggesting a sudden abandonment of the mine. A number of large unworked boulders, perhaps being stored for future use, were also located in a nearby hollow.

Some of the stone hammers discovered at Brynlow in the 19th century (Shone).

This site of Brindlow (today known as Brynlow to the west of the Macclesfield Road) was visited in 1874 by Boyd Dawkins, Professor of Geology at Manchester University. He discovered a few stray hammers on the ground and upon further investigation uncovered evidence for prehistoric open cast mining to a depth of between 2.5 and 3.5 metres below the surface. Over a hundred tools were unearthed in the debris used to back fill the mine, including the hammers and the oak shovel mentioned by Sainter. The finds attracted interest from a variety of antiquarians, some of whom were not convinced of their prehistoric provenance. One in particular, a Mr Plant, believed them to be nothing more than 'stones used for the attachment of tents, or for the rope-weights to hold the thatch on the roofs of the huts of the miners, and not perhaps gone long out of existence'.

Luckily for archaeology not everyone was of this opinion and the discovery inspired a local resident, Mr F.S. Graves, to undertake a systematic search of the entire Edge, revealing a whole host of interesting features (see Figure 6). Further hammers were detected in waste heaps in Windmill Wood to the north of the Brindlow levels and at the Engine Vein and its environs to the east (on the opposite side of the Macclesfield Road). Continuing in a north-easterly direction yet more came to light in Dickens Wood and also in Mottram St Andrew, but those from the latter were of highly inferior quality.

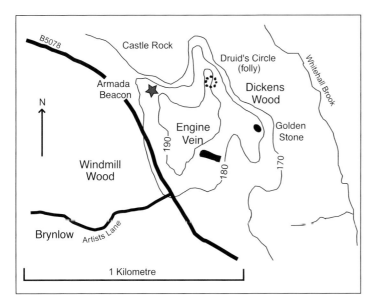

Figure 7 - The mines and other prehistoric features on Alderley Edge. Reproduced by kind permission of Ordnance Survey.© Crown Copyright NC/04/26823.

Before leaving Brindlow it is important to mention the 'oak shovel' described by Dr Sainter. This was lost for many years, but then fortunately rediscovered by local author, Alan Garner, under the stage in Alderley Edge School in 1953. He tried for several years to persuade various academic institutions to recognise its ancient provenance. The Manchester Museum was 'unavailable to comment'; The British Museum dismissed it as 'possibly a Tudor winnowing fan' and The Ashmolean declared it to be 'a child's toy spade: Victorian'. Luckily Garner did not give up and eventually revisited The Manchester Museum with it many years later. An inspection declared it to be a Bronze Age shovel which was later confirmed by radiocarbon analysis to have been produced between 1888BC and 1677BC. It is now on display in the newly opened gallery in The Manchester Museum.

Having established that the Engine Vein also dated back to prehistoric times, Mr Graves and his acquaintance, Mr Roeder, undertook further investigations in this area. They discovered that the Bronze Age miners had worked the exposures of malachite from the surface to a depth of approximately five metres by sinking small circular pits into the ore bed, and then knocking out the side to make a clear face. This was repeated until the whole of the bed was revealed.

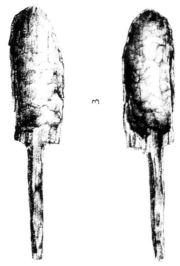

The Bronze Age oak shovel found in the prehistoric mine workings at Alderley Edge in the 19th century (Sainter).

71

These circular pits in the hammer-battered rock along the surface of the Engine Vein mine have been linked to an early phase of prehistoric mining.

On the eastern side of the Engine Vein, the rock face was blackened and cracked as if it had been subjected to fire setting in order to make it brittle. This was further supported by the discovery of large pieces of charcoal and decayed stems of gorse (fuel) found in what they believed to be fireplaces on the ground constructed from lead ore. Similar evidence of blackening was discovered on the western side of the mine where a large number of stone hammers were located in a spoil heap. A small deposit of crushed ore was also found on the southern side of the mine indicating that it was broken up, separated and heaped close by. Even more interesting is the report of 'lumps of smelted copper and slag' which was uncovered from a spoil heap to the west.

As mentioned previously, the discovery of a large dump of both new and old hammer stones suggests that the Alderley mines were suddenly abandoned, but why? By the Late Bronze Age the use of British copper was dwindling and the majority of finds are fabricated from Continental imports. Various reasons have been suggested as to why this occurred. It may simply have been that by this period the easily accessible ores had been exhausted and this coincided with readily available supplies from elsewhere. Alternatively, it could be down to the deteriorating climate which would have made the mines more susceptible to flooding and waterlogging. The former seems more likely with regard to Alderley Edge, as the ores here would have been easily won initially, because of the small veins and nodules of high-grade malachite. These were, however, soon worked out, leaving only the ores impregnated into the sandstone. Even in the 18th and 19th centuries this ore was extremely difficult to smelt because of its high sand content. It would have been an impossible task for Bronze Age people.

Bronze Age Metalwork in Cheshire

All in all it cannot be denied that copper mining operations at the Edge during the Bronze Age took place on a large scale, which suggests there must have been quite a populous community living in the vicinity in order to support this. However, it is interesting to note that in comparison to the amount of ore that must have been mined, relatively few bronze artefacts have so far been found in Cheshire, suggesting that the copper was perhaps traded elsewhere to be transformed into bronze or continuously recycled, reused and dispersed into later prehistory.

Evidence for Bronze Age metalworking in the county comes from one settlement site at Beeston in mid-Cheshire and also from just outside the modern Cheshire boundaries at Mellor hillfort in the east. At Beeston Castle a highly significant metalworking centre came to light during excavations between 1968 and 1973 (see Iron Age section for further details). At the turn of the 2nd and 1st millennium BC, in the area of what is today the Outer Gateway and Outer

Ward of the medieval castle, metal production appears to have been taking place on a moderately large scale. An unusual assemblage made up of complete artefacts, unlike those normally associated with debris from a domestic settlement (there were no personal implements or small tools), was found scattered within the topsoil of the Outer Ward. These included metalworking objects such as scrap bronze artefacts, clay moulds and pieces of crucibles used for casting, as well as high temperature hearths and a concentration of clay refractories perhaps used for building the furnaces needed to melt down the metal. The crucibles and moulds are very fragile and their survival suggests they must have remained *in situ* ever since. All this evidence points to the area being primarily associated with metalworking which is almost unknown from contemporary sites, the only exception being South Cadbury hillfort in Somerset where 'a group of furnaces', interpreted as an armourer's workshop on the evidence of associated scrap bronze and iron, was reported during excavations between 1966 and 1970.

Ten bronze objects were discovered in the metalworking area at Beeston in total. The majority of these were ribbed socketed axes dating to between 900BC and 700BC in the Late Bronze Age. Also uncovered were a socketed knife, a fragment of a sword blade and a spearhead along with various waste products from metalworking activities represented by a piece of an ingot, a blob of copper alloy and another unknown lump. Analysis of the recognizable metal artefacts showed that they were either made from one source or, more likely, from a regional pool where repeated recycling and re-melting had created a common mixture. Two of the larger bronzes had been scrapped and the others were very worn suggesting they were destined for the melting pot. It is unclear whether the objects were deposited together as a hoard or lost over a period of some time, as the area has been greatly disturbed.

What makes the site even more intriguing is the fact that beneath the earliest rampart close to the entrance, archaeologists discovered two carefully placed, newly cast bronze axes. It is believed that these may have been deliberately deposited as foundation offerings under the first phase of the defences to signify the importance of the hill as a metalworking site, and perhaps to ask for blessing from whatever forces they believed in. Interestingly there are sources of copper in Bickerton at the foot of Beeston Hill itself and in the nearby Peckforton Hills. These were worked in the 19th century and although no evidence has as yet come to light for prehistoric workings, it is possible that as at Alderley Edge these veins were exploited by Bronze Age miners.

Although the site appears to have primarily been a working area, the metalworkers and their families may well also have been living on the hill. The presence of a number of querns, spindle whorls and loomweights indicates that a range of domestic activities, such as corn grinding and weaving, was taking place there in the Late Bronze Age. A second site, providing evidence of early metalworking in the region, was discovered recently at the hillfort in Mellor near Stockport. This was primarily a settlement site, but several crucible sherds and a mould uncovered during excavations, may possibly have been used for metal production. A chemical analysis of the crucible revealed traces of copper, tin, zinc and lead indicating it was used for melting bronzes, possibly in the Late Bronze Age or Early Iron Age.

Bronze Artefacts

As to the metalwork objects themselves, of those known from Cheshire the earliest, in the form of flat bronze axes, date to the first half of the 2nd millennium BC. Examples of these have been found at Bickley, Burwardsley, Tattenhall, Grappenhall, Kinderton, Weaverham, Malpas, Newbold Astbury near Congleton and at Mottram St Andrew, with a marked concentration along the flanks of the mid-Cheshire Ridge. The four axes from Bickley, Burwardsley, Gorstage near Weaverham and Chowley near Tattenhall were discovered by metal detectorists between 1991 and 1993. All are very simple in form dating to circa 2000BC when bronze technology was in its infancy and objects were cast in one-piece stone moulds.

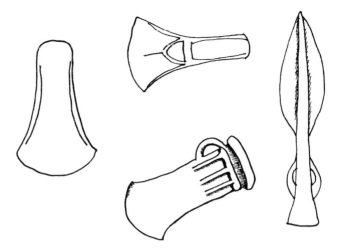

Examples of Bronze Age metalwork – Flat axe (left), palstave (top), socketed axe (bottom) and looped spearhead (right).

All of these axes have been chance finds discovered in isolation, but while prospecting in a ploughed field at Bridgemere near Nantwich a metal detectorist uncovered a very rare hoard of four Early Bronze Age tools in a ploughed field, close to what is believed to be the traces of a destroyed round barrow. The hoard, dating from circa 1700BC to 1450BC, comprised three cast flange axes, and a very rare and unusual long dagger broken into five pieces by recent ploughing activities. Hoards of this date are exceptionally uncommon and so far there is no exact parallel anywhere in the country for the long dagger (or possibly short rapier), making it a highly significant discovery. Other items of interest from this early period include a small fragment of copper from a cairn cemetery at Butley near Macclesfield, and a rivetted dagger accompanying a burial close to Wilmslow station.

After about 1500BC new developments and stabilised communities led to a more sophisti-cated range of tools and weapons being produced which included dirks and rapiers, socketed axes, spearheads with side loops on the socket and palstave axes. Palstaves were one of the earliest developments in this phase as advances in bronze technology led to the introduction of two-piece moulds. Bronzesmiths were now able to create more complex designs, with additions such as a projecting collar for strengthening (flange) and a stop ridge to prevent the axe from splitting its wooden haft when in use.

A beautiful example of a palstave axe found in Adlington by local metal detectorist, David Bailey.

Between 1985 and 1992 five Middle Bronze Age palstave axes were found by metal detectorists and reported to the *County Sites and Monuments Record*. The first, found in Twemlow during drainage operations and dating to between 1400BC to 1300BC, was 172mm long by 74mm wide and very similar to one found in a rabbit burrow at the hillfort of Kelsborrow Castle in 1810. Two other palstaves from this early phase came to light on plough land at Reaseheath near Nantwich in 1990 and in a garden on Hough Lane in Alderley Edge in 1991. A second type, a little later in date (circa 1200BC to 1100BC), was discovered in a ploughed field at Marbury in 1991 on a low terrace overlooking an old streambed. It was slightly smaller at 166mm long by 53mm wide, as was a fifth found at Iddinshall near Tarporley in 1990. An example of a shafthole axe was reputedly recovered from the mere around Tabley Hall during cleaning in 1725, but this has since been lost.

During the final phase, after approximately 1000BC, a new technique pioneered in North Wales resulted in lead being added to bronze, perhaps because of a need to economise on tin and to enable better casting. This saw the introduction of leaf blade swords, an example of which was reported from Pott Shrigley by George Ormerod but is now sadly lost, and new types of 'lunate-opening' spearheads such as those found in a hoard at Congleton dating to the 8th or 9th century BC. This hoard, which was discovered during the building of a new school on New Street in 1925, also contained a socketed axe and two bronze tubes believed to be spearhead ferrules, one of which was stolen from Congleton Library in 1942 and has never been recovered. During the 1990s the Cheshire Museums Services Unit cleaned and x-rayed the artefacts, detecting previously unsuspected casting flaws in the barbed spearhead, the lunate spearhead and the ferrules. This led to speculation that these otherwise beautiful items were part of a travelling bronzesmith's hoard, destined for re-melting and buried but never recovered.

A number of Bronze Age implements have been recovered from wetland contexts, such as bronze axes from the Rixton and Risley Mosses near Warrington in the north of the county, but it is unclear whether they were simply lost during clearance work in the area or placed there deliberately as ritual deposits. The depositing of items of value into watery locations began in the Neolithic period but became increasingly common from the Late Bronze Age onwards. It was perhaps linked to increased pressures on the farming communities caused by a deteriorating climate with increased rainfall. This focus on watery places is covered in further detail in the section on Bog Bodies at the end of the book.

With the expansion of metal detecting activities in recent years and the responsible reporting of finds, many more items of prehistoric interest have come to light. A full catalogue of all the bronze items discovered in Cheshire can be found in the *County Sites and Monuments Record*, while other more recent finds can be seen on The Portable Antiquities website. These represent only a fraction of the amount of copper mined at Alderley Edge, and so the question is – what happened to the rest of Cheshire's prehistoric copper? Perhaps it was simply reused and recycled, slowly disappearing during the course of prehistory, or maybe it was traded out of the area, but if so, then what was it exchanged for and where was it traded? In the Neolithic period monuments, such as the henges and earlier large stone circles, developed in the principal distribution areas of stone axe factories, for example in North Wales and Cumbria, close to Graig Lwyd and Great Langdale respectively. Unfortunately very little research has been undertaken on the correlation between prehistoric copper mines and the distribution of Bronze Age ritual monuments but we will now turn our attention to those remaining in Cheshire, of which there are many in the area around Alderley Edge, beginning with the stone circles which perhaps served a similar purpose to the Neolithic henges, but on a smaller local scale.

Stone Circles

There are over 1,000 prehistoric stone circles in Britain and Ireland, of which there are five or six possible known examples in Cheshire (see Figure 7). These may be outliers of the concentration in the Peak District where 26 circles survive. Apart from these, the nearest groups of any significant number are located some distance away in North Wales and the Lake District. It is possible that originally there may have been other stone circles in the Cheshire area which have long since been ploughed out or recycled into gateposts and stiles; this was the fate of the Henbury circle, near Macclesfield. However, unlike the neighbouring Peak District, in general, the landscape of Cheshire is not geologically conducive to stone circle construction, with a few exceptions. There are scarcely any suitable hard rock outcrops, reflected by the propensity for soft sand and gravel quarrying in recent years. In the lowlands glacial erratics are the only source of suitable stone. It is possible, therefore, that Bronze Age people may have erected timber circles instead, but as with the dwellings of the period, these survive only as postholes and are almost impossible to locate.

A reconstructed timber circle around a burial cairn at Llyn Brenig in Denbighshire, North Wales.

The stone circles in Cheshire, namely The Bullstones, Henbury, Delamere, Church Lawton III, Grappenhall and Butley, were constructed in the Early to Middle Bronze Age. In comparison to the huge stone circles of southern England and northern Scotland, they are characteristically small, both in stone height and diameter. Unfortunately, The Bullstones is the only example surviving in any recognisable form. Circles, whether of stone or timber, were undoubtedly constructed as some kind of special place, a focal point and sacred centre for the community. Exactly what they were used for, however, is a matter of conjecture. Archaeology tells us who built them and when, but it does not reveal the secrets of the mysterious ceremonies held within.

Figure 7 - Distribution map of current known stone circles in Cheshire.

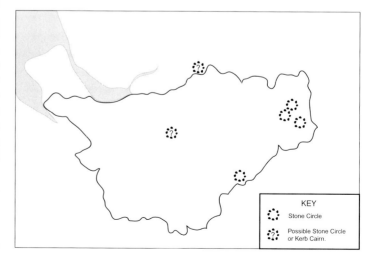

KEY

Stone Circle

Possible Stone Circle or Kerb Cairn.

They may have been connected with astronomy – many of the prehistoric sites in the British Isles show some sort of alignment with the heavens, particularly the midsummer and midwinter sun and moon rises. The annual rotation of the sun is significant in cultures the world over. Particular emphasis is placed on the four main divisions of the year – the summer solstice (around June 21st) and winter solstice (around December 21st) along with the vernal equinox (around March 21st) and autumnal equinox (around September 21st). At Stonehenge on the morning of the summer solstice the sun rises over the outlying Heel Stone. At Newgrange in Ireland, only on the day of the winter solstice do the rays from the sunrise shine through a special opening above the entrance and illuminate the 24 metre long, stone-lined passage of the chamber deep within the mound. At Nine Stone Close in Derbyshire the major southern moon, around midsummer, sets between the pillars of Robin Hood's Stride overlooking the circle, while at the Rollrights in Oxfordshire an entrance to the south-east is positioned almost directly in line with the rising of this same southern moon. In Cheshire a sight line through the Henbury stone circle near Macclesfield reveals it was aligned to the rising sun on the midwinter solstice.

Alternatively, stone circles could be the ancient places of worship where rituals associated with birthrights, unions, death and seasonal festivals were performed. Many have also been connected to fertility. So why circles? Many of the monuments are not true circles, but slightly longer in one direction making them more oval in shape. This indicates that they were perhaps laid out by eye and made to look round rather than being geometrically perfect. Nowadays living in our square houses with right-angled corners and straight walls it seems unnatural for things to be circular, but ancient man obviously had his reasons. Perhaps it is because a circle is the easiest shape to create well, or maybe it is because in a circle there is no hierarchy – everyone is equal in status, just like the Knights of King Arthur's Round Table.

On the other hand, perhaps we should look to nature for the answer. In the natural world there are few straight lines, but there are however many circles. The glowing orb of the rising and setting sun, the glimmering golden circle of the ripe full moon, the ripples on a lake, the rings on a tree, the centre of a flower, fairy rings of fungi, even the irises of the eyes. Nature is full of all things circular, suggesting that our ancestors recreated what was natural to them.

Today with light pollution, roads, cities, cars and our modern scientific understanding it is almost impossible to imagine just what it would have been like living in an outdoor world with nothing but the elements, and not really comprehending why everything happened as it did. As a farmer, man would have been more susceptible to the forces of nature than ever before. The passing of the seasons, the patterns of the weather, an abundant crop and healthy livestock are all essential parts of farming life. As discussed previously, some time around 2300BC a natural disaster, perhaps the result of an asteroid or comet flying close to or colliding with the earth, appears to have caused widespread disruption across the planet, perhaps blotting out the sun for a considerable amount of time. In a world devoid of science this must have been a terrifying experience for the farming communities, perhaps even powerful enough to cause them to abandon the 'spirits of the ancestors' and turn instead to a life and religion centred on the sky, worshipping in open stone circles looking up to the heavens.

For us the stones will always have a mystical appeal, probably because the reason for their construction will never really be known. Discussed here are the circles of The Bullstones, Henbury and Delamere in Cheshire and two sites in Grappenhall, now lying outside the county boundaries in Warrington. Church Lawton III and Butley both form part of a barrow cemetery complex and so for reasons of ease are discussed later in the barrow section.

The Bullstones

The Bullstones can be found high above the town of Macclesfield on the southern boundary of a moor called Cessbank Common, close to Clulow Cross in Wincle. Geographically and topographically this site lies within the Peak District National Park. The ring of small cobbles encircling a central standing stone is located on the eastern flank of Brown Hill, with an uninterrupted view through approximately 180 degrees. The vista to the north, east and south is stunning, taking in the sweeping moorland and the summits of Shining Tor and Shutlingsloe to the north-east, and the outcrop of The Roaches and Hen Cloud to the south-east.

The Bullstones looking towards the characteristic peak of Shutlingsloe.

According to the *Cheshire County Sites and Monuments Record* The Bullstones is classed as the 'site of a Bronze Age cremation burial' and as far as the *Victoria County History* is concerned its stones are 'obscured by vegetation'. This is not at all the case. The Bullstones is a spectacular monument in a breathtaking setting, and quite possibly one of the most important and unusual monuments in the Cheshire area, after The Bridestones.

The Bullstones, or Bullstrang as it is sometimes known, first came to the public's attention through the works of Dr John D. Sainter in the 1870s. The following extract was published in his *Scientific Rambles Round Macclesfield* in 1878:

'A short time ago, in a field close to the [Clulow] Cross, an ancient burial was investigated by myself and others. The interment proved to be that of a child or young person, and it was similar to that which had been found at Langley. The urn, which was also of Celtic type, had been inverted, and among the burnt bones was found a calcinated flint knife and a flint arrowhead.'

The flint arrowhead and knife unearthed at The Bullstones in the 19th century (Sainter).

Interestingly a badly damaged urn, reputedly retrieved from The Bullstones, is part of the reserve collection of the Congleton Museum. However, it was not the burial itself that was most interesting, but the setting in which it was placed:

'The circumstances connected with this burial were rather peculiar. It lay about three feet below the surface, and was surrounded by a stone circle 20 feet in diameter, with apparently a headstone, more or less mutilated, four feet in height and the same in breadth, placed not in the centre of the circle, but between two and three feet to one side of it, northwards. Directly opposite the headstone, the circle was entered northward by a short avenue of stones; a line of stones also ran up to the circle in an oblique curve from each corner stone at the entrance to the avenue, leaving a small semi-triangular space on both sides of sufficient dimensions to accommodate four or five persons standing upright in each'.

Dr J.D. Sainter's illustration of how The Bullstones appeared when the site was excavated in the 19th century.

Sainter and a team from The Macclesfield Scientific Society did investigate these triangles but 'upon a trial being made with a spade no burial was found in either of them.' The site survives today more or less as Sainter described it. The most striking feature is the central standing stone which dominates the monument. It is a square looking monolith measuring 1.4 metres wide, 0.7 metres deep and 1.1 metres tall. Its 'flat' top contains a bowl-shaped depression formed along the stone's natural bedding, similar to the weathering 'bowls' found on many standing stones in this region. This 'headstone' sits in a rough oval of cobble-sized stones. Surrounding the central stone is an incomplete outer ellipse of rounded cobble to small boulder-sized stones with a diameter of 7.9 metres by 8.5 metres which appears to mark the perimeter of a small platform. Parts of this ring are barely visible but can be followed or inferred through the encroaching grass. The entrance avenue, as described by Sainter, is difficult to make out amongst the mass of small boulders found today.

Being rectangular, the 'headstone' has a number of faces that could hold alignments. The long axis of the stone appears to be orientated in the direction of Roach End (the northern tip of The Roaches outcrop). The sight line takes the eye across the Dane valley, over Back Forest where the gorge of Lud's Church is situated and on to the northern end of the millstone grit ridge. The north-eastern long plane is orientated in the direction of Cessbank Common, past the characteristic summit of Shutlingsloe to the smooth featureless ridge of Shining Tor, the highest peak in the area. The south-western face of the stone points to the unimpressive flank of an adjacent hillock where the southerly end of Wincle Minn is just visible.

The Bullstones today with its ring of outer cobbles which can be traced in the grass. (Please note this site is on private land and permission must be sought from the landowner before visiting).

So what exactly is The Bullstones? It has been classified here as a stone circle, because on the face of it that is what it is – a circle of stones. As mentioned previously, the Cheshire *County Sites and Monuments Record* describes it simply as the 'site of a Bronze Age cremation burial', perhaps a barrow or cairn. Dr Sainter also postulated this when he suggested that the circle and standing stone may have been enclosed in a 'tumulus ten or twelve feet in height, with the circle of stones placed round its base'. However, just because a site has a burial there, this does not make it a burial monument. There are many examples of burials found at stone circles which were used as ritual monuments by the living. For example, at Doll Tor in the Peak District, burials and accompanying urns were found at the base of several of the standing stones, while at Arbor Low an inhumation was found close to the central cove.

The Bullstones shares many similarities with a group of monuments known as centre-stone circles which are commonly found in south-west Scotland. One of the best examples is Glenquickan near Kirkcudbright in Dumfries and Galloway. Reading the description of this site by stone circle expert, Dr Aubrey Burl, in his *Guide to the Stone Circles of Britain, Ireland and Brittany* one gets the feeling of *déjà vu*:

'Standing on level grassland it is composed of twenty-nine very low, closely set stones in an ellipse. . . the apparent gap in the ring at the south-west is filled by a stone whose tip just shows above ground. The interior of the ring is tightly laid with small stones like cobbling. At the middle of the circle is an immense upright pillar...'

In his larger volume, produced in 2000, Burl expands his description and explanation of centre-stone circles, which are also found in Shropshire, Wiltshire, south-west Ireland and Cornwall. He states 'circles with centre stones appear to be late and frequently have a cremation deposit at the foot of the centre stone' and that 'the circles are composed of unobtrusive, rounded stones whereas the interior pillar is distinctly bigger.' He adds 'such monuments can never have been conspicuous and were probably for local ceremonies'.

The stone circle of Glenquickan in Dumfries and Galloway which is uncannily similar to The Bullstones, apart from being much larger.

It is interesting to note that, located a few kilometres to the south of the stone circle of Glenquickan is Cairnholy, a fine example of a Neolithic Clyde cairn with its characteristic semi-circular forecourt and horned cairn, discussed earlier in relation to The Bridestones. As the Bridestones cairn lies only ten kilometres to the south-west of The Bullstones, could this have been planned or is it just coincidence? The site undoubtedly has more to uncover and may yet defy current classification theories, but following conversations with John Barnatt of the Peak District National Park Authority, we may be a little closer to revealing the mystery. He describes The Bullstones as 'a truly cracking site which does not fit with our normative typologies'. He believes it has affinities with the platform cairns found in areas such as Dartmoor and Bodmin Moor as well as the centre-stone rings in south-west Scotland.

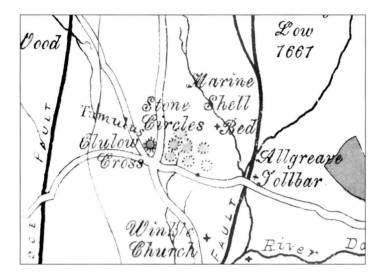

Left: Dr Sainter's 1878 map showing a number of stone circles in the Clulow Cross area.

The importance of the Cessbank Common area does not end there, however, for a close inspection of Sainter's text reveals that there may have been at least one other stone circle in the immediate vicinity. In addition to the 'small stone circles' in the adjoining field to the south, which might possibly represent the remains of hut circles as discussed previously, Sainter also briefly mentions that 'at a short distance to the north-east [of the hut circles], in a hollow, there is a traceable stone circle, 30 feet in diameter'. Approximately a 100 metres to the south of The Bullstones, a single standing stone still sits in a hollow today. The stone seems to be a glacial erratic with a face that is highly polished and very pale in colour, making it stand out quite noticeably from the surrounding vegetation. A plough scar can be seen at the top of the stone suggesting it has been buried and re-erected at some stage, but it may perhaps represent the remains of this second circle. The diamond-like profile of the stone is very noticeable on the horizon from the road to the south-east (A54 Congleton to Buxton road) at the point where the road crosses the tributary of the Hog Clough brook.

New Farm, Henbury

Unfortunately all that remains of the stone circle at Henbury near Macclesfield is a few stones scattered amongst the hedgerows of a field belonging to New Farm, to the east of Lower Pexhill Road. Attention was first drawn to this important site in the spring of 1970, when the field was ploughed for only the second time in recorded memory. During the tilling two stones were unearthed, one a small limestone boulder and the other a large millstone grit slab, both glacial erratics around 30 to 40 centimetres in diameter. A search of the field led to the discovery of several other stones, some lying in hedges, others incorporated into a nearby stile.

Large boulders are not commonly found in this locality, so the possibility of them belonging to some kind of prehistoric monument was considered. Investigations began in the north-western area of the field, where the ground rises slightly and the two buried boulders had been found. Trenches were cut across the crest, revealing a series of 13 pits, 11 of which lay in a circle surrounding one in the centre, the other being outside (see Figure 8).

The pits had been cut into the ground surface to a depth of about 60 centimetres. Most were filled with either cobbles or soil mixed with ash and charcoal. The only finds consisted of one tiny fragment of flint, two minute pieces of bone and a large chunk of charcoal. The excavators could not be certain that all eleven of the holes contained stones, but concluded that 'the site would be appropriate for a small stone circle'. The presence of a pit in the centre indicates that, as at The Bullstones, this site may also have been a centre-stone circle, highly unusual in this area of the country.

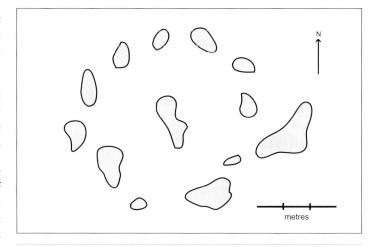

Figure 8 – Plan of the Henbury stones (after Rowley, 1982).

The most convincing piece of evidence that it was a ritual monument used by prehistoric people, comes from its positioning in the landscape. On the winter solstice (December 21st/ 22nd) it was observed that a sighting taken through the centre of the circle on a north-west/ south-east axis pointed to the rising sun over Sutton Common, 6.5 kilometres to the south-east. Intriguingly, placed on almost exactly the same alignment is the Bronze Age Beaker barrow at Woodhouse End just over 4 kilometres to the south-east in Gawsworth. Within this mound a beautifully ornamented Beaker was discovered in the 1980s, which had been carefully placed in the mound with its mouth pointing to the south-east, again in the direction of the rising midwinter sun over Sutton Common.

One of the glacial erratic stones, possibly from the Henbury circle, which can be found at the edge of the field where the monument once stood.

One stone of particular note, fitting the dimensions of Rowley's plan, is located to the north-east of the stile on Lower Pexhill Road, along the hedge line. The surface of this stone is very smooth suggesting it had travelled some distance, possibly via a glacier. It is interesting that the circle builders used a mixture of both limestone and millstone grit. In the nearby Peak District all the stone circles are composed of either one or the other, whichever rock was available locally. Dotted around this part of Cheshire there would have been a far larger proportion of millstone grit erratics than of limestone due to the proximity of gritstone outcrops, so the inclusion of the rarer limestone may have had greater significance to Bronze Age people.

Delamere Stone Circle

Moving on across the county, the *Victoria County History* records a site 'with a circular setting of stone' in Delamere close to Eddisbury hillfort. In 1937 a possible cist and cremation came to light during ploughing activities, leading to an excavation which revealed a circle of stones just over two metres in diameter. It is possible that a mound may originally have covered the site, as early sources report that several cartloads of stone and two wheelbarrow loads of 'soot' were removed. This could be what is known as a 'kerb cairn' rather than an open stone circle. Kerb cairns, or cairn circles, as they are sometimes called, were essentially burial monuments with an interior mound surrounded by a ring of large kerb stones. Excavations in Delamere uncovered three pits, outside the circle of stones, containing the cremated remains of an infant and an inverted urn, which proved to be a Collared Urn in which was found a small fragment of bronze. Burials are not unknown in and around stone circles, but in light of the other evidence the kerb cairn theory seems more plausible here.

The Grappenhall Circles

Two other sites with circular settings, possibly also kerb cairns, came to light during excavations between 1931 and 1934, in Grappenhall to the south of Warrington. These are now lost beneath a modern housing estate. Unfortunately the results were never properly recorded, but it appears that in the centre of one of the cairns a stone cist was uncovered. Several cremations lay outside the cist and others were discovered in the mound material, one of which was found in association with fragments of an urn and almost certainly a secondary interment. The second cairn contained a primary burial accompanied by a Food Vessel and a saddle quern, and secondary cremations again located in the surrounding mound. Other remains lay in the vicinity of the cairns in association with two Collared urns and another Food Vessel decorated with a maggot or whipped cord design. The indications are that this complex may have been a small cemetery with a multi-phased history.

The Druid's Circle, Alderley Edge

Finally there is one other stone circle still in existence in east Cheshire, but unfortunately it is relatively modern. The Druid's Circle on Alderley Edge is mentioned here, only because it is located in an area which is littered with Bronze Age remains and has been misinterpreted as being authentic in the past.

In her guide book to Alderley and its neighbourhood in 1843, the Hon. Louisa Dorothea Stanley wrote: 'On the road between stormy point and the beacon is a circle of stones placed in the form of a Cromlech or Druidical Circle. An author who was writing some account of Cheshire, put down in his book these stones as real remains of antiquity, and was far from being well pleased when he was undeceived.' The author in question is likely to have been William Marriott, who gave a detailed report of the Druid's Circle stone by stone in his *Antiquities of Lyme,* published in 1810.

In an article in *Cheshire Life* in March 1991 it is claimed that both the Wizard's Well and the Druid's Circle on the Edge, were the work of local author Alan Garner's great-great-grandfather, Robert Garner, a local stonemason. He apparently erected the circle, which is also known as the Hanoverian circle, last century because 'he wanted to get rid of some old stones'.

The Druid's Circle on Alderley Edge, constructed as a folly a couple of centuries ago.

Round Barrows and Cairns

Round barrows and cairns, or 'tumuli' as they are often called, are the most prolific prehistoric monuments in Cheshire, but they have suffered much in recent years due to modern agricultural techniques and quarrying. According to *The Monuments at Risk Survey*, almost half have been completely destroyed, while still more survive only as slight bumps in grassy fields. Nevertheless around a hundred sites are known, almost a third of which have been either excavated by archaeologists or disturbed by road builders and quarrymen. At a further 20 or so sites urns have been found which may once have been covered by a mound, or were perhaps buried in a flat cremation cemetery. This section will cover the most interesting barrow sites,

intriguing either because of their archaeological significance or because they are still worth visiting today. For the real enthusiast a gazetteer of many of the round barrows in Cheshire, both surviving and destroyed, can be found at the back of the book.

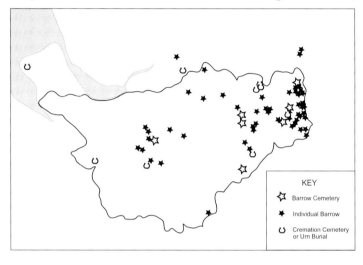

Figure 9 - Distribution of the barrows covered in the text.

In the past barrows have been essentially classed as five types: bowl, bell, disc, saucer and pond, but within each of these broad categories there is some regional variation. Most of the Cheshire sites fall into the first category being composed of a simple round mound resembling an upturned bowl, sometimes with a surrounding bank and ditch. Sizes generally in the UK range between 3 metres and 65 metres in diameter and between 0.3 metres to 6 metres in height, although many are

now considerably larger and flatter due to the actions of ploughing. Tumuli and cairns are usually found singly in Cheshire, although there are a few areas where cemeteries occur, such as Jodrell Bank, Old Withington, Delamere, Church Lawton and Butley near Macclesfield. Such barrow cemeteries are often evenly spaced, either in lines (linear cemeteries) or in clusters (nucleated cemeteries).

By the Early Bronze Age, the round barrow was the most notable type of funerary

An example of a linear barrow cemetery on Overton Hill near Avebury in Wiltshire, giving an idea of how some of the Cheshire sites may have looked prior to ploughing.

monument. Sometime during the Late Neolithic period chambered tombs and long barrows were suddenly abandoned. Their chambers were carefully blocked off and the façades closed. As the ritual focus of the living shifted from the large henges to the smaller localised stone circles, so those of the dead moved from the larger chambered cairns and long barrows to smaller, family-orientated round barrows and cairns. Although these were much smaller than their Neolithic predecessors, they were much more numerous, and so in terms of man-hours still required a similar amount of effort to construct.

Not everyone who died in the Bronze Age was interred under or near a barrow and, apart from the occasional chance discoveries of cremation cemeteries, the final resting-place of the majority of the prehistoric population is unknown. Only certain members of society were chosen to receive special burial. These people may have been selected because of their status or popularity, perhaps local chieftains and their families or people such as bronzesmiths who would have been revered as having magical powers for turning stone into shiny metal. A study of cremated bone from the time has revealed that a much larger deposit of ash was usually collected from the pyre of those who received a primary burial beneath a barrow than from those interred in a cremation cemetery, indicating a more careful search of the debris and burial of their remains. Another explanation, suggested by archaeologists such as Mike Parker Pearson, is that certain individuals may have been given carefully place burials to ensure that they did not come back to haunt the living, perhaps those who had been menacing or troublesome in life.

As with the chambered tombs of the Neolithic, although round barrows were primarily associated with the burial of the dead, they were also a symbol for the living. They are often found on the edge of areas which were under cultivation in the Late Neolithic/Early Bronze Age, between the lowlands and the uplands. In Cheshire the main concentrations lie around Macclesfield on the western fringe of the Pennine slopes, and around Delamere on the eastern flank of the sandstone outcrops of the mid-Cheshire Ridge. There are very few on the Plain itself and where they do occur, they are usually on the fringes of the major river valleys such as the Dee, Weaver and Mersey, indicating that the majority of the lowlands were still covered with dense forest at this period.

Bronze Age barrows were far more than just grave memorials and as Francis Pryor commented recently, 'They were a means of communicating with the higher forces that played a key role in the management of the landscape and people's daily lives'. During the Bronze Age pressures on the land increased as farming became more widespread and society became more organised. Pryor, a professional archaeologist of *Time Team* fame, has been studying Bronze Age landscapes for many years, and he believes that regular spaced barrows were the equivalent of 'spiritual electric fences'. At this time farmers were beginning to mark out the landscape by planting hedges, building fences and digging ditches. These kept the animals where they were supposed to be, but it required something far more powerful to control man. Barrows were thus constructed close to these boundaries where 'the ancestors' could watch over them in order to reinforce land ownership. In some cases they continued to be used for hundreds of years.

Although the mounds themselves can be interesting, it is often their position within the landscape that makes them more intriguing. Some tumuli have prominent hilltop positions such as Reed Hill in Lyme Handley and Nab Head in Bollington, while others, such as Sodger's Hump near Monk's Heath crossroads in Over Alderley, make use of a natural knoll. Many are also sited on hilltops and ridge tops in open country to maximise their visual impact and are often overlooking the banks of a stream or placed at the side of a modern road which probably follows the line of an ancient track. For example, the two barrow cemeteries of Jodrell Bank and Old Withington mirror the courses of the nearby streams; the Beaker barrow of Woodhouse End in Gawsworth overlooks the Macclesfield to Leek road, and the barrow to the north of Beech Hall school in Tytherington near Macclesfield had a commanding view of the Manchester Road before the modern housing estate was constructed. The fact that both were used by the Home Guard as dugouts during the war, testifies to their strategic positioning.

Throughout the UK there are many examples of barrows following the lines of waterways. They are common along the course of major rivers such as the Ouse, Thames and in the Upper Severn Basin. An example at West Deeping near Maxey in Wessex, studied by Francis Pryor, may give a clue as to why this should be so. Here a series of drove ways were discovered running down to the river flood plain along with a series of regularly spaced barrows more or less coinciding with them. It seemed that individual families held parcels of land and used their barrows to mark certain key areas, perhaps where land disputes were likely to occur. Similarly evenly spaced barrows close to rivers are found in Cheshire near Jodrell Bank and Old Withington (see Figure 10).

Archaeological investigations have revealed that barrows were often developed in more than one phase and had a number of burials within them. Some may have been used as 'open' monuments prior to the mound being constructed, with the original phase being a central grave pit (primary burial) surrounded by wooden stakes. Other burials (secondary)

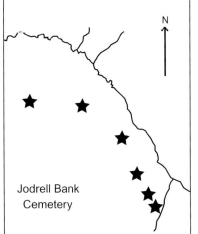

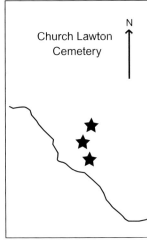

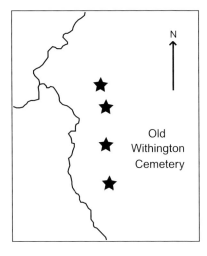

Figure 10 - Barrow cemeteries in Cheshire following the line of nearby watercourses.

were added either around this before and/or after the mound was constructed. Some, such as Church Lawton III, Grappenhall and a site in Delamere, even had circular settings of stone within them.

The material used during mound construction varies according to what was available locally. Technically those made from earth are known as round barrows and those constructed from stone are round cairns. Across Cheshire there is quite a diverse spread of material. For example the tumulus at Bearhurst Farm in Henbury near Macclesfield is made of sand; the mound at Mount Pleasant, destroyed during the building of the modern Macclesfield cemetery, was composed of a central core of boulders covered with alternating layers of sand and gravel; the barrow in the grounds of Sutton Hall close to Macclesfield Forest comprises boulders covered in soil, while others such as the Jodrell Bank cemetery are simply mounds of earth.

Often barrows were not just constructed from one or two materials, but built up in an elaborate series of different coloured layers, reminding one of the glass ornaments containing multi-coloured sands from Alum Bay on the Isle of Wight. For example, at one of the barrows in Old Withington alternating square layers of turf, sand mixed with gravel, and charcoal were carefully layered over the cremation before the overlying mound was constructed (see Figure 14). At Gallowsclough near Delamere excavations in the 1960s revealed a complex series of eight different strata including yellow and red clay, white and grey ash-stained sand and brown soils (see Figure 17). Some archaeologists, such as Anne Woodward, believe that the colours used may have had some significance, for instance red representing flesh and blood, white light and bones and black, darkness and death. In other cases as at Reed Hill, although suitable material was readily available close to hand, specific components were brought from elsewhere. Here, instead of using the soil and turf on this exposed hilltop, considerable effort was expended in hauling up river boulders from the valley below. This may simply have been down to practicalities. Perhaps the barrow builders thought the soil would wash away from the hilltop, or perhaps not. Maybe water held special significance for the person buried here.

As for the burials themselves, almost all discovered so far in Cheshire take the form of cremation. Quite often grave goods are associated with the ashes such as pottery, stone tools or other ornaments which would assist the dead in their journey to the afterlife. These include Beakers, as at Woodhouse End in Gawsworth and Food Vessels (coarse, thick, flat based pots with a decorated shoulder and rim, which are generally contemporary with, but also extending later in date than Beakers) as at Church Lawton II. Also common were Cinerary urns, particularly Collared urns made solely for funerary purposes, like the one found at The Seven Lows in Delamere. These had heavy rims with a tapering body, and in some cases could be as large as 50 centimetres. They were often decorated with 'whipped cord' patterns, resembling maggots in herringbone and lattice arrangements; or in some cases, as in the barrows at Gawsworth and Tytherington near Macclesfield, there was no decoration at all. Sometimes the pottery simply accompanied the burial, while on other occasions the cremated bones were found inside the vessel. Often the urns had been inverted over the remains, resembling the roundhouses of the living with their conical thatched roofs. In other instances, as at Church Lawton and Withington, cremations were even deposited inside leather bags.

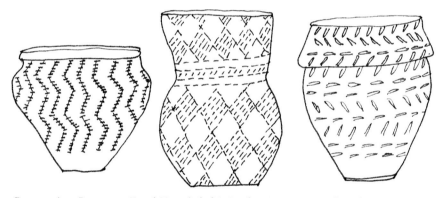

Bronze Age Pottery – Food Vessel (left), Beaker (centre), Collared Urn (right).

Other interesting grave goods include miniature cups, known as pygmy cups which sometimes accompany cremations in urns. Often perforated with one or more holes, they are generally accepted to be 'accessory vessels' which probably had some kind of ritual function, perhaps holding a form of incense which was made from fragrant gums and produced a perfumed smell when burnt. However, in one case reported by Lesley Grinsell, a pygmy cup was found to contain the cremated remains of a baby which may perhaps have been interred with its mother who died in childbirth. A fine example of an incense cup was found in the Cheshire barrow of Glead Hill Cob during building work in the 1870s.

Beaker Graves

The earliest known surviving round barrow in Cheshire is the Beaker barrow at Woodhouse End in Gawsworth near Macclesfield, constructed circa 2000BC. Around 500 years earlier a new phase of burial practice had reached the British Isles, following increased trade with the

Continent. Often referred to as the 'Beaker phenomenon', this development was named after a novel kind of pottery drinking cup, and characterised by burials with an accompaniment of rich grave goods. Beaker ware was a characteristically fine, thin-walled, well-fired drinking vessel, usually red in colour and covered with various zones of complicated geometric decoration over the majority of the exterior surface. Some had handles and a pattern inlaid with a special white paste. It was distributed widely across Europe from the Mediterranean to northern Scotland.

In the British Isles in general, the Beaker burials themselves usually consisted of a single crouched inhumation or cremation, either covered by a small barrow or cairn, placed in a flat grave or cave, or as a secondary interment within a Neolithic long barrow or chambered tomb. Woodhouse End is Cheshire's only intact example and it accompanied a cremation in a newly created round barrow. Sherds of Beaker pottery have also been found on the ground surface below the Church Lawton II barrow; in a pit at Oversley Farm during excavations in advance of Manchester Airport's second runway, and possibly at the Carden Park rock shelter in association with burnt human remains during excavations in 1998.

Another interesting find came to light during excavations at Beeston Castle between 1968 and 1985, when sherds of Beaker ware and other Early Bronze Age pottery such as Collared urns and accessory cups were unearthed from the rampart and the fill of Late Bronze Age/Early Iron Age postholes. A number of flints, including four knives and tanged arrowheads, objects commonly occurring as grave goods, were also discovered, leading to speculation that there may have been one or more round barrows associated with Beaker activity on the hilltop, levelled at a later date.

The closest Beaker concentrations to Woodhouse End lie in the Peak District, one to the south-east of the Arbor Low henge at Middleton and another at Hind Low, south of Buxton. In terms of the Beaker phenomenon, the Gawsworth burial is quite late in date and may represent an outlier of this group.

As well as being accompanied by distinctive pottery drinking cups, the Beaker burials usually also contained a variety of prestigious grave goods. Although copper objects and metalworking had been introduced to the British Isles by this period, stone implements still continued to be deposited with burials for several hundred years. As in the Neolithic, flint daggers, arrowheads, scrapers, stone maceheads, battle-axes and wristguards accompanied the dead on their journey to the next world. Only from circa 2000BC did bronze objects begin to appear.

Above: An Early Bronze Age barbed and tanged arrowhead similar to those often accompanying Beaker burials, discovered in Plumley by metal detectorist, David Bailey.

Woodhouse End Beaker Barrow, Gawsworth

This Early Bronze Age barrow lies at 160m (550ft) above sea level, on the edge of the geological boundary between the Peaks and the Cheshire Plain. It is not positioned on the highest point in the landscape, but overlooks the modern Macclesfield to Leek road, the Macclesfield Canal and the Cow Brook in the valley below which once housed a shallow but wide lake in prehistoric times. It forms part of a multi-phased ritual complex around Oakgrove, consisting of a possible henge to the east and a later Bronze Age round barrow and possible ceremonial avenue on Broad Oak Farm to the north-east. Further evidence for prehistoric activity in the area comes in the form of a fragment of a bronze dagger discovered in the locality by local metal detectorist David Bailey.

A fragment of a bronze dagger (right) found in Gawsworth by metal detectorist David Bailey, along with two pieces of a sword (bottom) and a spear tip (top left) from Bosley.

In the 1960s it was suspected that this mound may be a barrow, and as hedging and ditching operations were imminent, an examination of the site was agreed upon. Excavations were carried out between 1966 and 1968 by the late Gordon Rowley and a team of volunteers, but work was disrupted due to the first Foot and Mouth crisis. All finds were deposited in The Grosvenor Museum in Chester. After a close inspection of the excavation report, an interesting story unfolds.

Almost exactly 4,000 years ago someone of great importance within the local community died. Their remains were cremated on a funeral pyre and their final resting-place was chosen in a prominent spot overlooking a nearby brook and lake. Several centuries earlier, this area had been settled by their Neolithic ancestors and the remains of their domestic activities, broken pots, tools and other refuse, lay in the soil thereabouts. At sometime

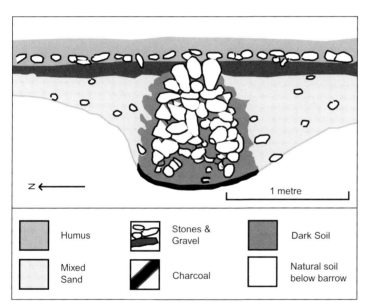

Figure 11 - The Beaker Pit at Woodhouse End (Redrawn from Rowley, JCAS volume 60, 1977).

during the intervening years a tongue-shaped channel had been dug. This was filled with numerous blackened pebbles, probably the remnants of some kind of fire ritual.

The local community worked together to prepare the site, stripping the turf and topsoil and digging a pit. The recently cremated remains, containing some of the pyre ash, were then placed at the bottom of this along with a flint knife and an ornate long-necked pottery Beaker. This highly prized, light buff coloured pot with red and black tones, had been decorated with a comb in hatched triangles and lozenge patterns. It was carefully placed at an angle of 45 degrees with its mouth pointing towards the south-east in the direction of the midwinter sunrise, and packed around with sand (see Figure 11). Once the pit was full, a large beehive-shaped pile of stones

An exact replica of the long necked Beaker found at Woodhouse End, carefully reconstructed by Applepot Pottery on Orkney.

was carefully stacked up over the top. This was then covered by a mound of sand which was excavated from around the edge to create a surrounding ditch, thus the mound contained fragments of pottery and other occupation debris from the earlier settlement activity.

The barrow was then left to stand proud for several generations, but perhaps due to some kind of crisis within the community, such as a land dispute, it again became the focus of attention for the living and the dead. A circular pit, just over a metre in diameter was dug through the barrow fabric. Within this pit, the bottom of which was lined with large cobble-sized stones, some kind of ritual fire was lit. This blazed with such intensity that it turned the surrounding sand red, eventually smouldering away to leave only a thick layer of black ash on the cobbles beneath. Around this time a second oval pit 2.5 metres by 2 metres was hollowed out almost exactly south to north towards the Beaker pit. This was used for burning something other than bone and was filled with cobbles and larger stones. A series of four satellite burials were then placed in an arc in the south-western quadrant, with a fifth close by.

The first burial was that of an adult female and a child over six years of age. They were both cremated on the pyre along with some of their personal belongings including a clay nose or ear stud and some flint tools. Once the flames had died down their burnt bones and personal effects were collected from the ground and deposited in an undecorated and poorly fired Collared urn. This was then placed in an upright position on the floor of the ditch. To some this coarse, gritty pot would seem shoddy and inferior, but it is actually highly unusual to find an urn of this type without decoration.

Andrew Appleby from the Applepot Pottery fashioning the replica Beaker using drawings from the excavation report.

At approximately the same time an adult male, who was perhaps the local potter, and a female who may have been his wife, also died. Again they were cremated with some personal belongings including a flint knife and a set of earthenware mouth bellows. These bellows would help the potter heat his kiln in the afterlife, just as they had done in life. The couple's ashes and cremated bones were carefully collected and placed with an accessory cup in another undecorated urn, which was then inverted onto a layer of gravel close to the first burial.

The third interment was that of a mature adult male between 39 and 45 years of age. He was to receive a different kind of burial with his cremated remains accompanied only by a flint flake and placed in a pit shaped like an inverted beehive, and cut into the floor of the ditch. Close by the cremated remains of another unknown individual were buried, again without an urn. Finally the burnt bones of an unidentifiable fifth person were placed in an urn which was inverted and inserted into the cobbles of the ditch. The Beaker mound was then enlarged with material scraped from another outer ditch and all the features, except this, were covered with a capping of cobbles. The ditch was filled with yet more cobbles (two of which were unfinished stone hammers), earth and refuse including bone, pottery, flint and charcoal. Some of the stones and pottery were deliberately flung into the ditch and broken with such force that archaeologists were still able to see the main points of impact thousands of years later. Barrows often have a surrounding ditch and it is possible that, as well as providing material from which to build the mound, it may also have served as a symbolic feature, separating the area of the burial from that of the living.

Domestic debris is frequently found in and around barrow mounds and ditches in the UK. In the past archaeologists have thought that this was evidence for pre-barrow settlement, but in most cases the structural evidence for buildings such as postholes and pits is not found. Current theories are that specially selected portions of domestic refuse were therefore brought from the settlement areas and deliberately deposited as part of the funeral activities. It seems more likely in this case, however, that the debris from the second phase represents the remains of a ritual feast where pots and flint tools were ritually broken. Perhaps if one of the men had been the local potter as the mouth bellows suggest, then some of his handiwork may have been ritually broken as a mark of respect.

Most of the other general finds unearthed at Woodhouse End were composed of flint. In fact flint objects represented some 90% of the total number of fragments and artefacts discovered. Many of the pieces were very small tools, some of which showed signs of having been refurbished for further use after being broken. Most were damaged and show considerable signs of ware. This highlights just how important flint was to prehistoric people. High quality flint was not readily available in Cheshire and would have to be imported from elsewhere making it a highly prized commodity. Even the smallest fragments were made into tools, and broken objects were reshaped and reused as far as possible. The only other artefacts of note were two jet rings, one found on the barrow surface and one below it. These rings are too large to fit on the finger and too small for the wrist but may have been used as girdle fasteners or belt rings.

The mound's story, however, does not end there in the Late Bronze Age. Almost 4,000 years later, during the Second World War, the Home Guard, realising the strategic positioning potential (but not the fact that it was a prehistoric barrow) used the site as a dugout. Excavators unearthed numerous fragments of Hessian mingled with metal, glass and earthenware including a portion of a clay pipe bearing the name and address of a local maker. Luckily their trench narrowly avoided cutting through the Beaker pit and damaging one of Cheshire's best examples of prehistoric pottery.

Barrow Cemeteries

The Church Lawton Complex

The barrow cemetery known as the Church Lawton Complex lies on land overlooking the watercourse of Hooze Hollow, a tributary of the River Wheelock near Alsager. It originally consisted of an arc of three Bronze Age mounds, but today only two (II and III) survive. Church Lawton I was cut through during the building of the A501 Newcastle to Sandbach road sometime before 1881, and what little remained was completely destroyed during the construction of a petrol station.

As with many of the barrows in Cheshire, Church Lawton III (or South as it is sometimes known) is now nothing more than a slight hump in a grassy field. It is, however, one of the county's most important sites, for beneath the barrow is one of the region's few known stone circles. The other stone circles are covered earlier in this chapter, but for convenience this circle is discussed here with the barrows.

Church Lawton III was constructed in a number of phases and was used as an 'open site' prior to the mound's construction (see Figure 12). Excavations were carried out by Robina McNeil in the early 1980s, revealing a circle, between 22 metres and 23 metres in diameter, of nine huge glacial erratic boulders with entrance gaps to the north and south. Two of the stones stood upright, while the other seven had been deliberately placed on their sides on the old ground surface. Within the circle stood a turf and daub structure around 2.5 metres by 1.5 metres. This appeared to have been burnt and a few fragments of cremated bone were found close by. What this structure was originally used for, no one can be sure, but it is possible that it may have served as an excarnation platform where the remains of the dead were 'exposed to the elements' so that the flesh decomposed before burial. This theme is common in many societies throughout the world where it is believed that the soul lies in the fleshy parts of the body. Corpses were often placed on high platforms in remote places where they were out of the reach of wild animals. Here they could be stripped by the birds and taken off into the sky, thus releasing the soul into the next world. Similar sites have been found across the UK such as at Stoney Middleton in Derbyshire, and the notorious 'Seahenge' discovered a few years ago at Holme-next-the-Sea in Norfolk.

Once it had served its purpose, the turf and daub structure was then covered by a low mound of sand, scraped up from the sub-soil within the circle of stones, and partially surrounded by a turf wall. No burials or cremations were found in association with this mound. Although seemingly strange, empty barrows are quite common throughout Britain, and archaeologists believe that they were perhaps built to commemorate the death of a person whose body could not be buried, for example someone who had drowned or been lost in battle. How-

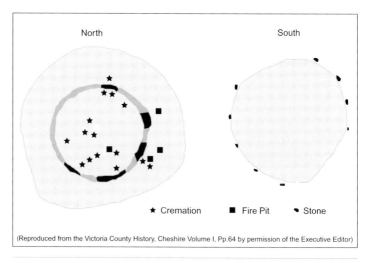

(Reproduced from the Victoria County History, Cheshire Volume I, Pp.64 by permission of the Executive Editor)

Figure 12 – Plan of the two surviving barrows in the Church Lawton Complex (Redrawn from Longley, 1987).

ever, in other cases it could simply be that the bones have been destroyed because of the acidity of the soil in which they were buried.

The second existing barrow, Church Lawton II (North), like its neighbour, was also constructed in two phases. The first consisted of a gravely sub-soil and sand mound surrounded by a ditch, approximately 16 metres in diameter and 1.4 metres high. A 'boat-shaped' pit sealed with a wooden lid was uncovered in the centre and proved to be filled with nothing more than sand. The excavator believed it could easily have housed a crouched inhumation, as any bones would have rotted away in the acidic soil. Eighteen cremation pits were discovered in the covering mound itself along with another four outside the ditch. A few of these hollows contained the tiny remains of foetuses and infants, but for the most part they were those of adults. Also found were two Collared urns, one with a cremation and one without, and two Food Vessels, one inverted and one upright. Two of the cremations outside the ditch were placed in leather sacks, one accompanied by a flint knife and the other by a battle-axe.

This small grassy hump is all that is recognisable of the Church Lawton Complex, one of the most important prehistoric sites in Cheshire.

During the second phase the mound was greatly enlarged with sand and turf to a diameter of around 30 metres. Only one cremation was associated with this development, although archaeological evidence demonstrated that a number of fire pits and pyres had clearly been located at one time in the eastern section. Pottery was also found close to the surface, but unfortunately this was badly plough damaged. Interestingly, according to Longley, sherds of earlier Beaker pottery, very rare in Cheshire, were apparently recovered from the ground surface upon which the barrow was constructed, suggesting the area had been a ritual focus for a great many years.

The Seven Lows

This famous cluster of seven earthen mounds at the head of the valley of Sandyford Brook, has suffered much in recent years. Damaged by ploughing, quarrying and landscaping only four now survive as slight bumps overlooking a valley to the south of Delamere, which was once an area of open water, as is suggested by the name of the nearby Fishpool Farm. Two of the others were so unrecognisable that they were descheduled in 1994.

The earliest mention of The Seven Lows comes from the *Itinerary* written circa 1540 by Henry VIII's chaplain and librarian, John Leland: 'there is a place in the forest of Delamere cawlid the VII Loos wher be seen VII Caste Dikes. The people there speak much of them. I think they were made by men of warre.' The Lows were later described by the local landowner and palaeontologist, Sir Philip de Malpas Grey Egerton, part of whose account appears in the works of Cheshire historian, George Ormerod, in the 19th century: 'The Seven Lows are ranged in form nearly semicircular, and are of different sizes varying in diameter at the base from 105 feet to 40 feet. Beginning at the highest tumulus and following the semicircle, the tumuli measure in diameter 105, 45, 40, 105, 66, 68 feet. One has been removed in the recent alterations of the forest, another was opened at a former period, both of which were composed of the dry gravely soil of the forest, and contained black matter, similar to that which appeared on opening Castle Hill Cob.'

Right: George Ormerod's 19th century plan of The Seven Lows in Delamere.

Egerton continues, 'A tenant of mine, being in want of material to level an old road, opened for that purpose No 6 in Ormerod's Plan. On digging into the mound on the north-east side an urn with bones was found. It was reversed on a flat stone, fragments of charcoal and earth were found over a great part of the floor of the mound. It appears that the *modus operandi* in its construction was this: A circular area of a definite diameter was first selected and floored with a layer of stones; on this the funeral pyre was erected. When the fire was extinguished, the ashes and bones were collected and deposited in the urn, and the latter reversed in such a position near the circumference as not to be crushed by the superincumbent structure. This being arranged the tumulus was formed by a covering of soil. The quantity of stones in this tumulus cannot have been less than 50 tons. The circumference was rather more than sixty yards, and the height in the centre six feet.'

He continues by describing the urn as 'of earthenware, apparently slightly baked or sun-dried. The marks of the latter are visible in the interior. Circumference at the rim 2 feet 7 inches; largest circumference, 2 feet 11 inches, diameter of the foot, 5 inches; height 1 foot 1 inch. At four inches below the rim a raised fillet surrounds the urn, and the portion between the rim and the fillet is rudely ornamented with parallel lines, drawn diagonally in various directions, but never decussating, they appear as if formed by a piece of twisted cord on the soft clay.'

Above: The collared urn discovered in the sixth barrow of The Seven Lows during extraction work in 1845 (Shone).

The further demise of the cemetery is recorded by antiquarian William Shone in the early 20th century: 'The writer visited, in November 1907, the VII Lows, only to find them almost levelled. A slight circular rise in the ground, in places, can be traced with help of the large scale Ordnance Survey map.' Fortunately the site does not seem to have deteriorated too much in the intervening years, but it seems criminal that such an important prehistoric feature has been reduced to nothing more than a few slightly raised grassy bumps.

As discussed in the introduction, the majority of barrow cemeteries in Cheshire mirror the line of nearby watercourses, but although The Seven Lows lie overlooking a dry valley, they do not. Instead they are clustered together in what is known as a nucleated cemetery. Upon studying Ormerod's plan and the relevant Ordnance Survey maps, it soon becomes apparent that the layout of The Seven Lows bears some resemblance to the constellation of The Pleiades, or the Seven Sisters as they are often known. The Pleiades have been noted since very early times and have appeared in the myths and legends of almost every culture on the planet including The Old Testament. In mythology they were seven maidens, the daughters of Pleione, the protectress of sailors, and Atlas, who held the sky on his shoulders. They were transformed into a flock of doves by Zeus and sent up to the heavens to avoid the lustful advances of Orion the Hunter. It is said that their name derives either from the Greek word *plein*, meaning 'to sail' or *peleiades*, translating as 'a flock of doves'.

In reality the Pleiades actually consist of hundreds of stars, but only a few are visible to the naked eye. In modern times with an increase in light pollution often only six are seen. One of the main reasons why this constellation is particularly significant is because it rises at dawn in the spring and sets at dawn in the autumn, traditionally marking the beginning and end of the farming and seafaring season. The Greek poet Homer also refers to its use as a navigation aid in *The Odyssey*, written in the 8th century BC, when he discusses the voyage of Ulysses who 'sat at the helm and never slept, keeping his eye upon the Pleiads'.

To Bronze Age farmers the appearance and disappearance of the star cluster would undoubtedly have been an important event in the annual agricultural calendar. In addition to appearing in literature, the Pleiades have also appeared on a number of ancient works of art, most notably on the Nebra disk, a Bronze Age artefact which was found by treasure hunters in 1999, and came into the hands of the State Museum of Prehistory in Halle, Germany in 2002. The disk has since been dated to 1600BC and chemical analysis has revealed that it was made from bronze utilising copper mined in the Alps. It depicts, in gold, a sun or full moon, a crescent moon, a cluster of seven stars believed to represent the Pleiades, the horizon showing the exact angle of the rising and setting sun at the solstices, and a boat which the ancients believed carried the sun around the world to rise once again after it had set. A number of other stars are depicted on the disk but these bear no resemblance to other constellations indicating that it was The Pleiades that were most significant.

The 3,600-year-old, Nebra Disk, showing what is believed to be the constellation of the Pleiades (between the sun and moon).

Further evidence uncovered recently in Britain indicates that prehistoric people may not only have used certain stars as a calendar, but also tried to replicate the constellations they saw in the sky in their monuments on the ground. For example recent research at the threatened Neolithic henge complex of Thornborough in North Yorkshire, by Glyn Goodwick and Jan Harding of the University of Newcastle, has revealed that the stars of Orion's belt played a key role there in ancient times. Not only did the constellation seem to have been the determining factor in the layout of these three almost identical, evenly spaced henges, but it also appeared to play a significant part in the ritual activities taking place there. Most notable was the framing of Orion in one of the henge entrances as it came into view on the horizon.

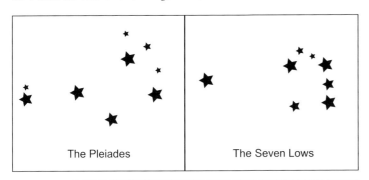

The Pleiades	The Seven Lows

Figure 13 – The Seven Lows compared to The Pleiades

To return to The Seven Lows, as discussed previously, they comprise a cluster of seven barrows, but more intriguingly also have at least one outlier at the nearby Fishpool Farm (Shone actually mentions two). Similarly although the Pleiades are actually referred to as the Seven Sisters, they also have two notable outliers positioned very close together and named after their mythological parents, Atlas and Pleione. The two plans by no means match exactly (see Figure 13) but it is interesting to note the combination of larger and smaller stars/barrows in each, as well as the significant outliers. As the Pleiades appear to have been important to other northern European Bronze Age farmers, is it possible that they also played a role in the lives of the communities living in Cheshire?

Jodrell Bank Cemetery

As at Delamere, this cemetery has also suffered much under the plough. Six barrows originally followed the line of the Redlion Brook in the parishes of Goostrey, Twemlow and Swettenham close to the famous Radio Telescope of Jodrell Bank, but now only four remain. Five of the mounds were described as early as the 19th century again by George Ormerod: 'In Twemlow are five of those tumuli which are of frequent occurrence at the sides of a British road, on which in this case probably the Roman one was grafted. They are nearly equidistant, and stretch along the banks of a small brook for about a quarter of a mile, the present seat of Mr Egerton Leigh standing between the second and third; the fifth is unusually large in its dimensions.'

Today barrows one and two lie to the west of the Chelford to Holmes Chapel Road in the shadow of the Radio Telescope. Both have been heavily damaged by ploughing which resulted in cremations being ploughed up from the largest mound (ii) during potato planting in 1977. On the other side of the road, the house of Jodrell Hall was erected in 1779 some 23 metres (25 yards) from tumulus number three. It is believed that this was done deliberately, because the mound 'would help to break up what might

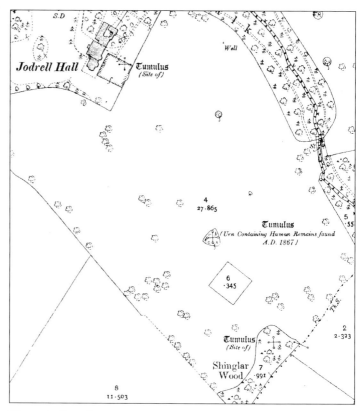

The Jodrell Bank cemetery barrows around Jodrell Hall, now Terra Nova School. (Reproduced from the 1909 Ordnance Survey Map Cheshire Sheet 42.3, scale 25 inches to 1 mile).

otherwise have been a flat and featureless view at that time'. Apparently this was quite common, as Lees-Milne states in his book with regard to Little Moreton Hall 'in the sixteenth and seventeenth centuries the owners of low lying or much enclosed gardens sought outlook, either by raised boundary terraces, . . . or by mounds, as . . . in Cheshire'. Some of these mounds can still be seen in the grounds of Little Moreton today, although it is likely that they are Tudor in origin rather than Bronze Age. Many other Stately Homes in the Cheshire area do, however, possess prehistoric mounds within their grounds; these include Capesthorne, Birtles, Swettenham, Astle Park and perhaps even Tatton. By the 19th century, such distractions were no longer in vogue; by 1897 the mound at Jodrell had been completely levelled during a general landscaping of the grounds referred to by Kaufmann as 'the horticolous execution'. Surprisingly the mounds at other Halls in the area do not appear to have received a similar fate.

As for barrow four, this was apparently opened in 1867 revealing an urn with accompanying cremation and marked as such on Ordnance Survey maps. The opening cannot have done too much damage to the mound, for it remained as a 'notable landmark' until 1950, when it was largely demolished to fill up a 'fosseway' dividing the boundary of the school fields from the outlying ones. Kaufmann noted in 1970, however, that 'it has not completely blended with the fields around it, for, if viewed at ground level, something of its former roundness is visible on the southerly side, which repeated ploughing has failed to eliminate.' Teachers at the school apparently kept a careful watch on things during operations, but no other artefacts came to light. The discovery of the urn in the 19th century was recorded in the *Object Name Book* of the Ordnance Survey Archaeology Division in Southampton. This book kept a record of all discoveries of archaeological importance vouched for by the finder or his agent, but was unfortunately destroyed during a bombing raid in 1940. The only other account comes from a book on the history of the Twemlow family: 'The fourth was opened some years ago, a small funeral urn being found in it which soon crumbled away: it is sandy and full of rabbit burrows.'

The fifth mound, Ormerod's 'unusually large' tumulus, still stands in a small plantation known as Shinglar Wood. Reputedly part excavated earlier this century without results and safe from the plough, it is possible that any burials may still be present. Finally, investigations undertaken by the Archaeology Division of the Ordnance Survey in 1968/69 discovered a previously unrecorded barrow (vi) to the rear of the one in Shinglar Wood. As with one and two this has suffered much under the plough and is now barely discernible.

Withington Hall Barrow Cemetery

This barrow cemetery, approximately three kilometres distant from the one at Jodrell, consists of a series of four Bronze Age barrows following the line of the Dingle Brook near Withington Hall. Again all are currently in agricultural fields and visible only as slight bumps, having been lowered and spread by ploughing over the years. A perforated stone axe-hammer, found two kilometres to the south-east in a potato field near Oakwood Farm in November 1959, was authenticated by The Grosvenor Museum as being 'a typical example of these Bronze Age implements'.

The tumuli in Old Withington were also described by Ormerod in his *History of Cheshire*: 'On entering Old Withington three tumuli lie to the left of the road, also along the course of a brook: the central one is much depressed by the plough, and would elude observation if it

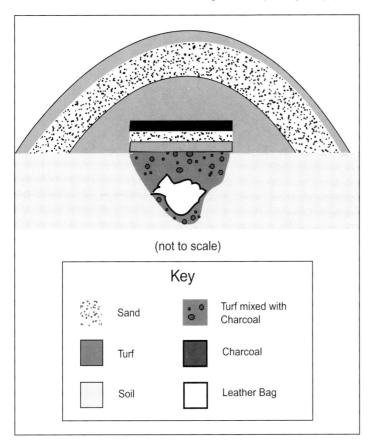

(not to scale)

Key

Sand

Turf mixed with Charcoal

Turf

Charcoal

Soil

Leather Bag

Figure 14 – Plan of the layers in one of the mounds at Withington.

had not been indicated by the others at the extremities. Further on to the right of the road, is a larger one at a distance of about half a mile from it'. The latter, not part of the cemetery, is located near to Brook House Farm, but when surveyed in 1990 proved to be entirely natural.

The first of the cemetery mounds is the most interesting. Excavations by David Wilson of Keele University during 1976 and 1977 on this previously un-dug barrow revealed an intriguing mystery. Within this sand and turf mound (18 metres in diameter and 0.6 metres high) were discovered the remains of an 18-year-old female who appeared to have died sometime around the middle of the 2nd millennium BC (radiocarbon analysis gave a date of circa 1490BC) after receiving a blow to the head. Her cremated bones, the largest ones of which had been carefully broken, had been placed in a leather bag within a D-shaped pit. This was then filled with turf scraped up from the cremation area and sealed off with an elaborate series of layers. Instead of covering the burial with a simple mound of stone or soil, a number of alternating coloured materials were carefully stacked on top. Firstly a square of turf, approximately 0.4 metres by 0.4 metres was placed over the pit containing the ashes. This was then covered by a 3 to 4 centimetre layer of sand mixed with gravel and a similar layer of charcoal, both following the same square shape. Once the ritual had been completed, the mourners set about constructing the barrow mound itself. A roughly circular turf stack was laid around the burial, filled with sand and then capped with turf (see Figure 14).

Around a century and a half later, two or perhaps three, further cremations in urns were added to the mound, one above the female and one to the north-east, accompanied by flint arrowheads, scrapers and blades. The story does not end there, however, for something even more unusual was discovered, just outside the confines of the burial mound, in a two metre long pit to the south-east. At the time of excavation this was thought to be Cheshire's only known prehistoric inhumation burial. Normally these bones would have been destroyed by the acidity of the sandy soil, but luckily for the archaeologists they were resting on the only patch of clay in the pit. A subsequent analysis of the teeth revealed that the remains were those of a child under ten years of age. According to the *County Sites and Monuments Record* radiocarbon dating indicated this burial was not prehistoric but Saxon, dating to somewhere between the 6th and 8th centuries AD.

Several intriguing questions remain – why was this female hit over the head and then buried with such an elaborate ritual. Was it deliberate or was it accidental? Who were the two people that were added later to the mound and what of the inhumation – was the child deliberately buried there because people thought the area was of spiritual significance, or were they buried furtively having died of unnatural causes?

Another interesting piece of evidence revealed during the excavations came from the analysis of soil samples taken from both the pre-barrow soil and the turf forming the mound. Pollen analysis of the soil revealed 'a sad picture of agricultural decline', suggesting that the barrow was constructed at a time when the cultivated land was losing its fertility and slipping back into wilderness. This was further confirmed by samples from the turf where herbs, alder and hazel were so prevalent that archaeologists deduced the site must have reverted to a woodland.

David Wilson also excavated the second smallest barrow (iii), from which an urn containing human remains was reported to have come, in 1982 and 1983. He re-examined a square excavation pit dug in 1835 revealing two main features, each surrounded by a ring of stakeholes. One of these stakeholes was radiocarbon dated to the Late Bronze Age, which was much later than the accompanying finds. These included the substantial remains of six decorated pots (not Collared urns), a Bronze Age barbed and tanged arrowhead, and a trimming flake from a Neolithic polished axe.

In comparison to the first two, little is known of the other barrows in the Old Withington cemetery apart from their size, which has been greatly reduced by ploughing in recent years. They are both barely recognizable, ranging in diameter between 30 metres and 35 metres and less than one metre in height. Perhaps these grassy humps hold similar secrets to the other two.

The Dark Valley Complex

Another supposed barrow cemetery known as 'The Dark Valley' is listed on the *County Sites and Monuments Record*. This lies at almost the same grid reference as the Jodrell Bank cemetery, so it is possible that some of the 'twelve barrows' listed as part of this complex are one and the same. The Dark Valley was discussed in a school project entitled *An investigation of the history of one of the richest archaeological sites in Britain* by J. Garner in 1986. In this work, Garner suggests there was a group of 12 barrows in the parish of Goostrey clustered around Toad Hall, with four outliers to the east. According to the *County Sites and Monuments*

Record one of these, located to the west of the railway line, was excavated by Keele University in 1987 and 1988, revealing a central cremation underneath an upturned broken pot which was radiocarbon dated to circa 1950BC. This central cremation was surrounded by a number of satellite burials, approximately 300 years later in date. The mound is now almost completely levelled by ploughing. Garner also suggests there may have been a henge around the site of the hall, but no evidence is given for this and there appears to be no other literature about this particular site.

Butley Cairn Cemetery

A further cemetery in east Cheshire was mentioned by antiquarians in the early 19th century. Little evidence of the site survives on the ground today, but from the description it appears to have been similar in plan to The Seven Lows in Delamere. In his *History of Cheshire*, Ormerod relates details of this find. The extract is included here in full as it makes an interesting read:

'An account of the discovery of this cemetery in the *Macclesfield Volunteer* newspaper for 1808 states that in that year some men searching for gravel in Butley in a field adjoining the high road between Stockport and Macclesfield discovered, a yard below the surface, what appeared at first glance to be a regular stratum of paving stones, but which on further examination proved to be an assemblage of tumuli, lows, barrows or cairns. The general position of the cairns appears to have been nearly circular, and the particular form of each of an obtuse cone. Around the circumference of the area occupied by these tumuli were placed at intervals large boundary stones, apparently a hundred weight or upwards. The most elevated of the cairns was about ten paces in diameter and about four feet from the base of the summit. Exactly in the centre was an excavation filled with stones.'

He continues: 'The whole of the uppermost stones of which this, but no other tumulus, was composed, exhibited every mark of having undergone the most intense fire, some being shining black, others as if sooted over. The stones underneath were most of them coated with a sort of film or pellicle, which resembled by its gloss and substance a thin coat of bright iron-coloured paint, approaching to a mahogany colour, and which, from fragments of bones among them, appeared to be caused by a plentiful effusion of blood. Near the circumference of this tumulus was found, covered with flat stone and surrounded by three large boulders, an urn containing exclusively ashes, and by the side thereof a collection of human bones. The urn, which was broken by the workmen, had the appearance of metal, being every mark of an iron crust, but was made of clay and coarse sand, and was capable of containing about two quarts English. Near it were some small bits of copper.'

The Food Vessel found in one of the cairns in Butley in 1808, illustrated by George Ormerod (Sainter).

The urn described by the workmen later proved to be a Food Vessel, a coarse, thick, flat-bottomed pot, named thus by antiquarians to distinguish it from the Beaker ware of the period (traditionally associated with holding liquid refreshment). This find is highly unusual, as Food Vessels are not normally used as containers for burnt bones; they just accompany them as grave goods. Interestingly this is not the only occurrence of such curious behaviour in Cheshire. In the Neolithic, people in the area around Eddisbury had used a type of pottery, known as Grooved ware, in a similar fashion. Here again pottery, which ordinarily accompanied burials, was utilised in the fashion of an urn.

Another tantalising snippet comes from the comment 'Around the circumference of the area occupied by these tumuli were placed at intervals large boundary stones, apparently a hundred weight or upwards'. Could this refer to a stone circle which has since been lost? Cairns and stone circles are often found together. Many examples can be seen in the neighbouring Peak District such as at Arbor Low, Stanton Moor and Barbrook on Big Moor.

There has been some debate as to exactly where this cemetery was situated. Longley postulated that it may have been located in the area of some sand quarries to the right of the main

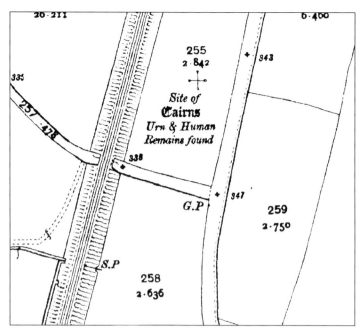

An old OS map showing the location of the cairns in Butley. (Reproduced from the 1909 Ordnance Survey Map Cheshire Sheet 28.16, scale 25inches to 1 mile).

Macclesfield to Poynton road, just past the drive to Hawlanehead. However, early OS maps mark a 'site of cairns, urn and human remains found' slightly further on in the field just after the Bonis Hall Lane junction. The faint traces of a scheduled bowl barrow can still be seen in the corner of this field. This would fit in well with Ormerod's final comments: 'The writer further mentions, that in a corner of the adjacent field, there seems by the gradual ascent of the ground, to be another collection of tumuli.' The remaining barrow has extensive views up through the Harrop Brook valley between Nab Head and Kerridge End, an area dominated by a number of prominently placed barrows (see Figure 15 on page 104).

Individual Barrows

Now it is time to consider some of the more interesting individual round barrows to be found in Cheshire, beginning in the far east on the Pennine slopes and moving across the Plain to Delamere Forest and the mid-Cheshire Ridge. It is not the intention to cover every single barrow in the county, merely to highlight those which are interesting either because of their position within the landscape or because they have been subject to investigation by antiquarians and archaeologists.

Lyme Handley

The area of Lyme Handley, the famous seat of the Legh family, once lay in the Forest of Macclesfield, a wonderful description of which comes from the pages of *Romantic Cheshire* in 1931:

'Macclesfield Forest, bleak, gloomy, desolate, almost savage in parts, retains plain evidence of what it was in olden days when wild beasts were hunted, and when outlaws made it their hiding place. Storms still sweep furiously over that darkling region, and there are guide poles on the high road, for weird tales are told of wanderers lost in the snow, and of furtive crimes long hidden in unpopulated parts. There may the Bowstones be seen, subject of endless speculation and legend; but despite all fantastic surmises there can be little doubt that they marked the boundaries of the Royal desmesne. They may also have denoted trysting places at the converging of pathways – "By a fforest gan they mete, Wer a cross stood on the street," as the old rhyme runs. The road over Sponds Hill branches off where the Bowstones stand, and that seems finally to dissipate the mystery of the why and the wherefore.'

The Bowstones are actually the upper parts of the shafts of double crosses, dating to the 9th or 10th century AD. The crosses were probably destroyed shortly after the Reformation in the mid 16th century. Two cross heads, now in Lyme Park, were ploughed up in a field near Disley Church in the 19th century and may belong to these shafts. The stones were probably erected in their current position at Bow Stone Gate by Sir Piers Legh in the late 16th century, perhaps as boundary markers or guide posts – they stand at the intersection of two long-established routes. From here a number of interesting Bronze Age barrows can be viewed.

The Bowstones located in a small enclosure at Bow Stone Gate in Lyme Handley.

Knight's Low Wood

According to the *County Sites and Monuments Record*, Knights Low Wood in the care of The National Trust on the Lyme Estate, is a barrow hotspot, home to a cluster of Bronze Age mounds. The most well-known is the so called 'Eastern Bowl Barrow', the reputed resting-place of the first Sir Piers Legh who died from wounds received at the Siege of Meaux in the 15th century. (The body of Sir Piers was, in fact, brought back from Paris to Macclesfield for burial, and the Legh chapel, now part of the Parish Church, was created as a memorial.) This enormous mound was discussed by local antiquarian Dr J.D. Sainter in 1878: 'Knight's Low in Lyme Park is a fine, conical and well-wooded hill about 250 feet in height. Its summit forms a rounded platform about 40 paces across it, and some obscure traces of stone and earthworks, (probably the remains of a cairn), are visible on the surface'.

Visits by the Ordnance Survey in 1962 and Longley in 1977 failed to locate this barrow, but John Barnatt describes it in his Peak District barrow survey in 1989 as 'located on a gentle sloping valley side in Knightslow Wood' and consisting 'of a circular earthen mound 7m in diameter by 0.6m high'. It has since been located and scheduled by English Heritage. A second scheduled mound known as the 'Western Bowl Barrow', is close by; it is a circular earthen mound about 5 metres in diameter and 0.5 metres high.

Three further barrows in the vicinity were discussed by the Reverend William Marriott in his *Antiquities of Lyme* in 1810: '3 small tumuli, just beyond the wall which forms the partition of the calf-croft from the Knight's Low. These are not particularly striking, yet have character enough in them to warrant the supposition that they may be composed for small barrows or sepulchres.'

The first, a flat-topped oval mound 0.9 metres high and 9 metres by 7.5 metres in diameter, is located east of the north-south aligned path through the wood. The second, also flat topped and of similar dimensions, can be found on the gently sloping valley side west of this path. The third, known as the 'Bowl Barrow in Knightslow Wood', was described in the 1988 barrow survey as being in poor condition, circa 12.5 metres by 10 metres by 0.3 metres high and located on the north slope of the valley side. However, a subsequent survey failed to locate it.

Finally a large mound to the north-west of Knights Low was also described by the Reverend Marriott in 1810 as 'a large hillock of the finest form. . . evidently not the production of nature, but of artificial formation. Its figure is that of a half-sphere, though considerably broader in the horizontal than the vertical diameter, which is 100 paces. . .no interpretation remains for it but that of having been a barrow or ancient sepulcre'. The mound is huge and therefore considered by modern investigators to be an entirely natural feature.

On a recent visit the authors only managed to locate one of the possible barrows close to the footpath through the wood. There were also a number of interesting stones in the area, one of which had obviously been in position for many years, as it was ensnared by the roots of a mature tree. Could these once have been standing stones or perhaps simply modern boundary markers?

Sponds Hill

Sponds Hill lies on the border between Cheshire and Derbyshire within the estate of Lyme Hall and is reputedly one of the most notable objects to be seen from the Cheshire Plain. The hill, which runs north and south at 411m (1348ft) above sea level with fantastic views across to North Wales, Snowdon and the Great Orme, is home to three Bronze Age tumuli.

Sponds Hill North, stands on the summit of the hill, with a second some 50 metres to the south, however, both are rather dilapidated examples and little is know of their history. The most notable lies on the spur of the hill on a natural mound, known as Reed Hill or Reed's Piece, midway along the ridge.

Breaking the skyline the Reed Hill tumulus is a prominent landmark for miles around, resembling a cherry on top of a cake. This barrow was excavated during the early 20th century, but was not marked on the Ordnance Survey map of that time, despite the fact that it had an Ordnance Mark on it proclaiming its height to be 385m (1263ft) above sea level.

The round barrow on Reed Hill (in the foreground) which stands out as a prominent landmark for miles around.

According to an account in the *Transactions of the Lancashire and Cheshire Antiquarian Society*, operations were carried out from Wednesday 11th to Monday 16th January 1911 (excluding the Sunday) with the permission of Lord Newton, owner of the estate.

The tumulus was found to be almost circular in shape, measuring 14 metres by 16 metres in diameter and standing between 1.5 and 2 metres high from the original ground surface. Around the base there were traces of what may have been a ditch 'but which may possibly have been merely the result of sheep treading for centuries around the mound'. A slight depression running exactly north and south was noticed, indicating that it may have been subject to examination previously.

The excavation team comprised Lord Newton himself, his son-in-law Mr John Egerton-Warburton, Mr Andrew (the author of the report) and one workman only 'because in such cases questions of time and speed are quite secondary to care and observation'. A trench was first cut east to west revealing a mass of tightly packed stones beneath a thin coating of turf. 'The stones were mainly brook or gravel pebbles, varying from the size of a man's fist to that of his head, but there was broken millstone grit also present'. As the author comments, this barrow was constructed in an area where turf abounded so why did they choose to bring up stones from the brooks and valleys below? Perhaps they did it for practical reasons, believing stone would last longer than soil, or maybe it was for spiritual reasons with water holding special significance.

Immediately inside the ditch, a retaining wall of large water-worn stones 'inclining inwards' was discovered. The explorers concluded that this must have been the original face of the tumulus. A little further in, a second retaining wall of natural sandy marl was found which 'represented the edge of a kind of saucer' and followed the contour of the hill. Within this bank on the eastern side, they discovered a few fragments of calcinated human bone with a tiny amount of charcoal. At 5.5 metres from the eastern end of the trench a circular cist composed of 'a circle of stones set upright' was discovered. To the annoyance of the excavators it looked as if this had been explored previously as the capstone was missing, the cist itself was filled with stones and three or four of the side stones had been thrown down. Not a single trace of human remains was to be found, so they concluded that any burial must have been in an urn which had been completely removed during previous investigations. The capstone of the cist was later found to be the large flat stone upon which Ordnance Surveyors had cut their benchmark.

The cist was built on the natural ground surface and its stones were standing on the level, the excavators therefore concluded that it must have been a secondary interment, dug some time after the mound was constructed. The ground must have been solidified before the cist was built, otherwise the weight of the barrow would have pressed the stones into the soil. Heartened by this discovery, the men pressed on in the hope that the main burial still lay undisturbed.

The third day, Friday 13th, lived up to its reputation and proved to be 'a blank day'. However, on the Saturday, whilst continuing work in the northern section, the explorers soon discovered a curious drain-like formation at floor-level. It was 'composed of a small trench about six inches wide, bounded by side stones of four or five inches high, covered over with cap-stones, like a stone drain. It slanted back towards the centre and a walking stick could not determine its length'. They immediately began to try and remove the stones, when a collapse revealed a second cist within inches of both trenches.

This cist proved to be very unusual – 'It was set in foundations about eight inches below the level of the floor, circular in plan, and dry-built of gritstone into the form of a perfect beehive, being two feet six inches in diameter and two feet high, inside measurements'. Within was a mass of cremated bones 'But it was now dark, and further examination was reserved for Monday'.

Upon their return the cist construction had collapsed revealing a heap of badly eroded bones but 'a most painstaking sifting of the contents of the cist disclosed not a trace of man's handicraft'. The excavators concluded their investigations by replacing the remains in the cist and restoring the mound to its original condition. A deposit of new copper coins and a scratched slate with details of the operations were left for posterity.

A modern beehive-shaped cairn in Rainow giving an idea of how the cist at Reed Hill may have appeared before collapse.

Bollington and Pott Shrigley

In the second edition of Ormerod's *History of Cheshire* only one line in a foot note is donated to a discovery in Pott Shrigley which tantalisingly could have proved most interesting: 'In Saltersford it is said that a bronze sword blade, and horns of wild cattle, were dug up, in or about the year 1874-5.' If this were the case it would have been a highly significant find as very little Bronze Age metalwork is known from the Cheshire area.

It is unclear where, exactly, this discovery came from, but the parishes of Bollington and Pott Shrigley were once home to a number of prehistoric barrows. Only two of any note, Nab Head and Further Harrop, survive today. Others included Big Low or Bug Low, which originally stood in Bollington between the railway and the canal to the north of Clarke Lane and south of the Adelphi Mill, before it was completely obliterated by quarrying activities.

A second known as Andrew Knobb at Pott Shrigley was described by Reverend Marriott in 1810 as 'a large circumference of earth, but so exceedingly defaced, as to leave only a probability of its having been a sepulchral barrow.' Surveys in 1978 and 1988 however failed to find any trace of this barrow, but there was a large amount of disturbance and quarrying in the area which may have accounted for its disappearance.

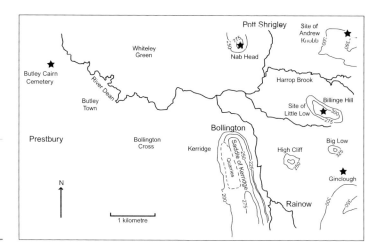

Figure 15 – Plan of the barrows in the Harrop Brook Valley. Reproduced by kind permission of Ordnance Survey.© Crown Copyright NC/04/26823.

The region around Pott Shrigley (and indeed the neighbouring parish of Rainow) is interesting from a topographical point of view. Many of the barrows in the area are placed in strategic positions on the watersheds overlooking streams and rivers and seem to be acting as territorial markers for individual parcels of land. One particular example of note is centred around the valley of Harrop Brook, which runs down from the Pennines to the Cheshire Plain and eventually joins up with the River Dean in Bollington (see Figure 15). In prehistoric times this pass would have been one of the main routes from the lowlands to the uplands.

Prominently placed examples around the Harrop Brook valley include the now destroyed barrow of Little Low on Billinge Hill, which lies in a parcel of land on the watershed between Mellow Brow Brook, Harrop Brook and the unnamed watercourse that passes through Oakenbank; the now destroyed barrow of Andrew Knobb to the north, which again lies on the watershed between Black Brook, Harrop Brook and an unnamed brook rising in Pott Shrigley; the prominent tumulus on Nab Head and the barrow on Black Rock Farm in Ginclough. Interestingly this leaves a convenient gap to the south of the River Dean on the saddle of Kerridge, with the ideal location for a barrow on the site of the recently modern folly of White Nancy. Another seemingly interesting fact about the mounds around the Harrop Brook valley is that they all have views looking down through the gap and out over the Cheshire Plain, across the area where the Butley cairn cemetery once lay on the floodplain below.

Nab Head

The barrow is situated in a prominent position on the top of Nab Head (hence the triangulation point) overlooking the east Cheshire town of Bollington. The now vandalised barrow has 360-degree views across the Cheshire Plain to the Berwyn and Clwydian Hills; across south Manchester to Lancashire, and east to the foothills of the Pennines taking in Windgather Rocks, Macclesfield Forest and Croker Hill. A visit is highly recommended. As for the mound itself, although scheduled, it has been damaged by stone quarrying and the erection of an Ordnance Survey trig point. In 1960 it was said to be 12 metres in diameter with an external ditch 27.5 metres in diameter and 0.3 metres deep, but by 1964 all traces of this had vanished.

The round barrow on Nab Head, capped today by an Ordnance Survey trig point.

Further Harrop

Within the Peak District National Park (but still in Cheshire) this well-preserved, scheduled Bronze Age barrow is found four kilometres north-east of Bollington, just below the top of a rounded knoll which forms part of a narrow steep sided watershed between Goyt Valley and the tributaries of the Mersey, the Bollin and Dean. It has almost 360-degree views, but with a bias towards the south and west where it looks across to Croker Hill and Bosley Cloud, then out to the Cheshire Plain through the Harrop Brook valley and over the saddle of Kerridge. To the north-east it looks up to the barrow of Reed Hill on the skyline, with views to the east opening up across the Goyt Valley towards The Cat and Fiddle. Described as a 'bowl shaped round barrow' in John Barnatt's 1996 *Barrows in the Peak District,* the mound is approximately 40 metres in circumference, 15 metres in diameter and just over one metre in height, having been spread by ploughing in recent years.

The barrow of Further Harrop in Pott Shrigley looking down through the
Harrop Brook Valley in the mist below.

Rainow

The parish of Rainow, in the hills above Macclesfield, houses a number of interesting tumuli, the most famous of which, Pike Low, was sadly destroyed by quarrying in the 19th century. A similar fate may have befallen that described by Dr Whitaker in his *History of Manchester,* the account of which is repeated by Sainter. This states that on September 27th, 1791, a tumulus was opened on Macclesfield Common, which contained 'some charcoal ashes and a few remains of burnt bones with no urn' and notes that 'perhaps if a more careful examination had been made, a flint instrument would have turned up'.

In addition to the scheduled sites listed below various other mounds litter the hillsides of Rainow, but it is believed that the majority of these are not prehistoric but probably slag heaps associated with coal mining activities on Macclesfield Common in recent centuries. One other discovery of note was referred to by William Shone in the early 20th century, when 'part of a stone saddle-back quern, 19 ³/₄ inches by 14 inches' was found by the side of a road near Rainow by T.C. Horsfall and donated to The British Museum.

Black Rock Farm, Ginclough

The first site of interest lies close to the main road through Rainow on a small terrace to the west of Black Rock Farm in the hamlet of Ginclough. Located on a south-west facing slope, the tumulus is almost untouched, apart from a hollow on the top and in the south-eastern section, which may have resulted from an undocumented excavation. As with the barrow at Further Harrop, it appears to have been strategically placed to take advantage of the view through the gap created by the Harrop Brook, looking down towards the Plain and the area of the Butley cairn cemetery. The view towards the barrow on Nab Head is blocked however by Big Low.

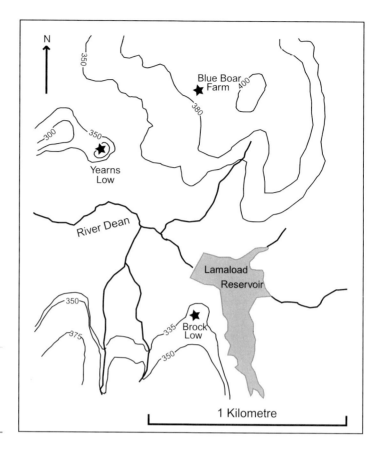

Figure 16 - The Rainow barrow triangle. Reproduced by kind permission of Ordnance Survey.© Crown Copyright NC/04/26823.

Blue Boar Farm

To the south-east of Black Rock Farm is an interesting triangle of barrows, which also seem to have been placed, for the most part, to be inter-visible with each other (see Figure 16). The first, mentioned by Sainter in his *Scientific Rambles Round Macclesfield* as being 'more or less disturbed', is the scheduled conical mound in a field opposite Blue Boar Farm. Standing on a naturally level platform on the ridge top, this tumulus was originally around 20 metres in diameter, but because of ploughing it is now closer to 31 metres by 26 metres. It was excavated in 1972, but unfortunately there are no records as to what, if anything, was found.

The large round barrow, visible from the road, close to Blue Boar Farm in Rainow

Yearnslow

A second intriguing bowl-shaped mound is situated on a knoll 358m (1175ft) above sea level close to the nearby Yearnslow Farm. Again, it is placed to look down across the Plain through the Harrop Brook valley and over the saddle of Kerridge to the west. To the north-west a gap opens up to Big Low and the view beyond but this is soon truncated by the spur of land in front. In the other direction, views extend across to Brock Low above Lamaload Reservoir and up

The barrow of Yearnslow (in the centre) under the line of a modern dry-stone wall.

to Cat's Tor, sweeping back round to the neighbouring mound of Blue Boar Farm to the north-east. The barrow was reputedly opened by some Derbyshire explorers in the 19th century and is also mentioned by Sainter: 'that near the Yanslow farm was investigated some years ago, when some Roman coins, glass beads, and bones were found in it.' Today the mound, which is around 19 metres in diameter and just over one metre in height, is covered by ruined dry-stone walls.

Brock Low

Also in the Parish of Rainow is Brock Low, a huge mound which is almost certainly natural, but may have been used by prehistoric man as a burial site. Located in a field to the right of Lamin Load Farm, it was described by Sainter in 1878 when it was reportedly 142 metres in circumference and 7 metres high. A survey in 1988 revealed that much of the mound had been removed by quarrying and was then only circa 58 metres by 48 metres in diameter. The interior had been robbed away. It was composed of sand and rounded pebbles and could possibly be glacial, but may have contained some secondary prehistoric burials. Interestingly Brock Low has clear views across to Yearnslow, but the sightline to the barrow at Blue Boar Farm is blocked by the slopes of Waggonshaw Brow.

The huge mound of Brock Low overlooking Lamaload Reservoir.

Charles Head Farm

Finally there is the scheduled Bronze Age bowl barrow built on a slight knoll on the northern flank of a saddle near Charles Head Farm, to the east of the main Macclesfield Road. Another typical example of a watershed barrow, it is placed to overlook the valley of Gnathole Brook, a tributary of Todd Brook. Approximately 14.5 metres by 13 metres in diameter, it is overlain by a dry-stone wall and remains largely undisturbed. Three grey flint scrapers were ploughed up in the field close by.

Macclesfield, Tytherington and Prestbury

Moving on down from the hills into the town of Macclesfield (famous for its silk) and the nearby villages of Tytherington and Prestbury, a few mounds of note can still be seen. There may have been many more in the area, which have long since disappeared under modern buildings and landscaping projects. One such tumulus was believed to have stood on what was known as the Castle Field at the lower end of Park Lane and adjacent to Old Park Lane in Macclesfield. Recent extensive building work in the area has revealed nothing to support this claim, nor the suggestion that a Norman Castle had once occupied the site. The 20th century historian Walter Smith also described two mounds mentioned in the 19th century – Great Lowe and Pye Lowe, close to Moss Lane on the edge of Danes Moss. All traces of these have subsequently disappeared.

The area around Danes Moss, the majority of which is now covered by a landfill site, must have been important during prehistoric times for in addition to the two tumuli mentioned above, the Beaker barrow, discussed previously at Woodhouse End, and a possible stone circle in Henbury, both lie on the fringes of the Moss. A number of prehistoric finds have also come to light over the years, found by the turf men digging for peat.

In addition to the bones and horns of an ox and the antlers of a buck, they have also unearthed numerous curiosities, most of which were probably relatively modern, such as swords, muskets, bridle bits, stirrups and coins. However, close to what is known as 'The Bone Works', a limestone hammer, an ancient iron crossbow and an iron spearhead were discovered. Sainter also mentions two querns, which he had seen in the Stoke-on-Trent Museum, found when cutting through the Moss for the railway. In his words 'They are of very rude workmanship, and must certainly date from a very remote period of art'. One has since been dated to the Iron Age.

Above: Red Deer tines and an oak paddle found in a peat bog in Tytherington in 1869 (Sainter).

Similar interesting finds have also been exhumed from the area around Tytherington Fields, most notably during the construction of the Marple Line in 1869. Again according to Sainter, workmen discovered two red deer tines (i.e. the pointed branches of deer's horns) in a bed of solid peat bog and an ancient oak paddle 'of early coracle age' close by. A perforated stone hammer dating to the Bronze Age was also found in the area by Dr W.H. Clarke.

Mount Pleasant, Macclesfield Cemetery

During the creation of the Macclesfield Municipal Cemetery in the 19th century, between Prestbury Road and Westminster Road, a number of interesting prehistoric discoveries came to light. Near the brook, which babbles along below the modern crematorium, a baked clay net-weight or net-sinker of 'early English date', according to The British Museum, was found about 2.5 or 3 metres below the surface; while in the valley gravel some bones and teeth of an ancient British ox (the *Bos longifrons*) were discovered. Evidence also revealed that the site of the modern cemetery had been the focus of a prehistoric burial thousands of years earlier. In 1878, Dr J.D. Sainter mentions an ancient mound that stood on the ground before it was levelled to make way for modern burials:

'Behind Mount Pleasant, Prestbury Road, there is to be seen a tumulus which when explored a few years since, yielded a Neolithic or later-stone age burial [now known to be Bronze Age]. At the foot of the mound westward, there are the remains of a peat bog; and an oblong block of greenstone, weighing 25 pounds, was taken out of it, that had been used by the ancient Britons as a hand-grain rubber or triturating stone...'

The barrow at Mount Pleasant, destroyed during the construction of the Macclesfield cemetery in the 19th century (Sainter).

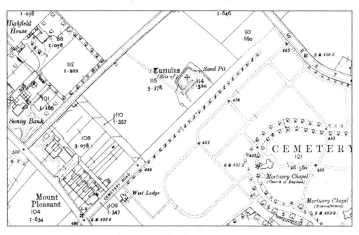

An old map showing the site of the barrow in the modern cemetery. (Reproduced from the 1909 Ordnance Survey map Cheshire Sheet 36.08, scale 25inches to 1 mile).

Sainter continues: 'The following is the result of an exploration of this barrow. Upon an oblong mound of the drift, 30 yards in diameter at the base, and 25 feet in height, 15 feet in thickness of earth had been added to form a barrow. After clearing off the surface soil, a depth of 18 inches of sand and gravel was removed. Below this came alternate levels of sand and gravel (partaking of an arched form), which were five feet in depth, succeeded by a heap of boulders that formed a cairn three feet in height and twelve feet in diameter; and some of the stones were split and blackened by fire. Upon the removal of the greater part of them, the following was the result; upon three stones placed in the centre and at the bottom of the pile, which rested upon the natural surface of the mound of drift, there was a collection of calcinated human bones and teeth, and between two stones placed on the north east side of the bones, there was picked up a highly polished flint saw, with a very fine serrated edge, that measured four inches and a half in length and one in breadth'.

Beech Hall Barrow and Urn Burial, Tytherington

Two interesting sites lie within a hundred metres of each other in the village of Tytherington on the outskirts of Macclesfield, in what today is a modern housing estate and internationally renowned golf club. The first, affectionately known as 'Tellytubby Hill' by the locals, is a Bronze Age round barrow located in a cul-de-sac on a knoll to the north of Beech Hall School. As at Woodhouse End, the site was used as a dugout by the Home Guard during the Second World War. In 1973 an investigation of a spoil heap from one of their trenches revealed 19 small fragments of pottery and a small quantity of calcinated human bones. The sherds were described as being red on the outside and black in the interior, some of which were decorated with dots and believed to be the remains of a Collared urn.

The Bronze Age barrow in the middle of a modern housing estate in Tytherington near Macclesfield.

A second burial site of interest was unearthed 92 metres south during building works in June of 1960. An account of the discovery comes from the *Transactions of the Lancashire and Cheshire Antiquarian Society* in that year. This states that 'during the construction of a new swimming pool at Beech Hall School, Macclesfield, the contractors exposed a Bronze Age cinerary urn containing a cremation burial'. The discovery was reported to the Headmaster and he, with the help of members of staff, 'took immediate steps to salvage the urn, which was recovered, practically complete'.

The urn was found 0.6 metres below the level of the present ground surface in the natural sand and had been inverted onto a layer of gravel. Now in the store of The Grosvenor Museum in Chester, the vessel is a rare undecorated example of a Collared urn with an overhanging rim and marked with an internal bevel. It is reddish brown in colour and can be dated to the Middle Bronze Age, perhaps circa 1400BC to 1200BC. A similar example was found in the Beaker barrow at Woodhouse End. The cremated remains were subsequently identified by Professor Cave of St Bartholomew's Hospital Medical College as those of an adult female around 20 years of age. Interestingly some of the bones had a greenish tinge as though they had originally been in contact with some kind of metal object.

It was impossible to say whether the urn was ever covered by a barrow, as the ground had been thoroughly levelled for tennis courts many years earlier. However, given its proximity to the barrow on the housing estate, it seems highly likely.

Sutton and Macclesfield Forest

The area of the modern day Macclesfield Forest is rich in prehistory with a variety of flint tools and weapons being found in the vicinity. Most notably is a fully polished flint axe found some years ago in a field near the Leather's Smithy public house, and a huge Neolithic ceremonial axe discovered in the River Bollin in Langley by a Macclesfield school boy a couple of years ago. (Even Stonehenge made an appearance in the parish during 2003 when it was depicted in a well dressing for Sutton village.)

Sutton Hall

Leaving Macclesfield in the direction of The Forest, the first parish visitors will come to is that of Sutton. Located on the boundary between the Pennines and the Cheshire Plain, in a field adjacent to Sutton Hall (just off Bullocks Lane) is a somewhat dilapidated Bronze Age barrow, now home to a water trough. Lying on a shelf of land above a tributary of the River Bollin, the barrow is overlooked by Tegg's Nose and Macclesfield Forest to the east and Croker Hill to the south.

The following account was related to a members' meeting of the Macclesfield Scientific Society by the Vice-President, Mr T.J. Smith, in 1877 in a paper entitled *Grave Mound Exploration near Macclesfield*: 'after a conversation with Miss Bent, and by the permission of

Mr Thompstone, the large mound at the rear of Sutton Hall has been opened; there has always been much speculation as to its origin and purpose, and I had hoped by to-night to have been able to say something definite about it, but all I can say is that we have entered it by a trench some twelve feet long, six feet wide and eight feet deep, and have up to the present time found no remains. It is entirely composed of boulders, some split by the action of fire. The investigation will be continued.'

The tumulus in a field adjacent to the grounds of Sutton Hall near Macclesfield.

It would be another 85 years before this happened when it was partially excavated in 1962 by James Forde-Johnston of Manchester University, who had investigated another mound in Cheshire at Gallowsclough in Delamere two years previously. He unearthed a few secondary cremations, but no primary burial. According to the *County Sites and Monuments Record* he revealed that the mound had originally been around 100 yards (91 metres) in diameter, but was since substantially reduced with many of the river cobbles having been removed to the nearby farmyard. This is unfeasibly large for a round barrow and would mean it was one of the largest in the country. It must therefore be presumed that this is a typing error. Despite being scheduled in recent years, in addition to the damage caused by cattle drinking from the water tank, the site has suffered from other local wildlife activity. A badger sett can be seen to the south-east, and elsewhere rabbits have made their burrows.

Langley

Moving onwards up into what was once the wild realms of Macclesfield Forest, where the lairs of wolves, wild boars and bears were prevalent, we come to a number of interesting mounds, some presumed natural, others not. One of the most notable areas is that around the Bottoms and Teggsnose reservoirs where visitors flock to admire the nesting herons and watch the jumping fish. An interesting discovery was made during repair work in Langley in the 19th century. Sainter gives a full account of what was found:

'a few months ago, as some labourers were engaged in repairing a reservoir, upon arriving about three feet below the surface, one of them struck his pickaxe into something which he took to be a drain-pipe, but it proved to be a sepulchral urn of the genuine Celtic type, containing a quantity of burnt human bones, apparently those of a young person, and a finely polished flint arrowhead of the leaf pattern, likewise some fragments of a barbed arrowhead that had been partially calcinated.'

'The whole had been deposited upon the bare soil, and formed into a heap, with the urn inverted over it, and its dimensions had been about 8 inches in height, 7 in breadth, gradually tapering down to 4 inches at the bottom. Upon examination of the natural surface of the ground where the interment had taken place, there was nothing unusual to be seen indicative of its site; around the urn, however, at the bottom of the trench, the soil had been deeply tinged with carbonaceous matter, bits of charcoal and blackened stones'. The urn found was highly ornamented with maggot type decoration, zigzags, lines, twisted cord impressions, and two rows of chevrons. Its whereabouts at present are not known.

The urn and arrowhead found during work on a reservoir in Langley in the 19th century (Sainter).

Sainter continues 'Near the head of the above reservoir at Langley, may be noticed a large conical mound which has the appearance of a tumulus; and a little further on the road towards the Leather's Smithy, close to a farm house on the left, there is another tumulus which has evidently been investigated.'

These two mounds can still be seen today. Neither has been investigated by modern archaeology so it is impossible to say whether they are authentic or not. However, the first conical shaped tumulus is located in a very prominent position over-looking the two former stream valleys which are now dammed to form the modern reservoirs. It can be seen from quite a distance on the roads overlooking the valley to the south and east. According to the experts it would be an obvious site for a Bronze Age burial. On the other hand, it could just as easily be a spoil heap from the building of the reservoirs. The second, known as 'High Low', lies on land belonging to a farm of the same name 300 metres to the south-east of the conical mound. The site has been heavily quarried and usually stands out from the surrounding pasture as a rough, overgrown mound.

The prominent conical mound between the Bottoms and Teggsnose reservoirs in Langley, very similar in profile to the one illustrated by Dr Sainter in Macclesfield cemetery. (see page 109).

Macclesfield Forest

Two further barrow candidates lie deeper within the forest area. The first close to Toot Hill was sketched by Sainter and referred to by the Macclesfield Scientific Society in 1878: 'In Macclesfield Forest, Warilow is the name of a site on the same hill where the Roman camp is situated, and which I imagine to be the site of a battle between the Britons and the Romans for the possession of the hill.' These earthworks of a so-called Roman camp have been the subject of discussion for many years, and theories, ranging from a Neolithic enclosure or Late Bronze Age/Early Iron Age hillfort to a medieval deer pound, have abounded. The latter interpretation is now acknowledged in the *County Sites and Monuments Record*. However, it is still possible that prehistoric man did use this area, for a telling piece of evidence comes from a manuscript by Dr Foote Gower dated 1774, now in The British Museum: 'About thirty years ago one of these implements of flint, which usually go by the name of British axes, was discovered within the vestiges of a Roman camp, in Macclesfield Forest, and presented to the late Earl of Falconberg, the proprietor of the soil.'

Left: The tumulus above Toot Hill in Macclesfield Forest illustrated by Dr Sainter in 1878.

The barrow itself is situated to the south-west of the summit of Toot Hill overlooking the Upper Bollin Valley, and is composed of earth and stones in an oval mound circa 8 metres by 13 metres in diameter and 0.7 metres high. A standing stone of gritstone 0.6 metres wide by 8 centimetres thick once stood in the centre. Experts believe it may be a natural knoll surmounted by a relatively modern boundary marker, but only an excavation will suffice.

Finally we come to the tumulus of Rains Low in Forest Chapel, the hamlet famous for its rush-bearing ceremony which still takes place at the local church in August. Sitting on a spur, on the watershed between the source of the River Bollin and the Clough Brook, a tributary of the Dane, this barrow has spectacular views through 360 degrees. To the south the tip of the triangular peak of Shuttlingsloe peeps out over the top of Buxtors Hill; to the east views extend across to The Cat and Fiddle sweeping round to Shining Tor, the highest peak in the area; to the west lies the prominent landmark of Toot Hill with its mysterious earthworks, mentioned above. Very little is known about the history of the barrow itself, except that it was supposedly opened by 'Derbyshire explorers' in the 19th century and has been greatly reduced by quarrying.

Wincle and Swythamley

In addition to The Bullstones (see the stone circles section) and the possible Neolithic long barrow at Bartomley Farm mentioned previously, there are a number of interesting mounds in the vicinity of Wincle. Finds from the area include a perforated flint object, possibly a macehead, which was discovered during the 19th century at the Old Wincle Grange when a portion of the foundations was being removed.

Another possible prehistoric feature was discussed by the Macclesfield Scientific Society in the 19th century in a field close to Clulow Cross. Described as 'a remarkable mass of stone . . by many considered to be the work of prehistoric man' this was believed to be what is known as a 'rocking stone'. It consisted of two parts: a large mushroom shaped stone, two metres in diameter, which was carefully balanced on a smoothly rounded stone stalk. The upper stone, weighing several tons, apparently bore 'unmistakable evidence of man's work', having been chipped away carefully so as to accurately poise it on its rounded point.

These so-called 'rocking stones' are fairly common and are generally agreed to be natural boulders which have weathered in such a way that they are poised in equilibrium. They may have been used by prehistoric men for ritual purposes, but were not created by them. Two famous examples, which could be easily rocked 'by a child', once stood on Rowtor Rocks at Birchover in Derbyshire.

Clulow Cross and Cessbank Common

The broken millstone grit pillar of Clulow Cross stands about 3 metres high on a large conical mound close to the A54 Congleton to Buxton road. Some, including Sainter, believed it to be an enormous tumulus: 'This wayside cross, once so common, is placed upon the summit of an artificial mound of earth. . .This mound, or tumulus, is 250 feet in diameter, 25 feet high'. This does seem unrealistically large for a barrow and is more than likely a natural feature, but that does not mean that it was not utilized by prehistoric people. Often secondary burials were added into the mounds hundreds of years after they were originally constructed. Who is to say that the Later Bronze Age communities did not mistake a natural mound for one built by their ancestors? It may have happened at Birtles Hall in Over Alderley where gravel diggers, quarrying a natural mound in the grounds of the hall in the 19th century, discovered a Collared urn. This may also be true of sites such as Brock Low and the Conical Mound in Langley.

The mound at Clulow Cross, believed to be of prehistoric origin.

The whole area around Clulow was examined in detail by Dr J.D. Sainter and the members of The Macclesfield Scientific Society in the 19th century. *The Proceedings* of the Society, of which Dr Sainter was the President, reveal that some members spent several days examining the area and discovered 'a well-defined grave mound' midway between Clulow Cross and the Four Lane Ends. 'In height it was about two and a half feet, oval, measuring from north to south about fourteen feet, and from east to west about ten feet. Around the mound was an irregular circle of stones, but most of them entirely covered with grass and bilberry bushes.' This site, now quite badly eroded, lies on the southern edge of Cessbank Common close to a public footpath and is surmounted by the grave of a dog named Rex.

During excavations a 1.2 metre wide trench was cut across the middle and beneath a layer of dark topsoil, a thin layer of sand and gravel was discovered covering a grave mound composed of boulders. The largest boulders had been placed around the base with smaller ones on the top and in the centre. The trench was further extended until it was two metres across revealing, in the words of the excavator, 'a soft mixture of white sand with a black layer in it'. Unfortunately 'it was raining very heavily at the time, and had been almost the whole five hours while I was in the trench, I could make but very little of this white and black puddle. I took out more of it and placed it in my specimen case'.

The white proved to be 'a calcination of the neighbouring grit and phosphates' and the black 'oak charcoal'. Further examination continued the next day, and after another widening of the trench, 'a funeral urn was discovered *in situ*'. Unfortunately it collapsed upon removal but enough fragments were preserved to identify it, particularly at the base where root fibres from plants had held it together. 'The urn measured four inches at the top, and the same at the bottom; it was eight inches in height and eight in width across the middle. The top portion is ornamented with the usual Celtic herring-bone pattern'.

Within the urn a 'good specimen of a sling-stone' and a number of smaller triangular shaped stones, which the writer suggests may have been broken arrowheads but were more likely to have been included accidentally. He concludes by stating 'Not far from the spot I have been describing are the remains of a cist under which our President (Mr Sainter) and others found a portion of an urn.'

Bartomley Farm, Swythamley

In the grounds of Bartomley Farm in Swythamley, not far from the suspect long barrow (The *County Sites and Monuments Record* actually places it at the same grid reference), is a tumulus which over the years has reputedly produced some high status treasures. The following account comes from the pages of *Scientific Rambles Round Macclesfield*: 'where the ground has been used for agricultural purposes, there has been turned up gold rings, chains, fibulae &c. The soil is of sandy character, with some small foreign pebbles in it, which denote its Glacial Drift origin. Of this deposit there may have been formed a small tumulus containing either a Roman or Saxon burial; and this, (probably for the object of plunder), has been levelled, and the above ornaments had escaped the notice of the marauders. Or, without any tumulus, the articles may have been stolen, and hid or secreted for safety by the owners'.

Sir Philip Brocklehurst, owner of the Swythamley estate, elaborated further in his book about the neighbourhood of Swythamley, describing a number of artefacts discovered following ploughing in the area: 'At Bartomley. . . have at various times been discovered in considerable number of Roman antiquities, consisting of gold rings, in one instance with a curious green stone called prez., together with gold ornaments: considered by Mr Meyer, the well-known antiquarian of Liverpool, to be bosses or shield ornaments, the last discovery being a very beautiful fibula of virgin gold.' Gold objects such as these are incredibly rare in Cheshire. The only other record that we have come across to such rich artefacts comes from William Thompson Watkin's *Roman Cheshire* where he reports the discovery in 1831 of two gold bracelets of twisted torque pattern, found while excavating for a cottage near the site of Egerton Old Hall near Malpas.

Newbold Astbury and Congleton

In 1931 Astbury churchyard was extended with the addition of a plot some distance from the church to the west of the main road from Congleton to Newcastle-under-Lyme. Whilst digging a grave here for Elizabeth Clift ten years later, the sexton unearthed a Bronze Age cinerary urn standing upright and containing some calcinated remains, four teeth and a small amount of charcoal. The find was reported immediately to the Parish Clerk, Mr Fred Cartlidge, resulting in the publication of a number of articles in the *Congleton Chronicle*, and the urn and bones were deposited in the south porch of Astbury Church. It is now on display in the recently founded Congleton Museum.

There was no trace of a mound on the spot where the urn was found, but it could easily have been ploughed or levelled in earlier years. The Reverend Gordon Cartlidge and Mr Fred Cartlidge reported that there appeared to be a brook running east and west to the south of the site. This was not visible from ground level, but when digging other graves the ground became very damp about two metres down and there were numerous stones which seemed to form part of a streambed. It was speculated, therefore, that any mound material may have been used to fill up the stream course.

The bones proved to be fragments of a skull and ribs, and were probably those of a female. The Collared urn was decorated only on the top portion with 'maggot' impressed designs and a herring bone pattern. It was composed of a brownish-pink pottery and burnt black at the centre. Some more calcinated bones were found about 1.5 metres away when digging the adjacent grave.

A second Bronze Age urn filled with calcinated bones was discovered in the area and kept in a cupboard at Astbury School for many years. Unfortunately it was never adequately recorded and its present whereabouts is unknown.

A third site close to Congleton was excavated in Somerford by David Wilson in 1984. No trace of a tumulus was discovered, but the excavator concluded that if there had been a mound, it had probably been deliberately levelled in the 19th century. However, after ploughing it did become visible as a circle of sand. One unurned cremation, pottery from at least seven different types of pot, and some flint, were unearthed.

Henbury Cum Pexhall

In addition to the stone circle discussed previously the village of Henbury, to the west of Macclesfield, once also boasted a number of prehistoric tumuli, but today only one at Bearhurst Farm survives. Three other mounds originally stood to the south of Lower Pexhill but were destroyed by mineral extraction activities. One of these was excavated in 1967 by D. Bethell revealing five cremations and a horizontal plank of carbonised wood at the centre.

The bowl barrow at Bearhurst Farm, marked on the OS Map as a 'tumulus', was examined by Gordon Rowley and D. Bethell in 1965 and 1966 and produced a number of interesting discoveries. Within the mound, which was 22 metres in diameter and 1.5 metres high, a Collared urn was found which was covered with a lid made from a round-based vessel. It contained the bones of a small-framed adult male about 18 years of age. The urn was of a very early date and closely related to a type of pottery known as Fengate ware, a variant of the Neolithic Peterborough ware found at Woodhouse End in Gawsworth. It was round bottomed and not originally intended for funerary use. The cinerary urn stood in an ash-filled cremation pit.

In addition over one hundred flint flakes were discovered, scattered on the upper surface of the barrow 'in an annular distribution, as if strewn around by a person standing in the centre of the mound' as well as a crude leaf-shaped arrowhead. The urns are now in the store of The Grosvenor Museum, Chester.

Capesthorne and Marton

The grounds of Capesthorne Hall, the ancient seat of the Bromley Davenport family, also appear to be home to a number of prehistoric mounds. The first, which appears on the *County Sites and Monuments Record* as a scheduled bowl barrow, lies to the north-east of the Hall. Consisting of a round earthen mound 25 metres in diameter, it now has a pedestal on the top. A second scheduled tumulus 17 metres in diameter by 1.5 metres high lies to the south-east, covered by trees and disturbed by rabbits; there is a possible third to the north-west.

One of the round barrows in the grounds of Capesthorne Hall, now surmounted by a pedestal.

A few kilometres down the A34 from Capesthorne lies the beautiful black and white, half-timbered medieval church of Marton, home of Cheshire's oldest oak tree. The church, which sits on a low mound, was built in the 14th century, but some have suggested that the site may have origins much earlier and was perhaps the original location of a Neolithic or Bronze Age barrow. Evidence of prehistoric activity in the area comes from a number of finds including a sandstone hammer, discovered on the surface of the nearby Cocks Moss in 1911, and flints uncovered by a local metal detectorist in 2003 in Cherry Lowe field. Other place names in the area with the suffix 'low' are also suggestive of a mound somewhere in the vicinity, with Pikelow Farm to the north-east and Mutlow Farm and Higher Mutlow to the east/south-east. Even more intriguing is research being carried out on solsticial alignments by local astronomer, Kevin Kilburn. He has shown that on the midwinter solstice (21st December) the sun, when viewed from Marton churchyard, rises over Bosley Cloud, and in 2500BC would have been sited exactly over a 'notch' in the Cloud in which The Bridestones sits.

Above: The half-timbered medieval church at Marton, reputed to be constructed on the site of a prehistoric barrow.

Left: Flints discovered in Marton by local metal detectorist, David Bailey.

Alderley and Birtles

As Ormerod once commented 'In both these townships, [Birtles and Over Alderley], the ground rises into numerous swells resembling tumuli, many of which are of proportions too gigantic to be other than natural; but some are certainly artificial; and in several instances fragments of urns, bones and ashes have been discovered, which appear to refer to the ancient line of the road from Kinderton to Rainow, and to some early settlement in the neighbourhood of Prestbury'.

The most famous of these mounds is Sodger's Hump or Soldier's Tump, located on a natural hillock crowned with trees close to the Monk's Heath crossroads. The mound was originally capped by pine trees, only one of which now survives. It has been so badly damaged by the removal of the trees and replanting and fencing that very little remains apart from the splendid name. Legend has it that a 'brass weapon of war' was discovered here suggesting the derivation of its name. It features in the children's novel, *The Weirdstone of Brisingamen*, by local author Alan Garner who whilst still a school boy was responsible for rediscovering the Bronze Age shovel from the copper mines at Alderley Edge.

A report from the *Proceedings of the Macclesfield Scientific Society* 1878 records that an urn was

found in the grounds of Birtles Hall: 'Some years ago in forming a carriage drive through the Park, a large tumulus was removed for the sake of the materials when several relics were found, particularly a Roman urn, about 6in, high and 18in in circumference.' This was almost certainly of Bronze Age date and may have come from one of the several apparently natural mounds located on the estate.

The wonderfully named barrow of Sodger's Hump or Soldier's Tump (under the tree in the background) close to the Monk's Heath crossroads in Over Alderley.

The Armada Beacon on Alderley Edge, erected on top of a Bronze Age barrow.

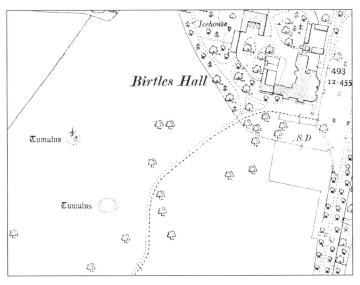

Tumuli in the ground of Birtles Hall. (Reproduced from the 1909 Ordnance Survey MapCheshire sheet 36.6, scale 25inches to 1 mile).

The Edge itself has a number of intriguing features, in addition to the prehistoric mines and the Golden Stone discussed elsewhere. Clues to its prehistoric past may lie in some of the place names such as Finlow Hill Wood and Brynlow, indicating the presence of ancient barrows. Particularly of interest is the mound on which the Armada Beacon was erected circa 1578. A subject of much debate by antiquarians, it has now been scheduled as a Bronze Age barrow. Elsewhere on the Edge several 'earth circles' have been reported. It is unclear at present whether these are ancient barrows or the result of more recent landscaping activities by the landowners, perhaps tree enclosure rings. The following was reported by Charles Roeder in the *Transactions of the Lancashire and Cheshire Antiquarian Society* in 1901:

'Then close to the Engine Vein, on its southern side, we have the distinct ramparts of an earthen circle or entrenchment, twelve yards in diameter, known popularly as the "Seven Firs"; another one, in proximity, six yards across; not far away on its northern side another one, seven and a half yards across and two feet high, near the Golden Stone, north-west of the Edge Farm in Dickens Wood, we distinguish another fine example in good preservation, sixteen yards in diameter; another at Windmill Wood; and south-east of the Wizard, in a field a little way from the Macclesfield Road, we encounter a much larger earthen circle, thirty yards in diameter and four feet six inches high in one place, which is also marked on the recent six-inch ordnance map.'

Shortly afterwards in 1904 the circle near Macclesfield Road was 'levelled for agricultural requirements', but before its destruction Roeder and his associate, Mr F.S Graves, had the site examined. Trenches were made in the centre at right angles but nothing was found, apart from the composition of the circle: 'We came first on a light soil, then stony clay, and below 4 feet sandy coarse loam. We were here on the original ground, and so abstained from further useless attempts.'

Wilmslow

Wilmslow is home to a number of prehistoric burials none of which appear to have been placed under a barrow, unless such mounds have long since disappeared. The latter is perhaps more likely, as the suffix 'low' is common in place names where tumuli once existed, such as The Seven Lows in Delamere Forest, Rains Low in Macclesfield Forest, Yearnslow in Rainow, or Arbor Low in Derbyshire.

The first discovery was described by the famous antiquary, John Parsons Earwaker, in his *East Cheshire: Past and Present* in Cheadle Parish, Edgeley (not strictly Wilmslow, but close enough): 'About 1872, in digging for the foundations of some new houses at the end of Massey Street, three urns were found, but, owing to the ignorance and stupidity of the workmen, they were broken to pieces. From the few fragments that remained, it seems probable that they were British urns, and very similar in character and general appearance to those found at Wilmslow'.

'Those found at Wilmslow' were unearthed during a period of twenty years in the middle of the 19th century. A description of the earliest find comes from the pages of George Ormerod: 'In making the railway, in 1839-40, an urn apparently British, was dug up in the neighbourhood of the present Wilmslow station, which contained the remains of a bronze dagger and human bones.' The bronze dagger is reported to have had a chevron on it, but unfortunately no one knows where it is located now. It is a highly important treasure as very little Bronze Age metalwork is known from the area of east Cheshire.

In 1857 a second urn containing calcinated human bones was found in the grounds of Ilex House in Wilmslow. A description comes again from Earwaker: 'Preserved in the museum in Peel Park, Salford, is another British urn found at Wilmslow in the year 1857. This urn is described in a paragraph in the *Manchester Guardian*, 1858, from which it appears that it was found in digging for gravel on land belonging to Mr William Goodier of Wilmslow, who presented it to the museum. The place where it was found is described as being near his house, on the east side of the railway, and about a quarter of a mile from the railway station. It was found buried with the mouth downwards, and covered with a piece of coarse cloth that fell to powder when touched. It was nearly full of small fragments of white calcinated bones. It also fell to pieces when discovered, but the fragments have been carefully put back together by Mr. John Plant, the curator of the museum. When perfect, it would be from 16 to 17 inches high and about 11 inches broad at the top, narrowing at the bottom to about 4 inches. It is of whitish-grey colour, of clay not baked but sun-dried, and consequently very friable. The upper part is ornamented with zigzag lines, each having four angles.' The site is now a housing estate and the urn is housed in The Manchester Museum.

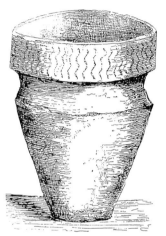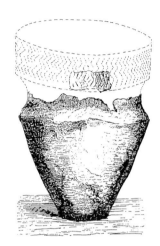

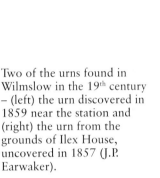

Two of the urns found in Wilmslow in the 19th century – (left) the urn discovered in 1859 near the station and (right) the urn from the grounds of Ilex House, uncovered in 1857 (J.P. Earwaker).

In 1859 a third urn was found in Wilmslow, of which the full account was sent at the time by the Reverend John Colston of Styal, to Mr Thomas Bateman, the well-known Derbyshire antiquary. Mr Bateman brought this account before the British Archaeological Association and the urn was described and illustrated in their Journal in 1860. Mr Colston wrote:

'The spot where the urn was found is about 100 yards distant from the Wilmslow railway station, in a ridge of gravel between the new and old roads leading to the village of Prestbury. The circumstance which first attracted the notice of the labourers employed in cutting down the said ridge of gravel, was the appearance of a quantity of soil in the gravel, a portion of which falling down led to the exposure of the urn . . . When found, the urn was placed with the mouth downwards, and on raising it up a quantity of dark earthy matter with bones fell out of it. The urn was considerably injured by the workmen. I send you a sketch of the urn, which was 16 inches deep and 13 inches broad at the mouth. At the top of the urn is a broad rim 4 inches deep, covered with an number of irregular zigzag lines. The materials of which the urn is composed are of a very coarse and friable kind, and seem to have been baked in the sun rather than in an oven or fire. The bones are much charred, and show evidence of traces of action by fire. The teeth are nearly perfect, and appear to be those of a young person about 14 years of age. A small bone stud, with perforations for attaching it to something by no means obvious, was also found in the urn.' The bone stud was later proved to be a sword pommel.

The tragedy of the workmen's haste appears in a paper read to the Macclesfield Scientific Society in 1877 which states that believing every urn must contain money 'The workmen with their spades soon reduced the urn to fragments; but its contents offered nothing to gratify their cupidity; and let us add that if they had preserved the urn entire, they would doubtless have earned a large reward.'

Vale Royal, Delamere and Frodsham

Moving on across the Cheshire Plain from Wilmslow, apart from the barrow cemeteries at Old Withington, Jodrell Bank (Twemlow) and the Dark Valley (Goostrey), there is a distinct lack of Bronze Age activity until the area around Delamere Forest, the only exceptions being the tumulus of Robin Hoods Butts near Great Budworth (now destroyed), and the bowl barrow close to the village of Whitley.

Very little is known about either of these two, but an unknown author, in a reference in the Bodleian Library, records that circa 1661 the tumulus of Robin Hoods Butts contained 'the armes of a man in an upright posture'. As for the scheduled barrow 120 metres east of the village of Whitley, this has suffered under the plough and is now approximately 32 metres in diameter and 0.6 metres high; although on a recent visit the authors failed to discover any traces of it. Fieldwalking in the area by local Mrs Pat Johnson revealed a small calcinated flint, probably a scraper 38mm long by 33mm wide, which may have come from the mound. A further flint and a small fragment of bone were found at a later date.

Delamere

One of the three great forests of the medieval period, Delamere takes its name from the numerous meres, mosses and pools found in the surrounding landscape. This area around the mid-Cheshire Ridge was obviously an important centre of population during prehistory and has one of the richest Pre-Roman landscapes to be found in the county. Within a radius of a few kilometres, as well as the tumuli of The Seven Lows, Castle Cob, Glead Hill Cob and Gallowsclough, and a possible stone circle, there were two later Iron Age forts at Kelsborrow and Eddisbury and a mereside enclosure at Oak Mere. In addition, the main Roman road from Chester to Manchester passed by Eddisbury, and was probably constructed on a pre-existing trackway.

A number of other barrows were mentioned in the vicinity by Ormerod in the 19th century: 'In its progress through the Hundred of Eddisbury several tumuli are raised on the high grounds of its neighbourhood. One of these is situated immediately to the left of the turnpike road leading from Chester to Tarporley at about half a mile distant from the latter place, and another to the right of the continuation of the same road within the township of Tiverton.' He continues: 'The Street proceeds along the high ground for two miles in a direction nearly parallel with the course of the Weaver. Two considerable tumuli, in a perfect state, remain close to the banks of the river, at the point where it deserts this line, and assumes its north west course towards the estuary of the Mersey.' None of these appear on modern Ordnance Survey maps and so presumably must have long since disappeared.

Several prehistoric stone tools have been found in the area including five wedge shaped stone hammers which were discovered at the foot of Eddisbury Hill in 1896 by Nathan Heywood of Urmston, and a number of good quality Late Neolithic/Early Bronze Age flint tools at Oak Mere during fieldwalking investigations for the North West Wetlands Survey in the 1990s. In addition a yellow sandstone grain crusher was found behind the Nurses Home, Crossley's Sanatorium, and close by a fragment of a disk quern. Patches of charcoal indicated that a temporary camp had been made in the area, leading some to believe that they may once have belonged to some Iron Age travellers or Roman soldiers who were camping there.

In addition to The Seven Lows discussed previously, four other barrows are known in the region of Delamere Forest. The only one of any note is Gallowsclough Cob, which is mentioned in detail below. Others include a bowl barrow at Forest Farm near Fishpool Lane and two close to Monarchy Hall, which are now destroyed.

Gallowsclough Cob, Oakmere

One of the best-recorded excavations in the Central Ridge area is that of the scheduled tumulus of Gallowsclough or Garruslow, prominently positioned on the salmon-pink sand of a hilltop contour. This mound lies close to a hedge on Gallowsclough Lane, to the north of the Chester to Northwich road, opposite a break in the mid-Cheshire Ridge known as the Mouldsworth gap, a drainage channel created at the end of the last Ice Age. The gravels and sands of this central ridge were undoubtedly the largest area of open land in prehistoric Cheshire.

Excavations were carried out during two weeks in August 1960 by James Forde-Johnston, who was later to investigate the barrow in the grounds of Sutton Hall near Macclesfield. The main barrow mound was found to be composed of layers of brown sandy soil of varying shades, defined within a circular bank or kerb of sand. Under this lay a clay cap or dome composed of a yellow sandy mass with patches of red clay. Below was a further layer of whitish sand, the bottom of which had turned grey. Next came another dome of yellow clay covering a mass of ashy dark grey sand with considerable amounts of charcoal and patches of bright red and orange sandy clay (see Figure 17).

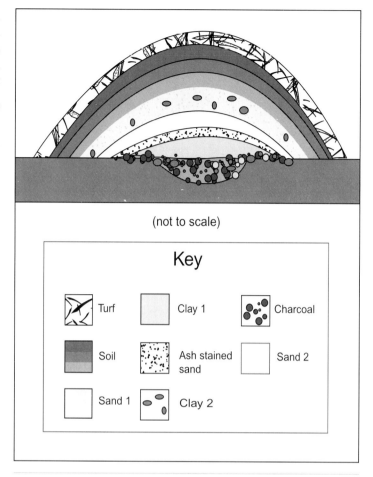

(not to scale)

Key

Turf   Clay 1   Charcoal

Soil   Ash stained sand   Sand 2

Sand 1   Clay 2

Figure 17 - Plan of the layers in Gallowsclough Cob.

Finally excavations revealed a roughly circular pit, approximately 30 centimetres in diameter, containing a cremation. No urn accompanied these remains, they were merely placed in a shallow scoop in the ground. Many of the bones were deeply embedded in the dark grey ashy material forming the sides of the pit. There was also a great deal of charcoal on the old ground surface and around the clay cap, indicating that the barrow may have been constructed on the actual site of the cremation. The main burial is unusual in that it was not placed in the centre as was normally the case. It is in fact approximately two metres south-south-west of the true centre as defined by the kerb. Could it be that the centre was reserved for ritual or was it simply because of the local topography?

As for the covering mound, the appearance of turf suggests that it was not made by digging soil out of a ditch as at some other sites, but from scraping the surface of the surrounding area. Other bones, almost certainly from secondary burials, were found elsewhere in the mound. Further remains may originally have been located in the upper portion of the barrow and have since been ploughed and dispersed elsewhere. The bones of the main burial were those of an adult male (over 21 years of age) who had a full set of teeth at the time of death. He was about 165cm (5 feet 5 inches) in height and was probably right handed and was quite muscular but not heavily built. The second burial was also that of an adult but the fragments were insufficient in quantity to determine age and sex.

There are a few other outliers to the Delamere group, namely High Billinge to the south of the Forest, and Glead Hill Cob and Castle Cob to the north-west. The scheduled bowl barrow of High Billinge is a prominent oval mound located on an exposed hilltop close to Utkinton. Unfortunately trees and fencing have encroached onto the tumulus which is now approximately 2 metres high and 35 metres north to south by 24 metres east to west.

The incense cup discovered in Glead Hill Cob during building work in 1879 (Shone).

Glead Hill Cob, also known as 'Houndslow' or 'Houndslough', once lay 6.5 kilometres to the north-east of The Seven Lows overlooking a stream. It was mentioned briefly by Ormerod who described it as being 'ninety-nine feet in diameter at the base'. In 1879 a Mr John Harrison of the New Pale (an area of forest enclosure dating back to the 17th century) was levelling this large tumulus for the foundations of a house when 'ten or twelve large urns (filled with burnt bones) were met with'. Unfortunately the urns fell to pieces upon removal, but a small incense cup did survive. A few of the relics within the urns were 'rescued by Mr Harrison from the workmen' including the incense cup, barbed flint arrowheads 'of good type', a flint scraper, a fragment of a flint knife and a bronze pin. The incense cup is described as being '2³/₄ inches across its base, 3¹/₄ inches high, 5¹/₄ inches across the mouth and 15⁷/₈ inches in circumference at the widest part'. These were all photographed by William Shone in the early 20th century.

The base of the incense cup showing a cross pattern (Shone).

Finally we come to Castle Cob in Kingsley. This mound 25 metres in diameter and 4 metres high is now located in a private garden, surmounted by a water tank and a summerhouse. It was photographed by Shone in the early 20th century prior to this construction, but even then it was covered in trees and encroached upon by a fence. Ormerod records in his *History of Cheshire* that the tumulus was sixty-six feet in diameter at its base and was opened during the 19th century. It was found 'to contain nothing but a quantity of black soil, which might be supposed to be either animal matter, or produced by the effects of fire'.

William Shone at Castle Cob in the early 20th century prior to construction of a water tank and a summerhouse (Shone).

Crewe and Nantwich

Finally, there is one other isolated barrow of note in southern Cheshire in the Borough of Crewe and Nantwich. Known as Robin Hood's Tump, the site was excavated in 1940 but no evidence of a burial was found, only a series of empty pits. Today it stands at approximately 17 metres in diameter and over 2 metres high. Despite being disturbed and covered with trees it is remarkably well preserved in comparison to many of the other barrows in the Cheshire area, and even has a Ministry of Works sign designating it as a scheduled ancient monument, a feature not found at any of the other barrows in the county.

The bowl barrow of Robin Hood's Tump in the village of Alpraham near Tilstone Fearnall.

Cremation Cemeteries

The majority of burials (from a minority of the population) discovered in the Bronze Age come from round barrows. For those not given this honour, rarely do we get to glimpse their final resting place. Occasionally flat cremations cemeteries come to light, but these are incredibly difficult to locate as they leave no obvious trace on the surface. One such cemetery was discovered by chance on a sandstone ridge overlooking the Dee at Grange Hill in West Kirkby on the Wirral during the enlargement of a garden in 1840. Workmen uncovered a number of inverted urns, one of which was cordoned (i.e. decorated with an ornamental cord), filled with burnt bones, charcoal, ashes and a flint.

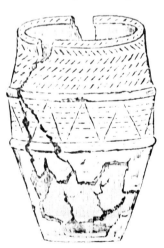

The urn found in a garden in West Kirby in 1840 as illustrated in the *TLCAS* volume 1 (Shone).

A second site was discovered recently in Cheshire during excavations of the medieval Abbey at Poulton near Chester in 2002. As a result of investigations carried out by the Poulton Research Project in the summer of 2002, a soil resistivity survey in the area revealed a feature 60 metres to the north of the chapel. A well-defined arc of darkened soil dug into the natural geology, perhaps a 'ring ditch' of Late Bronze Age/Early Iron Age date, was revealed. The ditch was estimated to be about 16 metres in diameter and after examining a small section excavators uncovered a few fragments of a horse skull and two fragments of coarse, handmade, pottery. Further sherds of this coarse pottery were found within the exposed area of the ditch, along with numerous fragments of cremated human bone directly associated with the pottery. On further investigation several small burnt areas were identified, circling fragments of cremated human bone. Excavations are continuing and it is early days, but all the signs point to a possible prehistoric burial site.

Standing Stones

Standing stones found singly (monoliths), in pairs and in long lines (stone rows) are dotted widely across the landscapes of northern and western Britain. Many remain hidden in the expanse of the countryside, only revealed by closely inspecting maps or entries on the *County Sites and Monuments Records*. Others are situated in popular localities, familiar to walkers using well-trodden paths. Many now form gateposts and field boundaries, as on Minn End Lane at Wincle in Cheshire or Nine Stone Close on Harthill Moor in Derbyshire.

No one can say exactly how many single or multiple standing stones remain in the UK, and a definitive explanation of their purpose has yet to be ascertained. There are many problems concerning their identification, so it is reasonable to assume that the answer may never be found nor their exact age discovered. It has been suggested that these stones, or 'menhirs' as they are sometimes known, are no more than scratching posts for livestock. Some may well have been put up solely for this purpose, or may have subsequently taken on this role, as at Higher Ridgegate in Macclesfield Forest, but it seems a little inconceivable that any farmer, irrespective of time period, would expend so much time and effort in shaping and erecting such stones in some of the most remote places. In any event, often the stone may actually be a metre or two taller than the beast it is supposed to assist, and therefore of unnecessary height.

It must be more than just coincidence that standing stones dot the lines of major routes to the upland territories. It would appear, therefore, that they were placed as way-markers, boundary stones or memorials, set at points where passers by could see them, perhaps marking significant points in the landscape such as crossroads or meeting places or marking out the lines of ancient tracks which would become overgrown with vegetation at certain times of year. As with the barrows, some standing stones are placed in prominent positions on ridge crests and the saddles of hills, adding weight to the suggestion that they may have marked territories and boundaries. In Cheshire three standing stones on Minn End Lane and one at Ginclough in Rainow all lie along the route of modern roads, which were almost certainly constructed along the line of much earlier trackways.

Often standing stones also appear to have had religious affiliations. Many prehistoric sites seem to have been aligned with prominent or important physical features in the landscape, such as mountain passes and hill tops, or to points where the sun or moon rise at important times of the year, in particular, the solstices or equinoxes. In some cases the stones seem to be the focus for ritual and spiritual activity within prehistoric communities. At one such site, at Stackpole Warren in south-west Wales it was found that seven well-used huts, clustered around a single standing stone known as the Devil's Quoit, suggested that this monolith was the central focus of this small community.

In addition, many independent standing stones are considered to be outliers of stone circles, for example the Heel Stone at Stonehenge; Long Meg and Her Daughters in Cumbria; the Pipers at The Merry Maidens stone circle in Cornwall; the two outliers of the Gors Fawr circle in Pembrokeshire or The King's Stone located a little way from the Nine Ladies on Stanton Moor in Derbyshire. These are again believed to be associated with certain astronomical alignments such as sunrises and moonrises.

One thing that is easy to explain is the reason why standing stones are generally only found in western and northern Britain. It is purely down to the geology – in these regions the rocks are hard enough to survive the elements. Millstone grit stands up reasonably well to weathering, chalk does not. Very few have been subject to modern excavation and even when they have, unless artefacts of some description are found in association with them, it is still impossible to prove their origin. Generally those that have been studied are found in context with stone circles, barrows and cairns which are Bronze Age in date. However, occasionally ritual deposits, such as flint tools and even Beaker burials, have been found at the bases suggesting that they may also fit into Late Neolithic ritual landscapes. This would make sense, especially if they were used to mark the lines of well-used trackways. Archaeologists believe that such tracks existed at an early period because of the long distance trade of items such as highly polished stone axes manufactured in The Lake District, North Wales and Cornwall, which may have been exchanged at henges and causewayed enclosures throughout the country. Roman roads often appear to have been subsequently constructed along the lines of these pre-existing trackways. For example, the henges of Arbor Low and The Bull Ring in Derbyshire have Roman roads running close by, which mirror the axes of the entrances, suggesting they were following an earlier prehistoric route. In Delamere the Roman road from Chester, known as 'The Street', runs along the base of the hillfort at Eddisbury Hill.

The Cheshire Stones

Foxlow Edge

This single standing stone is situated on a public footpath overlooking the famous beauty spot of the Goyt Valley, and is actually located just over the border between Cheshire and Derbyshire. As with many standing stones in this part of the world the view is fantastic. To the east the vista opens up over the two Goyt Valley reservoirs, obviously of modern construction, and further on into the Peak District National Park. The stone itself is a slim pillar, leaning heavily to the north-west. Erosion at its base, perhaps caused by sheltering sheep, has created a water filled pool (although it has been suggested that this is the result of a spring) which, in the right conditions, reflects the stone's elegant profile.

It is uncertain whether or not this stone has origins in the prehistoric period, but the reason for its existence could well be its prominent position next to the track taken to find it. As mentioned previously, some standing stones seem to act as markers along the lines of important routes; undoubtedly the Goyt Valley would have been an important, resource-rich area in the past and several hollow ways, Roman roads and medieval packhorse trails cross the area, highlighting its significance as an ancient trade route.

The standing stone on Foxlow Edge above the picturesque Goyt Valley.

The Murder Stone

The wonderfully named Murder Stone can be found on a long low hill near Cornfield Farm, two kilometres due west of the Derbyshire town of Whaley Bridge, but it is located in the Cheshire part of the Peak District National Park. This 'scheduled' stone, reported by County Archaeologist Rick Turner in 1993, stands 1.3 metres high, 0.5 metres thick and is roughly diamond-shaped. The ground around its base is partially eroded, perhaps again by sheltering sheep, but this does not appear to be threatening the stone. Composed of local brown gritstone it is pitted from centuries of exposure to the elements.

The stone is situated on a hillock which is not the highest point in the immediate area, but does have excellent panoramic views across the Goyt Valley and Reed Hill (topped by a round barrow) to the south, and Lyme Park to the north-east. It overlooks a small valley that feeds the Todd Brook, a tributary of the River Goyt, and is visible for a considerable distance from all directions apart from to the north-east. It is unusual in comparison to its other east Cheshire comrades. The broad 'diamond' of sandstone contrasts with the svelte examples at Foxlow Edge and Bosley Minn. The Murder Stone is clearly not located on a trackway and, although

it appears to be in a prominent position, it would not have been easily visible from other locations. For example from Reed Hill, it would merge into the background and from Higher Lane travelling north towards Disley it can only be seen with effort. Whatever The Murder Stone signified, its isolation has served to protect it from the forces which have caused so many other more accessible stones to lean so heavily.

Left: The wonderfully shaped Murder Stone near Whaley Bridge, as viewed from the nearby public footpath.

How the stone got its name is unknown; perhaps it has something to do with its fierce-looking, pointed shape – in the right lighting conditions, its shadow closely resembles a knife blade. Alternatively it may be linked to a local legend connected with an actual murder which took place nearby in the 19th century. Located on the wayside of the Old Buxton Road, on the north-eastern slopes of Black Hill (the road running to the east of The Murder Stone between Disley and Whaley Bridge), is a relatively modern 'Murder Stone'. It bears the inscription 'William Wood, Eyam Derbyshire, here murdered July 16th A.D. 1823, Prepare to meet thy God', and commemorates the death of a Derbyshire weaver who was mugged and murdered as he returned from selling cloth in Manchester. Three men, two of whom were later caught and tried, apparently smashed the unfortunate man's skull to pieces with a large stone. Legend states that there was a large hole in the ground where the skull had fallen and this remained despite various efforts to fill it in.

The Murder Stone of William Wood after which the standing stone may have been named.

The Minn End Lane Stones

Five standing stones are located near Wincle adjacent to the popular hikers' and cyclists' path, 'The Gritstone Trail' which runs for 56 kilometres from Disley to Kidsgrove. Three standing stones, believed to be prehistoric, and two possibly more recent additions, are all situated within two metres of the western edge of Minn End Lane. This would certainly add credence to the theory that standing stones were used to mark ancient trackways. The Gritstone Trail, passes close to a number of other ancient sites along its course, including several barrows in Knights Low Wood and two on Sponds Hill in Lyme Handley, and the Conical Mound overlooking Bottoms Reservoir in Langley. It also looks directly across to the barrow on the prominent outcrop of Nab Head, opposite the famous monument of White Nancy on the end of the saddle of Kerridge in Bollington.

Of the three scheduled stones, the southern single stone (Minn End Lane I) is a slim specimen that leans heavily to the east and, when vertical, would have stood at 1.2 metres high. The stone and the ground around it bear the hallmarks of its adaptation to a gatepost at some point in the recent past. The stone appears to mark the southern edge of a narrow, levelled entrance to the previously enclosed field to the west and has two hinge settings carved into its north face. Approximately two metres north of the stone the levelled area ends and a low bank starts, presumably marking the line of the former wall.

The standing stone of Minn End Lane I, later re-used as a gatepost.

The other 'genuine' stone pair (Minn End Lane IV and V) are located approximately 300 metres further north. These stones are also short and slim, leaning heavily and resembling gateposts. The southernmost stone of the two leans to the west, and would again have been about 1.2 metres high when upright. Its colleague, 2.4 metres to the north, leans southwards and would have stood about the same height if not for the list. All three of these scheduled stones have weathered, rounded edges suggesting they have been exposed to the elements for a great number (possibly hundreds) of years.

Between the single stone and the pair stand two unscheduled stones, probably more recent additions to the lane-side. Both of these stones (Minn End Lane II and III) stand vertical at one metre tall, almost two metres apart, and have sharp, 'freshly' quarried edges. The northern stone of the two has an Ordnance Survey 'benchmark' symbol carved into it.

The other pair of scheduled standing stones on Minn End Lane in Wincle.

All five of these standing stones could be said to mark the trackway that today is Minn End Lane, but also appear to have been used as gateposts. However, the antiquity of the middle two stones can be thrown into doubt immediately with their lack of lean, 'freshness' and carving, suggesting that they are far more recent additions than the other three. On looking carefully, a line of rubble can be traced linking the three now redundant entrances parallel to the lane. Historical Ordnance Survey maps confirm the evidence of a fully enclosed field on the western side of the track (currently between the two iron gates). The 1910 map of the area shows the lost field boundary which enclosed an area of approximately 11 acres (4.5 hectares).

The question is, of the six stones that were needed to make the gate post pairs, were the three Bronze Age ones already perfectly placed or were they moved a little from their original positions to save money, time and labour? Perhaps the answer lies in the lean. Only the three scheduled prehistoric ones are not truly upright, implying they were perhaps left in their original positions. As for the other two, although they appear to be more modern it seems strange that someone would remove all the other stones along the line of what was quite obviously once a dry-stone wall, leaving only those five. All that aside, the current location of each of the stones is perfect. This saddle is ideally placed to take in superb views to the east covering the Peak District, the Dane Valley, The Roaches and Hen Cloud and to the west across the Cheshire Plain, Bosley Cloud and Croker Hill. With such imposing vistas it is easy to see why our ancestors constructed so many ritual monuments on the Pennine fringe.

The Rainow Stones

There are several stones within the parish of Rainow in the hills to the north-east of Macclesfield, only one of which is currently authenticated as being genuinely prehistoric. For the curious, this rather unimpressive prehistoric standing stone, known as the Ginclough or Gin Clough stone, sits at the junction of the main 'Macclesfield Road' and the track to Cutlers Farm (a public right of way) at Ginclough in Rainow. This large stone or glacial erratic, 0.9 metres high and 0.9 metres deep at the base, is not typical of other standing stones in the area, being neither needle-like nor imposing. It is short, dumpy, crammed into the corner of a field by a busy road and surrounded by redundant agricultural equipment! Nevertheless it is scheduled as an ancient monument and may have acted as a way-marker on a prehistoric track from the Cheshire Plain to the uplands of the Pennines. It lies close to a Bronze Age round barrow located 300 metres to the north-east on Black Rock Farm, and marking the line of what is today the B5470 from Macclesfield to Whaley Bridge, it also lies opposite the gap created by the Harrop Brook valley between the saddle of Kerridge and Nab Head.

The standing stone adjacent to the main Macclesfield Road in the hamlet of Ginclough in Rainow.

Another curious stone pillar stands in a field close to a lane off the Macclesfield Road slightly further up, to the rear of the Highway Man public house. It is well positioned to be a prehistoric standing stone, but in the authors' opinion seems a little too well worked, suggesting it is perhaps the remains of a more recent wayside cross or even a scratching post for livestock. In its favour however, it is located close to a number of other Bronze Age features including the barrows of Black Rock Farm, Blue Boar Farm and Yearnslow, as well as the aforementioned standing stone at Ginclough.

Right: The stone to the rear of the Highway Man public house.

Below: The possible standing stone located on the footpath near to the tumulus of Yearnslow in Rainow.

The third interesting stone is not marked on the OS map but lies close to the footpath down to Yearnslow from Smith Lane. It does appear to be worked to some degree, but the fact that it is leaning and appears neither to be serving as a gatepost nor scratching post (being located rather awkwardly in the corner of the field close to a wall), makes it intriguing.

Macclesfield Forest

Regular visitors to Macclesfield Forest will be well aware of the curiously named 'Standingstone' car park at the eastern end of the forest. This must have been so named for a reason, but the question is where did the standing stone stand and how old was it?

On a recent visit the authors discovered two stones in the field to the west of the car park. These had obviously been used as gateposts at some time in the recent past, but one of the stones was much less worked suggesting it was of greater antiquity.

Various sources record a number of 'stones' in the area of what is today Macclesfield Forest, but unfortunately the majority have now disappeared. One remaining standing stone, pointed out by local astronomer Kevin Kilburn, which is undoubtedly used as a rubbing post today, can be seen in a field at Higher Ridgegate to the left of the road just past the Leather's

Right: The standing stone, obviously used as a rubbing post, at Higher Ridgegate in Macclesfield Forest.

Smithy pub. One of the best documented however, is 'a small standing stone' reported by Dr J.D. Sainter, W.T. Watkin and J.P. Earwaker located in the same field as the tumulus to the north-west of Toot Hill (see barrows section). According to the *County Sites and Monuments Record* a 'prostrate unworked stone post probably a rubbing post' was reported by the Ordnance Survey in 1964, but sadly this could not be located on a subsequent visit in 1972. The Reverend Marriott also described and illustrated two 'rude upright stones' on the characteristic summit of Shutlingsloe (often referred to as the 'Matterhorn of Cheshire') near Wildboarclough in 1810.

The Golden Stone

The Golden Stone lies close to the Engine Vein in Alderley Edge, where Bronze Age man worked the earth for its copper-rich ores. Displays in the visitor centre report that the Golden Stone was possibly a Bronze Age standing stone, later re-used as a boundary marker. Looking at this strangely-shaped, pebbly, sandstone boulder today, it is hard to see how it would have stood, but given its position in the landscape in close proximity to the prehistoric copper

workings and tumuli, it must have had some significance during Bronze Age times. Recent studies by Simon Timberlake in the copper mining areas of the Cambrian Mountains in Wales, have revealed that several groups of standing stones act as route markers along trackways which lead up from the coast and pass close to a number of ancient mines in the area. Perhaps the Golden Stone may once have played a similar role at Alderley Edge.

The Golden Stone located close to the Engine Vein mine on Alderley Edge.

Christianised Stones

In addition to the rough, unhewn pillars found in the Cheshire countryside, some have suggested that many of the carved crosses and inscribed stones may also be recycled Bronze Age standing stones. At many sites around the country pagan places of worship were used later by Christian churches. Particularly significant are those with round churchyards. The most famous example of this re-use can be found at Knowlton in Dorset, where a derelict 12th century Norman church stands in the centre of a large Neolithic henge. At Stanton Drew in Somerset, St Mary's Church lies 300 metres to the south-west of the great stone circle, close to the cove, while on Glastonbury Tor, the tower of St Michael's stands proudly at the centre of a prehistoric hillfort. At Toller Porcorum church in Dorset the 1400-year-old wall collapsed earlier this century, revealing two prehistoric standing stones that had been embedded deep within the structure.

Closer to home the church of St Edward the Confessor in Leek stands on a site of great significance, and according to a notice board in the church itself, was 'a site of great antiquity, of pre-Christian religious significance long before the Christian missionaries came here in the 7th century'. It has been suggested that the hilltop on which the church was built may have been a place of worship for over 5,000 years. On Midsummer's Day a unique event takes place when a double sunset can be seen looking from the churchyard towards the hill known as the Cloud. Local astronomer, Kevin Kilburn, has investigated this phenomenon and believes that this

alignment is 'much better than the famous midsummer sunrise alignment above the heel stone at Stonehenge'. Similar claims of pre-Christian activity are made for other churches in the Cheshire area, such as the half-timbered medieval church in Marton, which is reputedly built on top of a prehistoric barrow, and the small chapel at Forest Chapel in Macclesfield Forest lying close to the tumulus of Rains Low.

Just as the pagan sites themselves were reused, so were the stones. A number of edicts to this effect were passed by various church councils during the early Christian period. At Carthage (398AD), Arles (452AD), Tours (567AD), Toledo (681AD) and Paris (826AD) they denounced standing stones and condemned their worship, causing many to be destroyed and others to be Christianised. Sometimes crosses were carved into the stones or added to their tops. In France the official documents of St Cado, dating from Brittany in 1000AD, state that standing stones and other megaliths should be reduced to mere boundary markers.

Left: Stump Cross near Burnley in Lancashire, another example of a Bronze Age standing stone Christianised by the addition of a cross.

Throughout Cheshire there are a number of stone crosses, some of which may have been re-used standing stones or may have been used as boundary markers and memorials at important places in the landscape. Most of the crosses originally stood within the old boundaries of the Royal Forest of Macclesfield. There were four known pairs which include The Bowstones near Lyme, the Longside Cross (now destroyed), the Jordan Law Cross in Disley (now removed) and Robin Hood's Picking Rods at Mellor Moor End. According to Frank Renaud, in his *History of the Parish of Prestbury* written in 1876, these all appear to have been erected merely as boundary stones, and three out of the four stood in the heart of the forest where there were no boundary lines.

There are also a number of single crosses in the Macclesfield area including one at Fallibroome; one on Clulow Cross in Wincle (said to stand on a prehistoric tumulus), one on Greenway in Higher Sutton and three now in the West Park, Macclesfield. As Renaud comments when these stones were set up 'the country was a tangled forest, whereas now it is, for the most part, under cultivation. Whether woodland paths and roads intersected each other where the crosses stand cannot now be determined...'. One of the most convincing examples of a Christianised standing stone is that of the Greenway Cross or Plague Stone on the slopes above Macclesfield.

The Plague Stone

This stone wayside cross is located above Macclesfield Forest in the Parish of Sutton to the south-east of Macclesfield alongside a country lane. It is very prominently positioned to take in views of Shutlingsloe to the east, Croker Hill to the west and out across the Cheshire Plain to Alderley Edge and beyond, through the gap formed by the Bollin Valley and Rossendale Brook. On a clear day one can see as far as the sandstone spine of the mid-Cheshire ridge. The cross is essentially a rough, unhewn, flat stone with a cross carved on both sides and, although it has been used as a wayside cross in more recent years, it may originally date from a much earlier period, perhaps even being of prehistoric origin. This is not certain but it does fit well with one of the possible functions of a standing stone i.e. a wayside marker on an upland trail.

The Plague Stone or Greenway Cross, believed originally to have been a Bronze Age standing stone.

According to Frank Renaud, when Macclesfield was visited by the plague in 1603 and 1646, the stone was used as a plague cross, 'to which country people came to sell their provisions to dwellers in the town. The practice was for sellers to place their goods near the cross and then retire, after which the townspeople came and paid the price marked, letting the money fall into a basin or socket filled with water, by which process all infections were supposed to be destroyed'. By a strange quirk of fate the presence of a more recent 'isolation hospital' is shown nearby on old OS maps.

6 The Iron Age
(circa 700BC to 43AD)

Thriving agriculture continued in the British Isles until just before the turn of the 1st millennium BC, when in the Late Bronze Age there was a major climatic deterioration. As previously mentioned, in exactly 1159BC tree rings from many parts of the world indicate that a major catastrophe struck the earth; trees did not grow for a whole year and the planet was shrouded in dust, perhaps caused by a comet or asteroid travelling near the earth's surface. In Britain there was no sun for months on end, so crops failed as farmland flooded. This dramatic deluge was to persist for a further 18 years, resulting in far wider consequences. There was a prolonged deterioration in the weather which continued into the Iron Age. Increased rainfall and an accompanying drop in temperature of 2°C turned many areas of fertile arable land into useless blanket bog, while deforestation and continuous exploitation made the soils, even in newly colonised areas, deteriorate. The cooler and wetter climate also meant that there was often insufficient sun to ripen crops and excessive moisture would cause many to rot, often leading to food shortages.

The Greek historian Strabo commented on the farmers and the weather of the British Isles in the 1st century BC: 'Their cities are their forests, for they fell trees and fence in large enclosures in which they build huts and pen in their cattle, but not for any great length of time. The weather tends to rain rather than snow. Mist is very common, so that for whole days at a stretch the sun is seen for only three or four hours around the middle of the day'.

A century or so later the Roman historian Tacitus, writing in his work *Agricola*, confirms Strabo's observations: 'The climate is wretched, with its frequent rains and mists but there is no extreme cold'. He continues 'The soils will produce good crops, except olives, vines and other plants which usually grow in the warmer lands. They are slow to ripen, though they shoot up quickly – both facts being due to the same cause, the extreme moisture of the soil and atmosphere'.

The climatic deterioration put Iron Age people under new pressures. Food was now more valuable and needed protecting, so communities reorganized themselves in order to defend their agricultural land and their harvests. It is at this time that fortified sites, known as hillforts, developed. Other changes in society came as a result of Continental influences, which brought about a transformation in religious practices with worship centred on nature, and woodland and water taking preference over manmade constructions. As a consequence the creation of ritual monuments in the landscape declined, but the occurrence of the deposition of items of value, and even human sacrifices, into peat bogs, lakes and rivers dramatically increased. New types of weapons and highly stylized art, with elegant jewellery and delicately carved figures fashioned from bronze and other precious metals, also came from the Continent. These items are named after regions such as La Tène in Switzerland and Halstatt in Austria where the styles originated. Weapons of La Tène type have been found at Beeston Castle in Cheshire.

One of the most significant changes in the later prehistoric period in Europe was of course the introduction of iron. This was by no means a new technology as it had originated in the Middle East around the middle of the 3rd millennium BC (the beginning of our Bronze Age). Some of the earliest known iron artefacts dating to this period have been discovered near Ankara in modern Turkey. An iron dagger found in the tomb of Tutankhamen possibly originated from this area. After the collapse of the Hittite Empire around 1000BC, iron technology began to creep into the Eastern Mediterranean and was quickly embraced in Crete, Cyprus and on mainland Greece. Elsewhere in Europe bronze remained dominant until circa 800BC when the use of iron began slowly spreading across the Continent. By 600BC a scarcity of copper and tin led to its widespread introduction. Although iron was available at such an early age, it was regarded as an incredibly rare and precious metal. As Peter Firstbrook points out, in 1900BC clay tablets reveal that it was worth 40 times more than silver, whereas by the 7th century BC silver was worth 2,000 times more than iron. In just over a millennium it had depreciated in value 80,000 times.

Another characteristic of the Iron Age was the deposition of a large number of 'hoards' where prestigious metal and pottery items were deliberately concealed but never exhumed. Iron, as witnessed by the Indo European tribes' invasion of Anatolia, was also the perfect substance for creating strong, powerful weapons. All of these things point to an increasingly hostile society with warfare coming to the forefront. From the 2nd century BC onwards coins also began to appear in Britain. At first these were imported from the Continent, but by the 1st century BC the Britons had begun to produce their own currency and, for the first time in the history of these islands, the names of some of its inhabitants were preserved for posterity. Iron Age coins are common in the south and east of the country, but rare in the north and west. In Cheshire an exceptional selection of coinage has been found along the shores of Meols on the Wirral, perhaps the site of an Iron Age trading port which continued in use into the Romano-British period.

Although it is often the hillfort which springs to mind when thinking of Iron Age settlement, this was by no means the only type of habitation at that period. There are thousands of examples of contemporary non-defended settlements, in addition to the small-enclosed farmsteads occupied by single households, but unfortunately very little excavation has taken place in these. After about 150BC, the climate began to improve, and by the time of the first visit by the Romans to Britain it was more or less the same as it is today. In most areas hillforts were abandoned as Late Iron Age people were again able to settle on the lowland soils; then the pressures on the land eased. At a small number of sites, however, particularly those in southern Britain closest to the Continent and the ever-growing Roman Empire, defences were massively extended with multiple earthworks, ditches, long entrances and complex outworks constructed.

Daily Life

Of all prehistoric societies, the Iron Age is probably the most well-known thanks to programmes such as the BBC's *Surviving the Iron Age*. Apart from the new developments in metal technology and a more complex, socially ordered society, daily life for the average Iron Age person was essentially very similar to that of the Bronze Age. People still lived in roundhouses made of wood, wattle and dawb and thatch, although settlements were often enclosed by a ditch and low bank topped by a palisade fence. This was not so much for defence against human attack, but to keep children and animals in and dangerous wild animals out. A typical settlement consisted of one or more roundhouses occupied by members of an extended family with a granary, animal enclosure and storage pits within the compound.

Reconstructed Iron Age roundhouses at Castell Henllys hillfort in Pembrokeshire.

Food was still roasted and baked over an open fire or heated in water using potboilers. A large number of fire-cracked stones used for this purpose have been found during excavations in Mellor. Methods for grinding corn had advanced slightly with the development of the round or disc quern, which could be easily rotated using a handle. Two examples of these were recovered from Danes Moss near Macclesfield during construction of the North Staffordshire railway line in the 19th century, while the lower half of a rotary quern was unearthed in Tarvin. Animals were reared and eaten. Evidence in the region comes from Brookhouse Farm near Halewood in Merseyside, where cattle and pig bones showed signs of butchering. There were developments in pottery styles too, with finer wares appearing from the 7th century BC onwards, although the majority of vessels used on a day-to-day basis were coarse ware ceramics, such as large jars used for storage, or wooden plates and bowls. For most of the later prehistoric era pottery was handmade. Only on the dawn of the Roman Conquest did a fast

wheel for throwing pots come into use. In Cheshire late prehistoric pottery is very rare apart from the containers used for transporting salt.

The quern found in Danes Moss near Macclesfield during construction of the railway line in the 19th century (Sainter).

Evidence from clothing preserved in burials shows that Iron Age people wore colourful, chequered clothes, woven from wool on looms within the roundhouses. The typical outfit for a male consisted of a long tunic and long trousers fastened at the waist with a leather belt. They wore sandals on their feet and wore their hair long with carefully trimmed beards and

moustaches. The women wore a similar outfit with a full-length skirt instead of trousers. Strabo provides us with an interesting description of the British barbarian: 'The men of Britain are taller than the Gauls and not so yellow haired. Their bodies are more loosely built. This will give you an idea of their size: I myself in Rome saw youths standing half a foot taller that the tallest in the city although they were ungainly in build'. There were a few new introductions as far as personal hygiene went, with luxury items such as bronze or iron razors, mirrors and combs made from bone, wood and antler, but these were probably used only by the upper sections of society. One possible razor was found during excavations at Beeston Castle.

Compared to other regions in Britain the soils and rivers of Cheshire have rarely yielded items of significance from the Iron Age. There are few coins and metal artefacts and no hoards or items of highly ornamented metalwork, but as will be seen in the final section of this chapter, certain discoveries made in a bog in Wilmslow help to make up for the deficiency.

A reconstructed prehistoric loom at Castell Henllys in Pembrokeshire showing how the colourful chequered material of the Iron Age was woven.

Iron Age Cheshire

In the past many historians have portrayed Cheshire as an economic backwater, thinly populated by technically underdeveloped pastoralists until the advent of the Industrial Revolution. Recent research by Keith Matthews of Chester Archaeology, however, has suggested otherwise. One of the most significant developments in Iron Age Cheshire was the exploitation of the county's rich underground salt deposits and associated long distance trade networks. As mentioned earlier, during the last two centuries the eroding coastline of the North Wirral has brought to light a potentially highly significant site at Meols near Hoylake. From 1810 onwards, the inhabitants of the local area gathered numerous artefacts dating from the Mesolithic through to the medieval period. These were retrieved from a submerged forest on the beaches of the eroding coastline from which reports were made regarding the presence of timber structures, both round and rectangular, which had been preserved in the peat. Some of these are believed to have been Iron Age, but unfortunately any settlement remnants have now largely been washed away by the sea.

A number of exotic finds of Iron Age date have come to light on the coastline around Meols, particularly in the area known as Dove Point, although the whereabouts of these cannot now be traced. They include a small gold Celtic British coin from the 1st century BC, two swan's neck pins (pins with their heads bent into an 'S' shape); three Carthaginian silver coins from North Africa and two from the Coriosolites tribe (inhabitants of what is now Brittany in France) decorated with a head on one side and a horse above a wheel on the other. Most recently, a silver coin of Tigranes II of Armenia (20BC to 6BC) was found in 1987 at Leasowe Common to the south of Dove Point.

Elsewhere in the region other exotic artefacts include a 5th century BC amphora which was allegedly dredged up from the River Dee about 1900, and a high status leather drinking vessel with copper alloy fittings from Beeston Castle (see page 150). Some believe the former could be an illegal import of more recent date, but crustaceans on its outer surface are consistent with long-term submergence in the Dee, rather than in warmer waters such as the Mediterranean. Other high status finds have come from Beeston and include a La Tène type dagger and spearhead together with a swan's neck pin. Further imported coins include a Roman denarius dating from 211BC to 100BC which was found a few years ago just over the border (into Greater Manchester) in a farmer's field in Warburton; also a Carthaginian coin and coin of King Pyrrhus (king of Epirus in Greece between 318BC and 272BC) found in the bed of the River Irk in the 19th century. An unusual escutcheon in the shape of a bull's head was also unearthed in the not too distant past by metal detectorists in Crewe.

Coins of the types discovered around Meols are commonly found in the Channel Islands, and in the south of Britain at sites such as Hengistbury Head in Dorset which was known to have extensive trade links with the Coriosolites tribe of Brittany, and it is here that most Iron Age specialists have concentrated their research. Keith Matthews, however, points out that artefacts associated with the Coriosolites have also been found at a number of other coastal sites along the western margins of Britain. Carthaginian coins have been discovered in Wales at Caerleon, Monmouth and Towyn. Meols is therefore just one of a number of small ports from Cornwall to Ayr with such trade connections.

The bull's head escutcheon found by metal detectorists in Crewe.

Some historians have tried to explain the appearance of luxury goods in Cheshire as items transported along long distance trade routes from community to community, slowly making their way northwards. But Matthews believes that it is more than likely they came into the county directly through exchange with foreign merchants. Of particular interest are the coins, as these only have symbolic value to coin-using communities, something the North West of England was not. Matthews believes therefore that there must have been organised trade taking place in Meols between a local élite and foreign merchants, indicating a socially ordered society, hitherto unrecognised in Cheshire. It has been suggested that minerals from North Wales and salt from Cheshire were being exported to the Mediterranean, but as with the copper in the Bronze Age, what they were exchanged for remains a mystery. Perhaps the local tribal leaders liked unusual cattle or consumables such as wine, which would not show up in the archaeological record.

Salt Production

Throughout history salt, essential for human survival, has been treated as an important and precious commodity. To spill salt is still considered bad luck worldwide and superstition dictates that a pinch must be thrown over the left shoulder in order to ward off ill fortune. This folklore may stem back to ancient times when salt was considered sacred and precious due to its magical properties, and the fact that it was extremely difficult to get hold of. During prehistoric times it played a vitally important role in the preservation of food through the winter, as well as in cheesemaking and in the drying and preservation of hides. It may also have been used as an antiseptic for treating and healing wounds.

Cheshire is particularly fortunate in having a natural resource of rock salt which was laid down during the Triassic Period around 200 million years ago, when the area was submerged under a large, shallow sea. In locations such as Middlewich and Nantwich natural brine forms when groundwater reaches this rock salt and dissolves it into underground streams, which can be up to eight times saltier than seawater. As with most things in Cheshire, the Romans are often given credit for first exploiting these streams where they welled up to the surface as natural brine springs. However, evidence from the Iron Age, and possibly even from the Late Bronze Age, indicates that salt making was taking place on a reasonably large scale in the county during prehistoric times. The Romans did obtain the salt in the Middlewich area from the 1st century AD, naming it *Salinae* because of the rich deposits there, but they were merely continuing a long tradition of manufacture dating back hundreds of years.

The salt production methods employed by the Britons in the Iron Age, and indeed in the Romano-British period, were incredibly simple. In inland areas they collected the brine from natural springs and then evaporated it in open pottery containers, supported on cylinders over a fire to retrieve the salt crystals. Salt was also extracted from seawater in coastal areas. Extensive finds of Iron Age salt making vessels (known as briquetage) have come from Lincolnshire, the Fenlands of East Anglia and along the Essex coastline, where seawater was first concentrated by boiling in pottery pans 60cm wide, 120cm long, and about 1.2cm thick. Once strong brine was obtained it was channelled into tanks to allow the grit and sediment to sink to the bottom. The solution was then evaporated in small pottery vessels supported on pillars over a fire. These pots were constantly topped up until they were full of crystals and then broken open to produce a lump of finished salt, which was distributed in some kind of organic container such as a basket or leather bag.

In Britain generally, no major buildings directly associated with the salt industry have been discovered prior to the medieval period. Documentary evidence from the Middle Ages makes reference to the brine springs in Droitwich (Shropshire) revealing that they were only operated on a part-time basis from June to December, and that production was dependent on a variety of weather conditions such as the amount of rainfall and resulting groundwater. It is likely, therefore, that during prehistoric times salt making was also performed on a seasonal basis, perhaps only during the summer months. Salt makers could utilise the forces of nature, such as the sun and wind, as well as fire to assist in drying the brine. Salt working was probably part of the annual cycle of food production carried out by family groups, with women undertaking tasks such as the manufacture of the pottery vessels. Artefacts indicate that children may also have been involved from an early age. In the Fenlands a number of child-sized cups have been found in salt working areas and, even more revealing, a doll made from briquetage fabric unearthed in Addlethorpe, Yorkshire.

Excavations at salt making sites within Cheshire have produced relatively small amounts of briquetage in comparison to coastal sites. This is almost certainly due to the fact that the finished salt from the former was distributed in the vessels in which it was evaporated. In inland areas generally, salt containers comprised a type of coarse, funnel-shaped pottery known as Very Coarse Pottery or VCP. In order to enable the water to evaporate from the brine, the VCP had to be able to withstand variable temperatures and be of such a shape as to allow the vapours to escape easily. This was achieved by creating highly porous bodies fashioned from clay containing fragments of stone (known as temper) which created voids through shrinkage during drying, or by adding organic materials such as cereal chaff, which burnt off in the firing process.

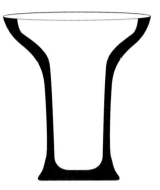

In Cheshire the glacial drift clays, which contain large fragments of sandstone and chert, were used to make a very distinctive type of bright orange, stony VCP. This was always handmade, possibly built up using coils of clay with no attempt to hide the joins, making it rough on the exterior. Dr Elaine Morris, a Research Fellow at the University of Southampton, has been studying consumer sites where ceramic containers from Cheshire have been found. Her research shows that in the Early Iron Age Cheshire salt containers were the only type to be found in the area north of the Severn, with pots from both Cheshire and the springs at Droitwich in the river's middle reaches. To the south however, only VCP from Droitwich has so far been discovered. By the Middle and Late Iron Age, Cheshire salt was being traded as far as Anglesey and the Lleyn Peninsula in North Wales, in the North Midlands and in the Welsh Marches. In some cases VCP containers have been found up to 125 kilometres from their probable source (more than double the distribution distance from that of the Droitwich salt

A typical example of Cheshire stony VCP used for transporting salt during prehistoric times (after Morris, 1985).

springs). Clay dug between Middlewich and Nantwich was used to make the VCP found at a number of Iron Age settlements across the Welsh Marches and Western England, and the counties of Derbyshire, Nottinghamshire and Leicestershire. Cheshire salt was reaching the hillfort of The Wrekin in Shropshire as early as the 5th century BC.

Closer to home one of the earliest discoveries of VCP came recently from excavations on a site at Brook House Farm in Bruen Stapleford, and at Irby on the Wirral. Fragments of the salt containers were found in context with Late Bronze Age pottery (circa 1000BC to 800BC) indicating that exploitation of the county's salt resources began much earlier than originally thought. Elsewhere, several types of VCP, dating to the Middle and Late Iron Age, were discovered at Beeston Castle during excavations in the 1980s, suggesting the hillfort was involved in the Pre-Roman salt trade network. Most of the pottery recovered was stony VCP but due to its soft and crumbly nature, the majority of the sherds were small pieces with the rim and base parts surviving best. It was therefore impossible for archaeologists to reconstruct a profile of a stony VCP from Beeston, but similar material from other sites indicates that such containers were tall and flared, with small flat bases of up to 170mm in diameter and rims of up to 250mm in diameter.

A second type of coarse pottery, tempered using sand and organic substances, was also discovered on the Beeston Castle site and proved to be more unusual. It had a very thick (30mm) and small (60mm to 80mm) base with rough smoothing marks on the exterior. The VCP from Beeston generally appears in the contexts of the Later Iron Age, but several fragments beneath the Early Iron Age platform to the rear of the rampart, and within the rampart itself, suggest that these VCP containers were of an earlier date than the Middle Iron Age rampart (which has been radiocarbon dated to circa 400BC). More recently 21 sherds of stony, orange Cheshire VCP were found in ten different contexts during recent excavations at the Mellor hillfort near Stockport. Other finds of VCP, similar to the second type from

Beeston, have come from Handbridge south of the Dee in Chester.

In Cheshire generally, the majority of evidence for Iron Age salt working comes from its distribution to settlement sites such as the hillforts mentioned above, rather than from the salt working sites (known as salterns) themselves. However, evidence for a possible early saltern came to light in July 1992 during the construction of a pipeline for British Gas between Crewe and Sandbach, when two pits were found to contain evidence of salt production activities. The first produced small quantities of Roman briquetage, possibly dating to the 1st to 4th centuries AD, but the second incorporated a few fragments of VCP 'similar to material recovered from Iron Age contexts at a number of sites in North West England'. This was the first discovery of Cheshire VCP in a salt working context. Unfortunately, as is often the case in the county, the majority of recent research into salt working areas has concentrated on the activities of the Romano-British period, so very little else is known of the Iron Age salterns.

Finally, one question often posed by archaeologists is why salt from inland areas was transported in heavy pottery containers rather than in lighter leather bags or baskets. The answer probably lies in the local traditions and the quality of the finished product. Recent studies have shown that VCP vessels were only made in regions where other types of pottery were fashioned and exchanged on a regular basis. In areas such as the Fens, where ceramics were not made for trade elsewhere, the only pottery associated with the salt trade is the troughs and pillars used for drying it. There is a distinct lack of evidence of the sort of packaging associated with transportation, indicating that the salt must have been packed and distributed within some kind of organic container such as a leather bag or basket. It seems likely therefore that in certain areas the container was as important as the commodity itself, perhaps signifying its regional source or the group of people who made and used it. For traders to lug Cheshire salt over long distances in heavy, fragile pots, which served no other purpose but to be broken up before use, it must have had some significance.

Settlement Sites in Cheshire

In Cheshire, as elsewhere during the closing years of the Bronze Age, the communities of the region, under pressure from the deteriorating climate and increased pressures on the land, began to enclose and defend their settlements. At the end of the 2nd millennium BC enclosed habitation sites began to appear in areas best suited to the environment, namely those which could take advantage of natural defence and had a suitable landscape for food production, together with a readily available supply of water. Some of the earliest

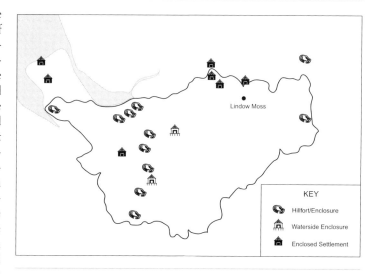

Figure 18 – The Iron Age tribes of England and Wales.

sites of this type have been discovered recently at Brook House Farm at Bruen Stapleford in the Dee Valley, and at Irby on the Wirral, both of which will be covered in detail later in this chapter.

140

In the following years, a number of heavily defended hillforts and promontory enclosures sprang up, mainly concentrated around the Central Ridge area. All of these, except Eddisbury, made use of natural features such as steep cliffs, rivers or lakes. The earliest, at Beeston, probably began life as an open settlement in the Bronze Age, developing its heavy defences much later. The forts at Beeston and Eddisbury are much larger than the others in the area suggesting they were key sites. Perhaps they were heavily developed hillforts inhabited by the élite, with control over the population and landscape in the mid-Cheshire area, especially the salt trade routes. At Beeston there is also evidence for large-scale grain processing and storage facilities. Other sites, for example the smaller defended enclosures at Helsby, Oak Mere, Kelsborrow, Maiden Castle, Bradley and Woodhouses, were probably only short lived and abandoned as the population outgrew them. In the Early to Middle Iron Age, settlement in the region is still primarily only known from these hillforts and enclosures.

A one-third size reconstructed roundhouse at Mellor hillfort, built by archaeology students from Ridge Danyers college in Marple.

By the Middle to Late Iron Age the climate had begun to improve again, and the majority of the defended enclosures were abandoned in favour of independent enclosed farmsteads. The hillforts of Beeston and Eddisbury may have continued in use for a while longer, but were almost certainly abandoned before the Roman invasion. In general, people began to move back into areas, such as those on the boulder clays, which had previously been unusable due to waterlogging. The most common form of settlement type in Cheshire in the centuries before the Roman Conquest appears to have been the double or single ditched compound of less than two hectares in area, often curvilinear and containing one or more circular buildings. These lowland sites often show evidence for mixed farming and small-scale metalworking activities. One of the most prolific areas discovered to date lies in the Lower Mersey Valley around Warrington, where 12 enclosure sites, mainly brought to light as cropmarks on aerial photographs, are suggestive of intensive valley occupation.

The People

In order to gain a better understanding of the nature of Cheshire during the Iron Age, it is necessary to take a look at the native tribes living in the area at the dawn of the Roman Conquest. There is no way of knowing when these tribal units first developed, but according to various classical sources and evidence from coinage, they were well established in the closing centuries of the 1st millennium BC, indicative of an earlier presence in the country.

The colourful British *barbari* (from the Latin meaning 'bearded ones'), or the *keltoi* as they were known by the Greeks, are mentioned in the texts of writers such as Julius Caesar, Strabo, Diodorus Siculus, and Cornelius Tacitus whose father-in-law, Gnaeus Julius Agricola, was Roman Governor of Britain in the 70s and 80s AD. It is very difficult to establish well-defined geographical boundaries from these descriptions, but Cheshire appears to have been on the fringes of three different tribal groups – the hillfort building communities of the Cornovii to the west and south of the county, and the largely non-fort building peoples of the Brigantes and Corieltauvi to the north and east (see Figure 19).

The Cornovii taking their name from Cernunnos, the Celtic horned god, mainly occupied the area of what is today modern Shropshire, but also extended into parts of Staffordshire, western Cheshire and north-east Wales. Unfortunately very little is known about this tribe as they never produce any coinage and only received the briefest of mentions in the classical sources. They did, however, build numerous large, powerful hillforts such as Caer Caradoc near Chapel Lawn, Bodbury Ring, Bury Ditches near Bishops Castle, Old Oswestry fort and, largest of all, The Wrekin near Little Wenlock. A so-called 'Celtic Head', said to represent the horned figure of Cernunnos, lies to the rear of the church in Rostherne in Cheshire. It has been suggested that this may have come from an Iron Age or Romano-British shrine overlooking the nearby mere. Alternatively it could be much more recent in origin, as a number of similar heads have proved to date from the 17th century.

Figure 18 – Iron Age Settlements covered in the text.

The 'Celtic Head' carving in Rostherne churchyard.

The Brigantes, whose name means 'hill dwellers' or 'highlanders', on the other hand are quite well documented in classical literature. Described by Tacitus as 'the most numerous people of Britain' in the 1st century AD, they were a federation of smaller communities who held most of the Pennines and the broad plains to the east and west. Unlike the Cornovii, the Brigantes constructed very few hillforts, but preferred to live in smaller defended hillcrofts. Settlement sites were characteristically quite small in the region, covering no more than a couple of acres. They were roughly circular or sub-rectangular in shape, with between two and four dwellings surrounded by a timber palisade. Their origins have been traced back to the 6th century BC and continued without change until the Romano-British period. Apart from the exception of the recently discovered hillfort at Mellor near Stockport, and earthworks of uncertain date at Eddisbury near Macclesfield, this is generally characteristic of east Cheshire.

To the south and east of the Brigantes, in the area of the Trent and Welland valleys, around Leicestershire, Lincolnshire and Derbyshire up to the line of the Humber, was a tribe known as the Corieltauvi or Coritani. They also built few hillforts and preferred to live in smaller settlements. A coin of the Corieltauvi, dating to the last few decades of the 1st century BC and decorated on one side with a boar and on the other with a horse, was found by a metal detectorist in plough soil at Brindley near Nantwich in 1992. Another was found at Halton Castle in Runcorn. At this time the Corieltauvi had begun to produce coinage bearing a pair of names, perhaps based on that from Gaul where the names of two magistrates were used. One name in particular 'VOLISIOS' appears on much of the later coinage, in the form of Volisios Dvmnovellavnos, Volisios Dvmnocoveros and Volisios Cartivel. These may represent the names of joint rulers or perhaps different members of the same family such as the sons of Volisios.

The coin of Volisios Dvmnovellavnos, discovered in Nantwich in 1992.

What is particularly interesting about these coins is that instead of being found in the tribal heartland of the Corieltauvi, they are found much further north, most notably from hoards in West Yorkshire dating to the post-conquest period. According to Malcolm Todd, it is possible that Volisios may have been a refugee chieftain who established a short-lived clan in the region of south-west Yorkshire, south Lancashire and parts of eastern Cheshire, after the majority of his tribe further south had succumbed without resistance to Roman rule. This may have survived until the Roman conquest of the Pennines around 71AD.

Apart from these few coins of the Corieltauvi, only one other coin bearing an Iron Age tribal name has so far been discovered in the county. In 1998 a gold stater coin, dating to the latter half of the 1st century AD, was discovered in Knutsford. It bore the name of 'BODVOC' and was beautifully decorated with a horse and chariot. Bodvoc was a ruler of the northern Dobunni tribe who resided in the Gloucestershire area, begging the question – how did this coin come to be in Cheshire?

Hillforts and Promontory Enclosures

In Britain there are over 3,000 hillforts or defended hilltop settlements, ranging from about 0.2 hectares (0.5 acres) to 320 hectares (800 acres) in size, with main concentrations in south-west Wales, Cornwall and the Welsh Marches, and reasonably concentrated distributions in North Wales, the Cotswolds and Wessex. Elsewhere hillforts are quite sparsely distributed, apart from in areas such as the Pennines where they are almost non-existent. The majority lie on hills, on a level below 305m (1000ft) above sea level, and are believed to have been created during a period of uncertainty and tension from around 650BC onwards. However, recent research has shown that the defence of hilltop sites has a much longer and more varied history, occurring at different times in different places.

Essentially a hillfort was a heavily fortified structure, protected by a number of defences, which could include earth and stone ramparts, palisade fences, ditches, specially designed entrances and natural slopes and precipices. Some appear to have been constructed as a place for temporary refuge and are almost completely devoid of occupation, whilst others were early forms of towns, with buildings and food stores carefully laid out; administration, trade, industry and craft also took place on site. These hilltop sites also provided the setting for ritual activity, with feasting and the sacrifice of animals, household objects and in some cases even people. Religious beliefs are also apparent in the laying out of many buildings such as roundhouses, and entrances are often orientated directly towards the equinox or midwinter solstice.

Evidence from Cheshire bears witness to the fact that hilltop settlements were not just an Iron Age phenomenon, but in some cases existed much earlier. Very few finds have come from the forts in the county and until more work is carried out one can only speculate on their dates of origin. It could be that the hilltop sites were occupied during the Bronze Age, but defended later at the beginning of the Iron Age. Of those that have been dated, all appear to be of Late

Bronze Age or Early to Middle Iron Age date, in contrast to the sites in the south of the country which continued on in use until the Roman Conquest. It appears, therefore, that in the centuries before the Roman invasion the majority of Cheshire hillforts had been abandoned.

As with the earlier Neolithic henges and funerary monuments, the amount of labour invested in the construction of hillfort defences was phenomenal. Not only did Iron Age communities quarry out large areas of soil and rock to create banks, ditches, and postholes but they also felled thousands of trees, needed to make up the main fabrication of the rampart, as well as palisades and cladding posts. The amount of effort required to cut and shape timber poles and then transport them up steep slopes is extraordinary. James Dyer notes that a study carried out on the construction of Ravensburgh Castle hillfort in Hertfordshire, with its 1190 metre circuit of defences enclosing 8.9 hectares, has shown that it would have taken approximately 175,000 man-hours to construct (the equivalent of 100 men working for 219 days). Of course the forts in Cheshire are much smaller in size than this, with the largest at Beeston measuring approximately 4 hectares, but nevertheless, it is still an incredible feat for what were essentially farming communities.

The Northern Forts

At the northern end of Cheshire's Central Ridge lies a cluster of three hilltop sites; they form part of a group of defended sites running from the Mersey Estuary in the north to the Malpas-Peckforton Ridge in the south. The first, marked on the OS map as a settlement, can be found close to the village of Bradley, a couple of kilometres to the south-east of Frodsham. Known simply as Bradley, this 0.7 hectare (1.7 acre) enclosure lies on ground sloping down from the mid-Cheshire Ridge to the River Weaver below. Most of the defences have been badly ploughed and disturbed by the addition of recent field boundaries, but traces of the bank and ditch can still be made out in the field to the east of the footpath. To the west of the site a sunken track, resembling a hollow way, runs down to a brook below which marks the northern extent of the settlement. The views are somewhat obscured by the modern hedge line, but in prehistoric times the inhabitants would have had a spectacular vista over the area of modern Frodsham and out across the Mersey Estuary.

The remaining earthworks of the Iron Age settlement at Bradley, near Frodsham.

Approximately three kilometres to the south-east of Bradley, lies the hillfort of Woodhouses on Woodhouse Hill. The 1.6 hectare (4 acre) enclosure lies on the sandstone at the northern end of the mid-Cheshire Ridge at 137m (449ft) above sea level. To the south and west it is protected by steep slopes, while to the north and east the ground rises gently and is defended by a rampart, but no ditch. The rampart has been quite badly damaged and broken in places yet where it can be traced, it ranges between 2 metres and 0.5 metres in height. Excavations in 1951 revealed that it was originally 4 metres wide and faced to the front and rear with dry-stone walling. The whole area is heavily forested, so in order to see the remaining defences a walk through the woods is required, but it is best not to visit in the summer months as it

One of the large ramparts of the unfinished hillfort at Woodhouses near Frodsham.

becomes heavily overgrown with bracken. The only finds from the area are a number of small rounded sandstones, possibly used as slingstones. Research has shown that a slinger, standing on top of a rampart, could throw a stone with accuracy about 110 metres downhill, while anyone trying to throw one uphill would have had their range severely curtailed by the addition of the defences.

The third hillfort on the northern end of the Central Ridge lies just under two kilometres from Woodhouse Hill in Helsby. In the care of The National Trust, this 2.3 hectare (5.7 acre) promontory fort lies at 140m (459ft) above sea level overlooking the Mersey. The site is defended to the north-west by sheer cliffs which drop almost vertically to the marsh land below, and to the north by two subsidiary banks on the cliff ledge below. To the south the land rises more gently and is protected by a double arc of ramparts and a ditch. The ramparts are quite badly damaged, but the inner one can still be traced along most of its

Helsby Hill as viewed from the services on the M56 motorway.

length and is best preserved to the west. The outer bank and ditch are almost impossible to see on the ground, however. The former was recognised on aerial photographs taken in the 1930s while the latter is only apparent as a parch mark at certain times of year. The entrance appears to have been at the western end of the inner rampart where the bank has been widened, heightened and provided with an inturn.

Small scale excavations were carried out on a section of the inner rampart at Helsby by J.D. Bu'Lock in 1955, revealing that the bank was composed of a central core of rocks, rubble and sand, and faced front and back with dry-stone walling made up of sandstone blocks just under one metre wide. The rampart was at least 3.5 metres thick at the base and must have stood at least 2.5 metres high. To the rear of the bank Bu'Lock uncovered a layer of burnt sand containing charcoal and fire-cracked potboilers representing an occupation layer.

Castle Ditch, Eddisbury

The earthworks of Castle Ditch lie at 152m (499ft) above sea level on a sandstone outcrop on the eastern edge of the Central Ridge close to Delamere. Unfortunately the defences to the south and east have largely been destroyed by stone quarrying and ploughing, but the fort is estimated to have been approximately 3.5 hectares originally, making it the second largest in Cheshire after Beeston.

Eddisbury Hill has a long and complex history, with the earliest activity taking place in the Neolithic, when cremations in pottery vessels were placed in a flat cemetery in the vicinity (see page 39). It is likely that the settlement site began life as a defended homestead and was later transformed into a hillfort during the Iron Age. In addition, pottery and roof tile dating to the 2nd century AD have provided evidence for Roman activity (which is not surprising as the old Roman road from Chester to Manchester runs along the bottom of the hill). Furthermore an occupation floor, over a silted up ditch in the western area, appears to date to the Saxon period, perhaps when the hilltop was reused as a defended burh by Aethelfreda in 914AD in order to protect the kingdom of Mercia from the Vikings.

The earthworks at Eddisbury were described and illustrated in the early 19th century by George Ormerod in his *History of Cheshire*, 'The form is nearly oval, and it situation within the inclosure called the old pale, on the summit of the hill which gives the name to the Hundred. It contains 11 acres, 3 roods and 10 poles, of statute measure; and extends 250 yards in breadth and 400 in length, exclusive of the projection of rock at the south east angle. The eastern side is irregular, being defended by a natural precipice; the other parts, being accessible

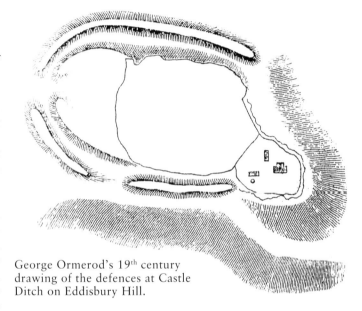

George Ormerod's 19th century drawing of the defences at Castle Ditch on Eddisbury Hill.

by a gentle slope, are defended by a ditch and double rampart with an entrance to the West. The ditch is about twelve yards wide; the ramparts which are constructed with red stone, now buried under the soil accumulated by the lapse of centuries, are still fourteen feet high in some places. No other vestiges of buildings are distinguishable'.

The fort was excavated by Professor W.J. Varley of Liverpool University between 1935 and 1938. His findings confirmed Ormerod's description of a double line of ramparts to the north and west, and a single bank to the south and east (the latter was somewhat hard to discern having been badly damaged by the addition of a medieval building and later field boundaries).

Varley published an article on the excavations in the *Transactions of the Lancashire and Cheshire Antiquarian Society* in 1950, concluding that the area to the east was enclosed first, and was later strengthened to the north by the addition of a second outer rampart. The original entrance had been overlain by later archaeology, but Varley believed it had possibly been revetted with timber and had a wooden guardroom to the south of an internal corridor. Later, an additional area was enclosed to the west with double (bivallate) ramparts made of clay laid on a stone footing to the north, and a timber entrance with an inturned gateway added to the western end. The latter appeared to have been burnt at some stage.

The ramparts of Castle Ditch viewed from the minor road to the south (there is no access to the hillfort itself).

The next phase saw the addition of 'timber-lacing' features as at Maiden Castle. Stone revetments were added to the front and back of a rubble and sand core, interlaced with timber along the entire length of the double line of ramparts, and twin stone-lined guard chambers may have replaced the earlier timber one at the entrance. Four posts, found near to the guard chambers, were believed to represent the footings of a timber bridge or raised walkway connecting the ends of the two ramparts, with a gate hung between the back pair. At this point, the ditch between the two had been re-cut. Varley concluded that the east and west sections of the fort had eventually been joined together. The final phase had come with the refurbishment of the outer defences when the ditch was re-cut, and a new rubble rampart with stone revetments was constructed along the line of the earlier one.

Varley's interpretation that the hillfort developed from a smaller site was accepted for many years, but a survey carried out by the Keele Office of the Royal Commission on Historic Monuments in England (RCHME) in early 1987 called into question the evidence and the excavation methods of the 1930s. Unfortunately neither the original site documentation nor any of the finds have been found, so all they could use was Varley's article in the *Transactions of the Lancashire and Cheshire Antiquarian Society*. According to the RCHME team, however, this report is 'in the form of an extended essay with minimal use of plan and section' and contains no details of the excavated pottery or other finds, making their task extremely difficult.

During excavations Varley had only examined four small areas, and evidence from only one of these trenches led him to his conclusions. The supposition that the hillfort was enlarged, was based solely on one tiny area in the northern section of the rampart, where the defences seemed to pull in slightly. Varley concluded that this 'pull in' was either associated with an entrance or represented the join between two sets of defences. He settled upon the latter interpretation, discounting the possibility of it being a blocked up entrance, because he noted that the ditch swept straight across where there should have been an entrance gap. Later on, however, he contradicted himself by concluding that the original rampart probably did not have a ditch after all.

Following fieldwalking in the 1980s, the Royal Commission surveyors surmised that Varley's conclusions were either unsubstantiated by modern field evidence or that he was simply wrong. No definite reinterpretation could be reached, but it was decided that the 'pull in' feature could just as easily represent a blocked up entrance within a larger fort. This seemed especially likely, as an entrance in this particular location would have meant that people approaching the fort had to pass a large section of rampart before arriving at the gate. The final statement in the Royal Commission report concludes, 'Unfortunately the very field evidence that might have allowed a deduction to be made is now missing, destroyed by the excavation trench...that was meant to investigate it', - what more is there to say?

According to Ormerod there was also a further hillfort in the Delamere region known as Finness Hill. He writes, 'Of the other supposed British work of Finborrow or Finness, no traces have been discovered. Erdswick (H.MSS. 473 p.5) speaks of it occupying one of the elevations of the forest.' This has now disappeared without trace.

Kelsborrow Castle

This fort lies on a promontory formed by two dry valleys on the western edge of the Central Ridge at 122m (400ft) above sea level, and is overlooked by higher ground to the east. It was mentioned again by Ormerod in the 19th century and described as 'a strong British camp, formed for the protection of the pass', the pass referring to the gap in the mid-Cheshire Ridge at Kelsall. The site is defended naturally to the south by steep slopes, and to the north by a single arced bank and external ditch which

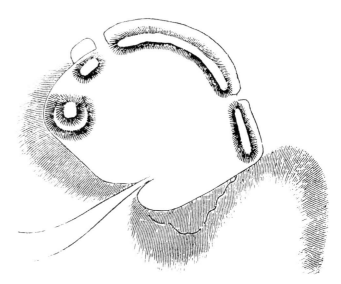

Ormerod's 19th century plan of the hillfort at Kelsborrow.

remains today only in the eastern section. According to Ormerod, the rampart was 'fourteen yards thick at the base' and the ditch 'about eight yards wide'. At the eastern end of the rampart a small gap between the defences and the break of slope may represent the remains of an entrance. Ormerod's plan indicates, however, that there were two entrances, one to the east and one to the north, about a quarter of the way down from either end. As with many hillfort sites, Kelsborrow has suffered much in recent years with its earthworks badly damaged by ploughing. A resistivity survey was carried out on the western part of the site in March 1996, revealing a number of roughly circular features around 15 metres in diameter. These may represent house foundations or trampled clay floors.

Ormerod also refers to the discovery of two significant artefacts within the defences of the fort in the early 19th century, 'The claim of the Britons to the erection of this fortress is strengthened by the discovery of a brass celt [palstave], found within the inclosure in the year 1810, and now in the possession of Mr Barrit of Manchester. It measures six inches in length and weighs 1lb. 3 3/4oz'. He continues 'At the same time a fragment of an iron sword was discovered which makes it probable that the works were the scene of warlike contention...'.

Beeston Castle

One of the most well-known and intensively excavated sites in Cheshire lies on a rocky summit at the northern end of the Peckforton Hills, the southernmost group of hills in the mid-Cheshire Ridge, at 160m (500ft) above the Plain. Today the 13th century ruins of Beeston Castle, under the care of English Heritage, offer stunning views from the Pennines in the east to the mountains of Wales in the west; to the north across the Mersey Estuary and south to the gothic castle at Peckforton and The Wrekin beyond. Evidence has revealed however that the hilltop was occupied as early as 1000BC in the Late Bronze Age and was later crowned by an Iron Age hillfort.

The site is protected to the north and west by vertical rock faces and steeply sloping sides in other directions. It is virtually inaccessible apart from to the south-east where the entrance of the later castle still survives today. Excavations on the site, carried out in two phases, were directed by Laurence Keen between 1968 and 1973, and by Peter Hough from 1975 to 1985. They revealed that the early site had a long and complex history from the Neolithic through to the Late Iron Age.

The earliest phase, discussed previously, consisted of a possible Neolithic settlement in the area of the Outer Gateway. At some time in the Late Bronze Age (before circa 900BC) the first defences were constructed on the hilltop in the form of a palisade, represented on site by a number of postholes in the Outer Gateway and Outer Ward. This was then replaced with a slight bank, interlaced with timber, sometime between 900BC and 650BC when metalworking activities were taking place on site (see page 72-73). At this point, there was no ditch and the entrance was very simple. Beneath this first rampart, close to the entrance, archaeologists discovered two carefully placed, newly cast bronze axes and it is believed these may have been deliberately deposited as foundation offerings, signifying the importance of the hill as a metalworking site. An analysis of the soils and pollen showed that this initial phase of defence took place in an environment of mixed woodland with local clearance for crop cultivation.

The original rampart was eventually overlain by two more complex phases of defence. The initial phase comprised a larger bank made from timber with a sand core, a steep-sided ditch, and a defended inturned entrance created by building banks on either side of a narrow passageway. Evidence from postholes and a cache of slingstones suggests there may also have been twin-fighting platforms at the entrance. By later prehistory with the disappearance of the woodland, the site had become increasingly open. Sometime, between 450BC and the 1st century BC, the final phase of defence occurred when the sand and timber rampart was overlain by a rubble bank created in boxed sections, and revetted by two lines of large boulders. On top of this a large palisade fence or timber walkway was constructed from oak and ash timbers. A considerable quantity of heavily burnt material throughout the excavation site suggested that the defences might have been deliberately vitrified, as at Eddisbury and Maiden Castle. All evidence from the prehistoric defences indicates that they merely cut off the promontory to the east. It is possible, however, that there may have been further additions to the north, south or west, which were buried under the later medieval phases.

In addition to the metalworking centre discussed in the Bronze Age chapter, one of the most significant discoveries at Beeston Castle came from a number of pits and postholes, possibly representing structures rebuilt following a disastrous fire. Associated with these was a large distribution of charred emmer and spelt grains dispersed over a wide area, suggesting the presence of a large grain storage complex or communal parching facilities used to make the grain easier to dehusk. It is believed that this phase may represent a transition from the closure of the metalworking site to the exploitation of the agricultural potential of the area, with the hillfort serving a central role for the communal storage or dehusking of crops grown within the local environs. If this is the case, it could be the first evidence for large-scale crop storage in Britain at that time. In the Outer Ward over 146 postholes, many of which had a filling of stone, had been cut into the bedrock, and it has been hypothesized that these represent the remains of nine roundhouses. Unfortunately the area has been badly disturbed so it is impossible to state categorically whether or not they are of Late Bronze Age or Iron Age date.

The fact that the fort was certainly of great significance and of high status is supported by the discovery of a number of other rich artefacts. During excavations in the Outer Gateway various pieces belonging to a rare, highly ornate, leather drinking vessel, with a bronze rim and fittings, were found. It was undoubtedly fashioned by a highly accomplished craftsman and was well finished down to the last rivet. Different alloys had been used for different parts, chosen for their casting properties, although the differences would not have been noticeable in the finished vessel. It was oval in shape, approximately 135mm long by 75mm across, and probably held just over a pint. Visitors to Beeston can see a replica on display in the English Heritage shop and exhibition area.

Also unearthed was a copper alloy bracelet decorated with round knobs, possibly imported from France or Switzerland. Similar jewellery has been found in the Arras graves in Yorkshire where members of the élite were often buried with their chariots. In addition six different types of shale rings were found, four of which were large enough to be worn as bracelets, armlets or anklets. Two of these were of Bronze Age date, whilst a third was assigned to the Iron Age. These were probably also imported onto the site but from slightly closer to home – many sites in the Pennines have produced isolated finds of partially worked shale rings, suggesting production was quite common here. Other luxury items included two beads, one of amber the other dark blue glass with white decoration dating to the 2nd century BC; also another fragment of an undecorated cast bracelet, a broken horse harness link and a piece of scabbard binding. Iron objects were represented by parts of a dagger in the La Tène style; a spearhead or javelin which still contained fragments of preserved wood; an adze with a curved blade; another small blade, perhaps used as a razor; and a swan's neck pin.

Reconstruction of the leather and copper alloy drinking vessel found in the area of the Outer Gateway at Beeston Castle(after Foster, in Ellis 1993).

Many artefacts associated with domestic activity were also uncovered, including part of a sandstone saddle quern; several green siltstone whetstones; a number of spindle whorls and loomweights of baked clay, and rubbing stones or pestles made from hard volcanic rocks. The range of material indicates that the inhabitants of the fort used a wide variety of stone and recognised the best properties of each. Studies in the area have revealed that over 80% of the stones could have been quarried in the vicinity with the rest acquired locally as glacial erratics. The presence of querns and spindle whorls indicates that corn grinding and weaving were taking place on site in the Late Bronze Age. Further evidence for domestic activity comes from pottery in the form of irregularly fired, handmade vessels fashioned from clays, again readily available in the Beeston area. As with the VCP associated with salt transportation, these pots contained large fragments of rock to prevent too much shrinkage during drying. They were fashioned by building up the sides with coils or collars of clay on top of a flat base. The Late Bronze Age pottery was comprised mainly of large barrel-shaped jars, between 18cm and 22cm in diameter, and a few flat-rimmed bowls.

It would appear from all this evidence that Beeston played a significant role in the area of the mid-Cheshire Ridge throughout prehistory, but particularly during the last millennium BC. It was used temporarily by Mesolithic hunters, settled by the first farmers in the Neolithic, possibly used as a burial ground by Beaker people in the Early Bronze Age, was the focus for metalworking activities in the Late Bronze Age and by the Iron Age was an important tribal centre where local communities came to store and process their grain and trade salt. The presence of a number of rich artefacts suggests that the hilltop was inhabited by members of the local élite. Many other defended sites in the region seem to have been abandoned by the Middle to Late Iron Age, but evidence from the glass beads suggests that Beeston may have continued on in use until the 1st century BC, vacated eventually sometime before the coming of the Romans. Only the hillfort of Castle Ditch at Eddisbury seems to have been of similar size and significance.

Maiden Castle

Maiden Castle is what is known as a plateau fort, with a double row of ramparts cutting off the 0.7 hectare (1.7 acre) sloping sandstone summit of Bickerton Hill, one of the highest points on the southern end of the Central Ridge at 211m (692ft) above sea level. The hilltop has fantastic views to the west over the Dee Valley and guards the pass in the ridge between

Bickerton Hill and Rawhead. It is protected to the north and west by the steep cliffs of a scarp edge, while on the more gentle slopes of the south and east, two curving ramparts defend the easier approach.

As with several of the other hillforts in the area, Maiden Castle was described by George Ormerod in the 19th century. In his opinion it is 'one of the most perfect specimens of British castrametation in Cheshire'. He continues, 'The earth works are on the accessible side of the hill, which is approached by a steep ascent, and form a perfect semicircle, the chord of which from rampart to rampart is about 140 yards. The width of the ditch is fifteen yards, and that of the summit of the rampart eight yards, which descends to the area by a slope of thirteen yards. The only avenue to the camp is by a narrow passage on the north side, near the precipice, and the sides of this passage are cautiously guarded by parallel earthworks. Notwithstanding the elevated situation, and the perfect state of the works, they are so completely overgrown

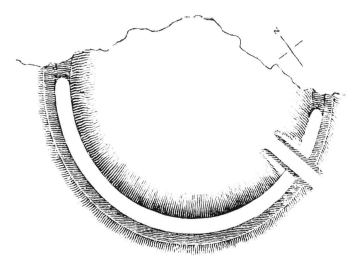

with furze and heath, that a stranger would experience some difficulty in finding the site of the encampment'. The final statement is still true today, and the earthworks are best avoided during the summer months when a sea of bracken overwhelms many of the archaeological features.

Left: George Ormerod's 19th century sketch of the double ramparts at Maiden Castle on Bickerton Hill.

One of the most interesting features at Maiden Castle is the inturned entrance which is located approximately two thirds of the way along the ramparts. This essentially comprises a long passage constructed from dry-stone walling and was designed to protect the fort's point of greatest weakness. It narrows, from circa 5 metres at the outer rampart, to 2.5 metres at the end of the inner rampart and was protected by a gate, about two thirds of the way down, the

postholes of which were discovered during excavations in 1934 and 1935. Within the southern side of the entrance a piece of plain pottery from a high-shouldered jar, a whetstone and a hammer stone were also discovered. In 1980 a subsidiary entrance was found at the southern end of the ramparts.

The inturned entrance at Maiden Castle, once protected further by a wooden gate.

Excavations on the defences revealed that within the inner rampart lay a core of sand along with layers of oak branches and logs, which were 'the colour of charcoal' according to the excavators and appeared to have been fired. These were of various sizes and had been laid across-ways, sideways and horizontally in distinct layers, alternately with the sand. This type of rampart is known as 'timber-lacing' and was common in

The double line of ramparts at Maiden Castle, now overgrown with bracken.

forts from North Wales to Yorkshire. In some cases, as here, the timbers were vitrified by burning. This often created such heat that the surrounding stones fused together. It is unclear whether this was done deliberately to prevent the timbers from rotting, or whether it is the result of attack. A similar method of construction can be found at Eddisbury and Beeston.

The outer rampart has a much more complex history, with the earliest phase consisting of a timber palisade supported by a clay bank. This was later replaced by an earthen bank, which was eventually revetted on its outer face, requiring the bank to be cut back to make it level. A rock cut feature behind the line of the original palisade may represent a quarry for the revetment stones of the inner rampart. Interestingly, despite Ormerod's reference to a '15 yard' (13.7 metre) ditch, nothing was uncovered during excavations.

The Western Forts

Located on a low, rocky promontory overlooking the Dee Estuary is a small enclosure known as Burton Point. Protected by a single bank and ditch which run in an arc approximately 60 metres long, from the bank on the north to the cliffs on the south, the promontory now overlooks the salt flats. The base of the hill was undoubtedly once lapped by the waters of the Dee, however, and these may have eroded away some of the former area of the enclosure. Unfortunately the site has suffered in recent years with a track cutting through the rampart to the east, the ditch badly ploughed and the interior overgrown with trees and riddled with rabbit burrows. The bank now stands to a maximum of 3.5 metres from the base of the ditch and is composed of fine-grained sand and small sandstone boulders.

In the extreme west of the county on the border between England and Wales another possible hillfort candidate lies on a defended spur overlooking the steep-sided Wych Brook. Known as Oldcastle Hill to the south-west of Malpas, the neck of the spur is defended by a triple row of ditches to the south. The site was investigated in August 1957 following the devastation of the surrounding woodland by a fierce storm. Eight trenches were dug revealing evidence of a patch of cobbles and a possible associated hearth, perhaps representing a settlement. However no finds were recovered, and the question as to whether it is prehistoric or medieval remains unanswered.

The Eastern Forts

On the Pennine edge a harsher climate with higher levels of rainfall and woodland clearance, led to the erosion of soils during the Middle and Later Bronze Age. The Pennine communities of east Cheshire seem to have barely invested in defences apart from two possible sites overlooking Macclesfield. On Eddisbury Hill near Rainow, a small univallate, hilltop enclosure, as yet undated, appears to be the only surviving feature in the region. The *County Sites and Monuments Record* also refers to a possible hillfort on Big Low in Rainow, but this has long since been destroyed. Antiquarians such as Dr J.D. Sainter also discussed two further hillforts in the Macclesfield area, on The Cloud near Bosley, and at Toot Hill in the forest (mentioned previously in the Neolithic section). However, the former has been dismissed due to its straight-sided trapezoidal shape and location away from the scarp edge, and the latter is now considered to be a medieval deer pound according to *the County Sites and Monuments Record*.

Mellor Old Vicarage hillfort

The village of Mellor, originally in Cheshire but now part of Stockport in Greater Manchester, lies on the fringes of the Peaks of Derbyshire. In the area of St Thomas' Church the land rises up to 222m (728ft) above sea level, with spectacular views to the west across the Mersey Basin and the Cheshire Plain to the foothills of Snowdonia. The ground on the hilltop falls steeply away to the north, west and south. The site was first mentioned by the Reverend William Marriott in his *Antiquities of Lyme* in 1810, when he commented on building work on the church and the construction of the Old Vicarage:

'Some years ago, in sinking deep into the soil of the churchyard for the construction of a vault, the progress of a cavern was discovered. It no longer, indeed remained hollow; but the line of it was as distinct as ever from the vein of the factitious soil, which had been introduced, in opposition to the native stratum at that depth, for the reparation of the cavity. The same vein was brought to light, many years before, in sinking the foundation of the adjacent dwelling house, now occupied as the residence of the clergyman of the place'. He summarized that this 'deep fosse was constructed originally for the inclosure of the position' and had since been filled up.

It was to be another 185 years before evidence for early settlement in the area came to light during the drought of 1995, when photographs taken by local historians, John and Ann Hearle, in the gardens and fields surrounding their home, the Old Vicarage in Mellor, showed what appeared to be cropmarks on the lawn and in the field below the back of the house. These parch marks were originally believed to represent the foundations of some medieval buildings but archaeologists were soon to be pleasantly surprised.

During the summer of 1998 an excavation was undertaken by Manchester University Archaeological Unit, and archaeologists soon discovered that a hillfort had once enclosed the sites of what are now the Church, the old and new Vicarages and the Glebe Cottage, an area covering over 2 hectares (5 acres) in total. The fort appeared to date originally to the Late Bronze Age or Early Iron Age but was later occupied by the Romans around 180AD. It is one of the very few hillforts to have been found in the whole of the eastern Cheshire/Greater Manchester area and is therefore of major archaeological significance. Further excavations have unearthed flints of Mesolithic and Bronze Age date, revealing that the site has a long and colourful history. Investigations, which have so far only covered a fraction of the site, are still continuing. The results of these will be published in detail by The Mellor Archaeological Trust, therefore the information included here is just an overview of what has been discovered, and revealed at the annual Open Days up to this time.

Right: Excavations at Mellor hillfort in 2003 showing the depth of the ditch.

Results from the first season of excavations in 1998 revealed that the hilltop was enclosed by a single ditch. This had been painstakingly cut through the earth and rock, between 1.5 and 2.2 metres wide and on average 1.6 metres deep. Large quantities of Iron Age pottery and fire cracked pebbles (used as potboilers) from within the ditch fill indicated that the fort had been occupied from approximately 900BC to 200BC, while a number of sherds of 1st and 2nd century AD pottery, roof tile, glass and a silver denarius dating to circa 78AD, suggested it was reused later by the Romans, perhaps as a station post. Archaeologists continued work on the ditch the following year, uncovering part of an Iron Age horse harness and over 20 pieces of pottery. Much to their surprise they also discovered several flints from the Late Bronze Age (circa 1200BC) and 15 Mesolithic flints, discussed previously, which could be as old as 10,000 years.

Over the last three years excavations have continued apace, revealing many other significant features including postholes and arcing drainage ditches from an Iron Age roundhouse in the garden of the Old Vicarage. These were later cut into by a stone lined gully into which rows of stakes were set, and may represent the footings of a stock enclosure post-dating the roundhouse. A number of samples were taken from the various features for radiocarbon analysis. One of the curvilinear ditches produced a date of between 520BC and 380BC, whilst two samples from the stone lined gully gave results of between 410BC and 360BC for one and 280BC and 240BC for the second.

Postholes and an arced drainage ditch representing the eaves drip from an Iron Age roundhouse (2003).

In 2003 the most exciting discovery came when a second deep ditch was uncovered close to the driveway of the house. This was comparable in size to the one found in 1998, but as to its purpose archaeologists are left to ponder the alternatives until further investigations can be carried out in 2004. It is possible that the site was protected by a double enclosure, with a substantial ditch surrounding the roundhouse in the centre, and a much larger, but less substantial, ditch further afield. The latter perhaps enclosing an area for stock.

One of the most interesting and rare artefactual finds to date is 'The Mellor Pot', carefully reassembled from 140 sherds found during excavations in the ditch. The barrel-shaped vessel with inturned rim appears to have been made locally, perhaps around the Castleton-Hucklow Edge area of Derbyshire. The pot was worked by hand from slabs of clay and the fingerprints

The eaves drip of the roundhouse at Mellor (reconstructed to one-third size) showing where the archaeological features above fit in.

The Mellor Pot (courtesy of Ann Hearle of The Mellor Archaeological Trust)

of its maker are still visible over most of the surface. It was then smoothed with a slightly rough object, resulting in a perceptibly shiny surface. This is a fantastic find, as Iron Age pottery, apart from VCP, is very rare in this area.

Another significant find comes in the form of slag and several sherds from crucibles and a mould, possibly used for metal production on the site. Chemical analysis of the crucible residuum has revealed traces of copper, tin, zinc and lead indicating it was used for melting bronzes, possibly in the Late Bronze Age or Early Iron Age, while the slag appears to represent waste from ironworking activities. The Mellor Dig has an annual open weekend each year and is well worth a visit for anyone interested in prehistory.

Defended Waterside Enclosures

In addition to utilising hilltops with steeply graded slopes, Iron Age people also made use of other natural forms of defence in lowland areas, such as rivers and lakes. An Iron Age enclosure, defended by a single earthen bank and external ditch, once stood on a promontory of sand and gravel on the eastern bank of Oak Mere in a relatively low-lying area. The settlement was protected on three sides by water, with only the neck of the promontory requiring man-made defences. In prehistoric times the bank would have stretched to the water, but evidence indicates that water levels have since dropped, as there is now a slight gap to the north. A causeway breaks the ditch almost halfway along.

Another small sub-rectangular, ditched enclosure lies on a low hill adjacent to Peckforton Mere, close to Beeston and Maiden Castle. The site, which has been heavily damaged by ploughing, remains undated, but is believed to be of Iron Age origin. The *County Sites and Monuments Record* also refers to two possible crannogs (circular timber-framed huts built on islands in lochs and lakes and joined to the mainland by a timber walkway, usually found in Southern Scotland) discovered on the site of the former Thomas Lockyers Factory in Warrington. However, recent excavations by archaeological consultants, L-P Archaeology, uncovered about eight timbers from the same area which were dated to the post-medieval period by associated pottery and woodworking. These were compared to the timbers, supposedly from the crannogs, with the records in Warrington Museum and found to be identical, thus dispelling the myth.

Enclosed Farming Settlements

As discussed, for the most part evidence for Iron Age settlement in Cheshire comes from the hillforts of the Central Ridge area, but like the long barrows of the Neolithic and the round barrows of the Bronze Age these were only a small piece in the prehistoric jigsaw. The majority of the population would have lived and farmed elsewhere. As with the whole of the prehistoric period the majority of buildings were composed of wood, so they leave little trace in the archaeological record. The remnants of associated prehistoric field systems and ridge and furrow lines do, nevertheless sometimes survive.

A few such field systems have come to light in the county, one of which, near Kelsall, was the subject of a paper in the *Transactions of the Lancashire and Cheshire Antiquarian Society* by J.D. Bu'Lock in 1954. Located to the north of Longley Farm on land between 91m and 122m (300ft to 400ft) above sea level, a number of earthwork ridges divide the hillside into a series of rectangular plots. Unfortunately, because of their nature, earthworks such as these are very difficult to date, but it is believed, as they closely resemble other known Iron Age and Romano-British field systems in Britain, they may also be of this date. Further examples have come from Chester where plough marks were sealed beneath the Roman parade ground on Frodsham Street, and traces of domestic waste were found within the area of the fortress at Eastgate Row. At Rawhead Farm near Bickerton, cropmarks showed up circular and rectangular features, possibly representing a prehistoric settlement.

Additional areas of Iron Age activity have been identified during the course of research into the wetlands of the area. One of the most important sites in Cheshire, and indeed in Britain as a whole, lies at Lindow Moss near Wilmslow, where ancient human remains have been exhumed from the sphagnum peat deposits on several occasions in recent years. Although no settlement has been directly linked with these they are a hugely significant discovery and will be covered in more detail later in this chapter. Elsewhere a few farming enclosures of Early and Late Bronze Age date have come to light by chance during pipeline construction and aerial surveys. Excavations carried out on these during the last decade or so, have added greatly to our knowledge of life outside the hillforts, both before and after their construction. Those that have been subjected to detailed archaeological excavations are discussed below.

The Brook House Farm and Irby Settlements

During the construction of a gas pipeline by Transco from Birch Heath to Mickle Trafford in the west of the county, a prehistoric settlement dating from the Middle Bronze Age to Late Iron Age (circa 1000BC to 50BC) was uncovered recently in the parish of Bruen Stapleford, near Brook House Farm. Subsequent excavations were carried out by Network Archaeology and funded by Transco.

The settlement, which is the first of its type to be found in the hinterland of Chester, lies on a plateau of high ground at 41m (134ft) above sea level, on the western side of a tributary of the River Gowy between the hillforts at Beeston and Kelsborrow and, as at the site at Oversley Farm at Manchester Airport, close to a ford in the river conspicuous in the name of the nearby Ford Farm. The soils in the area are heavy and prone to waterlogging, but gentle slopes on all sides of the settlement help to assist in the drainage and give some natural protection. An analysis of pollen sources from the site indicates that in later prehistory it was largely wooded, predominantly with oak and alder, although ash, hazel, willow, hawthorn and poplar were also present. Emmer and spelt grains, found in association with some of the structures, showed cereal cultivation was also taking place somewhere nearby.

The excavations uncovered a multi-phased site with a long history containing the remains of six structures – five roundhouses and one bow-sided or oval roundhouse – a large boundary ditch, and pottery from the Late Bronze Age and Iron Age. The earliest phase of activity on site was centred on a roundhouse circa 8 metres in diameter. Finds included a number of fire-cracked potboilers and a large collection of pottery fragments from simple, undecorated bucket-shaped jars or urns. Carbonised food debris, from the surface of one of these containers, was radiocarbon dated to the Late Bronze Age between circa 1050BC and 800BC. Inside the building there was a fire pit containing charcoal, VCP used to hold salt, burnt bone, and several degraded fragments of emmer and spelt wheat, which produced a date contemporary with the food debris on the pottery. The site was possibly enclosed by a large boundary ditch 1.4 metres deep by 6.8 metres wide, the charcoal from which gave a radiocarbon date of between 1130BC and 800BC.

The second phase of settlement activity is characterised by the construction of two larger roundhouses. The first is 19 metres in diameter with an entrance around a metre wide facing the south-south-east. This is represented in the archaeology by two gullies, one probably a slot for the wall and the other drainage for the eaves drip. Charcoal from the inner one of these features gave a radiocarbon date of between 920BC and 780BC. A pit inside the building, full of debris including charcoal and a grain of wheat, however, produced a much later date (circa 520BC to 170BC) suggesting further activity after the building's demise. A large collection of salt container fragments (VCP) was discovered within various features in and around the house, including pits and postholes. Large roundhouses such as this appear to have been quite common in the Bronze Age to Iron Age transition period. One particularly interesting feature of this structure is the discovery of two large piles of stones used as pads beneath the doorposts. These were much larger than was necessary to support timber posts, and it is possible that the frame may instead have been made of stone, leading to speculation that the house belonged to a local chieftain with a desire to impress. The second structure belonging to this phase was a smaller double-ringed roundhouse circa 9.5 metres in diameter, possibly with an internal partition. Radiocarbon analysis on two poorly preserved grains of barley from this produced a date of between 800BC and 350BC.

Following this second phase there appears to have been a lull in structural activity from circa 700BC to 400BC, but this may simply be down to the selection of radiocarbon samples chosen and analysed by archaeologists. In the Middle to Late Iron Age building work restarted with the construction of a roundhouse 12.5 metres in diameter around 390BC to 160BC, together with the rebuilding of the eight-metre roundhouse from the earliest phase of activity. Finally, with an improvement in the climate and the expansion of farming settlements in general, three new structures were built in the Late Iron Age. The first was a domestic structure, a bow-sided or oval roundhouse circa 11 metres in diameter. Very few finds were discovered in association with this apart from a few flecks of charcoal, grain and heat shattered rocks which were radiocarbon dated to between 390BC and 90BC. To the east, a number of associated postholes and pits, of unknown use, were also discovered. The second structure was another roundhouse approximately 12 metres in diameter with two construction phases. Unfortunately this was badly damaged by the later removal of topsoil so its use remains unclear. The eight-metre roundhouse was again replaced at this point with an overlying smaller structure. Evidence points to an abandonment of the site before the arrival of the Romans.

A second site with a similar multi-phased history has been discovered at Irby on the Wirral. Lying at 60m (197ft) above sea level near the top of one of a series of low sandstone ridges, the majority of the settlement lies on well-drained brown soils, fringed with boulder clays. Known as 'Mill Hill Road', the enclosure first came to light when someone brought a Roman bowl, found in a garden during the Second World War, into Liverpool Museum for identification in the early 1980s. Further finds came to light during the digging of a trench in 1987 and excavations were carried out by The Field Archaeology Unit of Liverpool Museum between 1992 and 1996. Archaeological evidence revealed that the site had witnessed several phases of activity indicating frequent replacement and rebuilding within a fairly constrained area, enclosed by ditches with a gate to the north. Occupation had occurred from the Late Bronze Age through to the Iron Age and included three phases of roundhouses built on the same spot, probably used for a generation each.

The earliest phase is associated with double-ringed roundhouses similar to those found at Brook House Farm and with similar coarse, handmade pottery, possibly barrel-shaped jars, radiocarbon dated to between 1400BC and 1100BC. The site provided one of the largest groups of pottery from the region, with seven or eight different types discovered in total. In addition to the Late Bronze Age material, at least two types of Cheshire stony VCP were unearthed. Another unusual artefact included a soapstone bead, found in a later Roman wall, which may have been deliberately deposited as an offering. The nearest source of soapstone (or steatite) is located on Anglesey.

The Mersey Basin Settlements

The majority of Middle to Late Iron Age settlement sites so far discovered in Cheshire, lie in the region of the Mersey Valley, with over 50 examples discovered in the last couple of decades during aerial surveys carried out jointly by Cheshire County Council and The National Museums and Galleries on Merseyside. This may simply be due to the soils in the area, which are particularly conducive to aerial photography. It is believed that similar examples may have existed across much of lowland Cheshire, but because of the nature of the water-retentive soils and the fact that much of the area is used for pastoral farming, there is generally little potential for crop or parch marks in other areas.

In general, these enclosure sites are located on gently sloping ground in the minor river valleys, overlooking a stream at between 5 metres and 150 metres above sea level, although the majority are placed below the 50-metre contour. Approximately half of those discovered so far are sited on sand and gravel with the other half on boulder clays, indicating that competition for the lighter well-drained soils was such that some communities were being forced into more marginal areas. The enclosures, which are sub-rectangular in shape, are usually found singly and are defended by a single bank and ditch. Environmental evidence from the Basin indicates that there were two major episodes of woodland clearance during the Iron Age, separated by a brief period of regeneration. During the first (circa 795BC to 420BC) there is a marked absence of cereal pollen, suggesting pastoral farming was the main focus, while in the second (sometime between circa 430BC and 250BC), there are high levels of weed and cereal pollen indicating a shift to arable farming.

One of the best-known settlements in this area lies just 50 metres over the Cheshire border at Great Woolden Hall in Greater Manchester. Limited excavations were carried out on this one-hectare, double-ditched enclosure by Michael Nevell in the 1980s and radiocarbon analysis provided a date in the 1st century BC. There appeared to be several circular features within the enclosure, but the most significant find was the discovery of a number of later prehistoric pottery fragments. The site was located on a patch of mineral soil at 16 metres above sea level and bounded on three sides by Chat Moss, the Rixton/Risley Mosses and the Glazebrook, a tributary of the River Mersey. It may therefore have been placed to take advantage of the natural defences provided by the wetlands.

Further enclosures in the Mersey Basin lie at Leghs Oak Farm in High Legh, with others close to Winwick to the north-west of Risley. The two enclosures at High Legh, one rectangular circa 30 metres by 15 metres, and one oval, around 60 metres in diameter, were shown up as crop marks by aerial photography in 1981. Both sites lie on the flanks of the ridge in 'Stoney Field' at 60 metres above sea level on boulder clay, close to what was once the bog of Sink Moss.

Limited excavations were again carried out by Nevell between spring 1986 and spring 1988, as well as a number of resistivity surveys, fieldwalking and soil samples in order to try and establish a date for the enclosures. Very few artefacts of any period were discovered, but results seem to indicate that they were of late prehistoric and Romano-British date. Within the smaller enclosure there was a circular structure with a stone wall circa 3.5 metres in diameter internally and 4.5 metres externally. The floor was composed of red clay mixed with many pebble-sized stones. Brown staining to the south of the wall indicated that iron panning had taken place on site. In the larger enclosure, small excavations revealed evidence for an earthen rampart and a stone pathway. No definite buildings were identified, but a number of postholes indicated structures of some description within the compound.

Death in the Iron Age

The activities of daily life in the Iron Age are probably the most familiar of all prehistoric societies, thanks to the writings of classical historians and the discovery of numerous artefacts at sites throughout the UK. But very little is known about how the majority of Iron Age individuals were treated once their lives had come to an end. In the Early Iron Age there is a dearth of evidence for burial in general, suggesting that large numbers of people were perhaps cremated, with their ashes scattered or buried without accompanying grave goods of any kind. Alternatively they may have been 'exposed' allowing the forces of nature and wild animals to dispose of their remains instead. Only very occasionally are cremations found buried in cemeteries close to the sites of Bronze Age barrows, or under small mounds.

From about the 5th century BC inhumations seem to have made a come back. These are still quite rare in the archaeological record, but examples are occasionally found in disused storage pits, in the ditches and ramparts of hillforts and, particularly in the South, in stone cists sometimes laid out in cemeteries. The most well-known burials of the Later Iron Age are those from the area around Arras in Yorkshire, where crouched burials, orientated to the north, were placed under earthen mounds, often grouped together in cemeteries. Some of the dead, presumably from the higher strata of society, were even accompanied by a chariot and horses. In many areas of Britain, however, there is very little evidence for the careful disposal of the dead during any period of the Iron Age. Cheshire has yielded no barrow or cist cemeteries and no rich chariot burials, but what it has brought forth is one of the most important Iron Age discoveries in the UK to date.

The Bodies in the Bog

Almost 6% of the British landscape is still covered with some form of peat deposit. Over the centuries the wetlands or 'lowland peat deposits' of Britain have provided a valuable source of prehistoric archaeology with stone and metal artefacts, trackways, boats and even ancient human remains recovered. The main type of wetland is what is known as the raised bog, which formed in hollows created by melting blocks of ice thousands of years ago. In Cheshire some areas of wetland have formed where depressions have been created by dissolving underground salt deposits.

Unlike the sprawling Fenlands of East Anglia and the Somerset Levels, the wetlands of North West England are very diverse in character, being broadly scattered and interspersed with areas of dry land. Surprisingly the North West has more surviving peat than any other region (approximately 37,000 hectares), but this is under constant threat from commercial peat cutting, agricultural drainage, forestry, road building and in areas such as Danes Moss near Macclesfield, from waste disposal. In Britain as a whole, about 96% of the raised bog which existed in 1850 has disappeared. This is mainly due to the fact that peat has been dug as a source of fuel (in fact since the medieval period), and in more recent years for animal litter and plant compost. Sphagnum peat in particular is renowned for its antiseptic qualities and was used as recently as the First World War to treat casualties on the battlefield. It is in the sphagnum peat layer, which is usually the first section to be cut due to its superior burning qualities, that bog bodies are occasionally found.

Lindow Moss, which takes its name from the Welsh *Llyn Ddu* meaning the 'black pool', is just one of many wetland sites in Cheshire. Lying between the parishes of Wilmslow and Mobberley, Lindow is one of the most important of the eastern mosses, together with Danes Moss. The earliest description of the site comes from a local resident and portrait painter to Queen Charlotte, Samuel Finney, who described the parish in the 1780s. At this time, local inhabitants were beginning to drain and enclose the Moss; continued activity means that today only about a tenth of the original wetland remains which once covered over 600 hectares. Peat was dug by hand until the 1970s, when the local extraction company began using mechanized excavators to cut trenches. It was then stacked and left to drain, eventually being taken by narrow gauge railway to the nearby mill for shredding and dispatch.

The Discoveries at Lindow

The earliest reference to possible prehistoric discoveries on the Moss comes from an article in the *Transactions of the Lancashire and Cheshire Antiquarian Society* in 1884 entitled 'Lindow Common as a Peat Bog - Its Age and Its People'. Concerned by the fact that the moss was rapidly disappearing due to widespread peat cutting, the author, William Norbury, decided to write this paper as in his own words 'in a few more years all that can be said will be – "this once was Lindow!"'. The article provides a general discussion on Lindow with reference to the Romans, but one mention, of what appears to be a prehistoric trackway, is of particular interest:

'. . . one Peter Cash found, somewhere on the Mobberley side of Lindow, what appeared to be a roadway made of logs of timber placed end to end, with sleepers across laid close together, and this I am told continued for some length up the Moss, and I think it was at the bottom of the bog, but of this I am not sure.'

For almost a century the Moss lay largely ignored by historians and archaeologists alike until the 1980s, when two (or possibly three) ancient bodies were unearthed during peat extraction works on its southern fringes. The quiet backwater of Lindow was suddenly catapulted into the national and international press with what was described as an 'archaeological sensation'. On the 13th May 1983, two men were working by the elevator carrying the freshly cut peat to the shredding mill, when they noticed an object resembling a 'burst foot-

The area of Lindow Moss where human remains were unearthed during peat cutting on several occasions during the 1980s.

ball'. Upon closer inspection, it appeared to be the remains of a human head. The police were immediately called in and a full search of the area was carried out but to no avail – no other body parts were found.

The discovery prompted a local man, who had lived on the edge of the Moss, to confess to the murder of his wife some years earlier. The police however had doubts about the age of the skull, and decided to send it to Oxford University for assessment. It proved to date to the Romano-British period between 130AD and 290AD. A further search was undertaken on peat from the same section, which had been dispatched to Somerset for mushroom compost, in the hope of finding further remains, but all that came to light was a single iron pin of unknown date.

On the 1st August 1984, one of the same peat workers who had chanced upon the ancient head, removed what he thought was a piece of wood from the extraction belt, only to discover that it was part of a human leg and foot. The police were again called in. Investigations had to be very diligent as detectives were still missing the body of the murder victim from the confession of the previous year. The following day Rick Turner, the then Cheshire County Archaeologist, visited the site and spotted more of the body protruding from the peat.

By the 6th August a detailed investigation had begun. The area of peat around the body, which lay 250 metres to the south-west of the previous discovery, was in danger of collapsing, so rather than try to examine it on site, the team decided to lift out a block which was then taken to Macclesfield District General Hospital for further analysis. Now in the hands of the Coroner, the body was X-rayed to check for signs of any metal (nearly all modern bodies have metal fillings in their teeth) but no traces were found. The Coroner insisted that The British Museum provided a radiocarbon date before he would release the body, so samples, including some tiny bones from the hands and a small section of the detached leg, were duly sent to London. The Museum's scientists pronounced the body 'to be at least 1000 years old' and it was immediately transferred down to them.

Lindow Man just after his discovery in 1984 (copyright Doug Pickford).

A team of experts was formed to carry out a detailed scientific investigation on the body including County Archaeologist, Rick Turner, and Don Brothwell of the Institute of Archaeology at London University. Their primary consideration was to preserve the corpse, whilst at the same time examining it as thoroughly as possible. It had to be kept cold, at approximately 4°C, so it was stored in the mortuary at Middlesex Hospital. In September a cautious investigation began with the peat gently removed section by section to reveal the body of Lindow Man, known then to the media as 'Pete Marsh'.

The body had virtually turned into leather, tanned in the acid environment of the peat bog, and many of his features had been flattened by hundreds of years of overlying peat growth. Unfortunately the lower half had been severed during the cutting process and was missing, apart from a section of the lower right leg and foot. Most of the internal organs and the bones had rotted away in the acid conditions, but the stomach and upper intestines remained intact. Various medical examinations were carried out including detailed scans, X-rays and an analysis of a sample of the stomach contents. At the time no other ancient body had been subjected to such a detailed investigation by so wide a range of scientists and medical experts. Even now, the only other remains to be put under more scrutiny are those of Ötzi, the ancient man recently discovered frozen high up in the Alps on the Austro-Italian border.

The next amazing manifestation came from Lindow in February 1987 when what was believed to be a third set of human remains, those of an adult male now known as Lindow III, were also recovered from the Moss. Although equally as important as Pete Marsh, this body has had very little coverage in the national media. Yet again the elevator at the peat extraction works provided the key when a section of a human back was found on its way to the shredding mill. A subsequent excavation of the surrounding area and a search of the trucks revealed over seventy different pieces of the body. With grant aid from English Heritage work continued throughout February and March of that year with many tons of peat being dug by hand. This was followed in the summer by further excavations on the peat layer itself to assess the environmental evidence.

The final piece of the jigsaw came to light in 1988 when the buttocks and part of the left leg of an adult male were unearthed on an elevator, 15 metres to the west of where Lindow II was found, and the right thigh and ends of a femur were discovered by a digger driver in his bucket. These pieces are referred to in the literature as 'Lindow IV' but are almost certainly the lost parts of Lindow II, meaning that the majority of his body, apart from the left foot, has now been recovered.

Lindow Moss was further examined between 1993 and 1995 as part of the North West Wetlands Survey, a project based at Lancaster University Archaeological Unit and funded by English Heritage. The jawbone of a *Bos taurus* (cattle) possibly of Iron Age date was found, but nothing more. This is more than likely due to the fact that the majority of the layer of peat, in which the bodies were found, has almost disappeared from the area being worked, making further discoveries highly unlikely.

Who was Lindow Man and how did he die?

A close examination by medical experts in 1984 revealed the body of Lindow II, or Lindow Man as he was officially known, to be that of a fully developed, heavily built, adult male between 25 and 30 years of age who died sometime between 2BC and 119AD (either in the Late Iron Age or Early Romano-British period). Apart from slight traces of arthritis in his back, he was generally fit and healthy at the time of death without any sign of disability. Well nourished with little fat deposit, he would have been very muscular and powerful, standing at approximately 168cm (5ft 6 inches) tall. Evidence from his teeth and nails suggests that he led quite a privileged life. Of the normal 32 teeth present, 30 were identified, all of which were well formed and healthy. His nails were well manicured, almost totally smooth and undamaged, particularly along the edges, suggesting he had not recently carried out any type of manual labour.

Bog environments are ideal for the preservation of hair, and Lindow Man boasted a full head of relatively short brown/ginger locks, varying in length between 10mm and 90mm. He also had a roughly cut, slightly darker, moustache and beard on his small, rounded chin. Tests seem to show that it had been cut using some kind of implement such as cutting tweezers or shears, rather than with a single blade. All the evidence points to him being of high status and in his prime. Given this it seems strange that he was wearing nothing but an armband of fox fur – there were no other wool or fabric objects near the body which would have preserved well in bog conditions. However, a chemical analysis of the skin revealed an excess of certain metallic substances such as copper, aluminium, titanium and zinc. These may have resulted from ingesting food grown on soils with a high copper content or contaminated water from minerals veins along Alderley Edge, but because of concentrations in certain areas of the body, scientists believe they may represent some kind of copper-based pigment which was painted onto the skin.

The fact that ancient Britons decorated their bodies is well attested in the classical sources and one reference from Julius Caesar's *De Bello Gallico* (V, 14) is particularly pertinent: 'All the Britons stain themselves with *vitrum* which gives a blue colour and a wilder appearance in battle. They let their hair grow long and shave every part of their body except the head and upper lip'. Writers have often assumed the *vitrum* to be blue woad, but translated as 'glass-like' from the Latin it could just as easily refer to some kind of pigment made from copper ore. Azurite, a blue copper ore, was not discovered in the Alderley Edge mines until the 19th century, but it is possible that Lindow Man could have stained his body green with the copper ore malachite, which had been mined on the Edge since the Bronze Age.

The Last Supper

An examination of the stomach contents of Lindow II revealed not only what he ate for his last meal, but also gave archaeologists an insight into the area where he lived. His final meal consisted of a mixture of cereal bran and chaff from emmer wheat, spelt wheat and hulled barley, as well as small quantities of weed seeds including dock, fat hen and cow parsley. All these weeds grow alongside cereal crops and could easily have been included accidentally even after processing. The low number of weed seeds, and the fact that the wheat and barley had been ground prior to consumption, indicates that the grain had been threshed, winnowed, cleaned and ground before cooking. In fact the inclusion of a small quantity of fine sand in the stomach contents may have resulted from a grinding stone or quern used for this purpose. Emmer, spelt and hulled barley are a characteristic combination of the cereal crops grown in the Late Iron Age. By the Romano-British period spelt was the main cereal and emmer had been ousted.

Further tests were carried out on these cereals to try to establish whether they had been eaten as porridge or baked into bread. The results showed that the grains had been heated for only a short time and at temperatures above 200°C, indicating that the mixture was probably made into some kind of flat, unleavened wholemeal bread and cooked quickly on a griddle over an open fire. The inclusion of two charred heather leaves suggested that the last meal may have been prepared in a settlement on or near heath land, using the heather as a fuel. It was quite common during the later prehistoric period for people to settle on islands of dry ground within the mires, often only a few centimetres higher than the surrounding marsh. At the time of the 1987 excavations, a survey was carried out on two sand islands projecting out from the peat to the west of the Moss. No finds contemporary with the bodies were unearthed, but a scatter of approximately 29 flints indicated that the area had been used several thousands of years earlier in the Neolithic. The nearest sites of Iron Age date currently known lie several kilometres away at Arthill and Tatton Old Hall.

In addition to the food, slight traces of sphagnum moss were also found in the stomach. It is highly unlikely that these were swallowed in the pool in which he lay for reasons discussed later. They may therefore have been consumed in a final drink of water with the meal acquired locally on the Moss, suggesting a settlement near the peat bog where he died. Unfortunately there were no seasonal foods to indicate the time of year when this occurred.

Small animal hairs were also found in the stomach contents. These may be debris from diary products or meat, which would not have survived in the acid conditions, or alternatively could have come from small rodents, accidentally included if the cereal had been stored for a while. There was also evidence for a relatively high infestation of internal parasites including whipworm and roundworm, but this is to be expected, as these were common until the introduction of modern sewage systems. There was, however, no sign of external parasites such as fleas or lice.

Another more interesting inclusion was a number of mistletoe pollen grains. Mistletoe, often associated with the Druids, grows on lime, hawthorn, apple and, less commonly, on oak trees. According to Richard Mabey in his *Flora Britannica* to early people 'it was entirely magical – a plant without roots or obvious sources of food, that grew way above the earth and stayed green-leafed when other plants were bare. It seemed the supreme example of spontaneous generation and continuing life'. It was commonly used in herbal remedies, but if used for this purpose one would have expected there to be much more pollen within the stomach. Nevertheless, it shows that the food he had eaten was either stored or prepared close to this sacred plant.

The Execution

After examining the number of wounds inflicted on the body, it soon became apparent that Lindow Man had suffered a gruesome 'three-fold' death. Perhaps when kneeling or standing, he had first received two blows to the back of the head from a blunt weapon, possibly a small axe. The force of these was so strong that fragments of his skull had become embedded in his brain and one of his molar teeth was cracked. This alone would have been fatal, but not immediately – he may well have survived for a further few hours in a dazed and painful condition. At some point close to the time of death he also received a heavy blow to his back, fracturing one of his ribs.

Following this beating, a garrotte of twisted animal sinew was placed around his neck and tightened by inserting a stick into a loop at the back and turning it around until the neck broke. A mark on the right hand side of his throat indicated that his jugular vein had also been cut with a sharp-edged weapon. There appears to have been no sign of a struggle and bearing in mind that he was a powerful, muscular man, we can only assume he must either have been a willing sacrifice or was rendered unconscious by the initial blow.

One of the numerous boggy pools on Lindow Moss where Lindow Man was executed around 2000 years ago.

Within a few hours of death, his body, naked except for a fox fur armband, was deposited face down in a pool of surface water, possibly when the weather was cold as the low temperatures would have prevented the body from bloating and rising back up. Environmental evidence suggests that for several decades before the body was inserted, the surface of the bog would have been spongy and could have been walked upon, but not easily and not without getting wet feet. However, for a short time before and for some years afterwards, the top of the Moss was a great deal wetter with widespread peaty pools, fringed with wetland plants and other bog vegetation such as cotton grass, mosses and heather, indicating a cooler and wetter climate. Lindow Man's assassins would not have been able to walk on the bog without frequently sinking up to their knees, and bearing in mind he was buried several hundred metres from the nearest dry land this would have been no easy task.

The body was found in a layer of peat dating to around the 3rd or 4th century BC, but it is more than likely that if it was pushed into a pool, it may have settled in the mud at the bottom which predated the deposition. An examination of the layers of peat corresponding to this period, has revealed that the region surrounding the Moss was mainly composed of mixed woodland. By the time the body was deposited, agricultural activity was gaining importance and the appearance of cereal pollen reveals that the death of Lindow Man coincides with the beginning of a major phase of forest disturbance, burning and occupation for farming.

Lindow III – the not so famous Cheshire bog body

As already mentioned for some reason the discovery of a second ancient body in Lindow Moss has not received the same attention as that of Pete Marsh, although it is equally as important. This could be due to the fact that it had become unrecognizable, shredded into approximately seventy different pieces and thus not as attractive to the public. The soft tissues still survived but the internal organs had largely been destroyed, apart from a small section of the intestines. There was no sign of a head, but a radiocarbon date for the body in the Early Romano-British period and the fact that it was found fifty metres north of Lindow I, led archaeologists such as Rick Turner to believe it was part of the same individual whose head had been discovered four years earlier and originally thought to be female.

Following detailed scientific analysis this body, known as Lindow III, was characteristically very similar to Lindow Man. It proved to be that of an adult male, who was thirty-five years or older at the time of death, and again apparently of some status. He was slightly taller than

Pete at 175cm (5ft 9 inches), of strong build and had well manicured fingernails. Tests on the skin again revealed high concentrations of copper, particularly on the torso, suggesting he too may have been painted with green copper-based pigments. Another interesting feature was that he had what is known as a 'vestigial' or extra thumb on his right hand.

Hazelnuts, the final meal of Lindow III, were an important food source from early times.

Investigations on a small sample of the stomach contents revealed that he had eaten a meal of raw hazelnuts, perhaps partially crushed or ground, along with some cereal bran of wheat and rye. Again there was a range of common weed seeds such as fat hen, brome grass and wild radish, but not in any large quantity. The presence of hazelnuts in the area of the Moss is proven by pollen analysis, but as they have good preservative qualities they cannot unfortunately indicate a season of death.

The environmental evidence from the surrounding peat was also very similar to Lindow II indicating that the body (which was naked and had been decapitated) was rapidly submerged into moist, boggy ground with pools of stagnant water very shortly after death; the date sometime between 25AD and 230AD. Again there were no fleas or lice on the body but there were whipworm eggs within it. This corpse proved much more difficult to radiocarbon date than its predecessor, due to the fact that it was badly fragmented and may have been contaminated by groundwater.

Bog Bodies in Context

The bodies of Lindow II and III are just two of many such finds from Northern Europe. In recent centuries approximately 2,000 bog bodies have been found in countries such as Ireland, Germany, Holland and particularly Denmark, dating to a variety of different periods. Just over a fifth of these come from Denmark and have been radiocarbon dated to the Late Bronze Age and Iron Age. In Britain over 220 individuals, dating from a variety of eras, have been discovered in the last 300 years. Many of the bodies have simply died from natural causes, perhaps travellers losing their way on a misty night and sinking without trace into a watery grave. There are many others, however, who like the Lindow men, appear to have been the victims of an unnatural death. Three bodies are of particular interest, and the similarities between their deaths and that of Lindow Man is uncanny.

The first is known as Tollund Man, an ancient body dating to circa 250BC (in the Late Iron Age) discovered in 1950 in a peat bog in Central Jutland, Denmark. He was between 40 and 50 years of age and had a noose made of two strips of twisted leather hide tied around his neck, with a slipknot at the back. As with Lindow Man he was naked apart from an oxhide belt and a pointed sheepskin cap. He is one of several bodies with a noose left around the neck and experts believe this may have been done deliberately in order to somehow retain the symbolism of death.

The second body, Grauballe Man, was found in 1952 in Nebelgard Fen again in Central Jutland, Denmark by peat cutters. He was completely naked and had a deep cut across his throat more or less from ear to ear. X-rays showed he had also received a blow to the upper temple from a blunt instrument. There were signs of rheumatoid arthritis in his spine and he was estimated to be over 30 years of age. Radiocarbon analysis dated him to the Late Roman Iron Age sometime between 210AD and 410AD. As with Lindow Man he also had well manicured hands, showing he had not performed any kind of manual work, and had an infection of whipworm.

Of particular interest is the fact that both Tollund Man and Grauballe Man had eaten an intriguing last meal of wild seeds, cereal grains and cereal chaff. As previously mentioned, wild seeds often grow alongside cereal crops and are occasionally incorporated accidentally when processing, but with these individuals they are found in unusually high proportions. Until fairly recently, in certain areas of the world, wild seeds have been used on occasion to supplement the diet during times of crop failure. Mixed with grain and certain palatable parts of the chaff, they form a coarse but filling porridge. Some archaeologists believe evidence from these two men may represent communities on the verge of famine.

Another constituent of the last meals of these Danish bog bodies was a fungus known as ergot. This is well known for its hallucinogenic properties and is the plant from which the LSD drug is derived. As with the weed seeds it could either have been ingested accidentally as a by-product of the cereal crop, or deliberately introduced as part of the death ritual. Some have suggested that the tranquil expression on Tollund Man's face suggests he was comatose, or perhaps even dead, before the noose was applied, although in the early stages the ergot would have caused severe abdominal pain and burning in the mouth.

The third individual of interest is called by the name of Borremose I. His method of execution is almost identical to that of Lindow Man in that he had a hole in the back of his skull and a hemp rope tied with a slipknot around his neck. He also had fine hands and was naked apart from a scrap of cloth under his head and two rolled up sheepskins at his feet. Closer to home, another bog deposit dating to the Romano-British period, which had been decapitated and strangled, was found 20 kilometres from Lindow in a bog in Worsley near Manchester, on the 18th August 1958. Only the skull was ever found and this was re-examined in 1987. It proved to be that of an adult male, between 20 and 30 years of age. Like Lindow Man he had a fracture to the back of his head and a cord of sinew around his neck.

Ritual Sacrifice?

The common theme linking these deaths is the fact that a number of different methods of violence, all of which would have caused death in their own right, are often applied to the same body. These include hanging or strangulation, throat-cutting, blows with a blunt instrument, decapitation, stabbing and drowning, in some cases by pegging down with stakes. Most of the victims have fine hands and feet suggesting they were not engaged in manual work, and most were buried naked apart from a small piece of animal skin clothing.

The question archaeologists frequently ask is whether or not these people were killed because they had committed some kind of crime and thus become social outcasts, or whether they were the victims of ritual sacrifice. Human sacrifice is well attested in 'Celtic' religion for various reasons including warding off disease or bad harvests, appeasement of the gods before going into battle, and the use of criminals, prisoners of war and hostages and the manner in which they died, to foretell the future. Ritual drownings to venerate pools and springs, often seen as 'entrances to the other world', were also common.

Evidence to support this theory of ritual drowning comes from a silver bowl, known as The Gundestrup Cauldron, which was discovered in the Raevemose peat bog in Denmark in 1891. Dating to the 2nd or 1st century BC, the cauldron was made up of a series of 13 highly ornamented plates, depicting mythological scenes, and had been carefully disassembled before interment. One of the depictions shows an army of two lines of infantry and cavalry soldiers alongside a much larger figure who appears to be deliberately pushing one of the soldiers into a vat or bucket as if to drown him. Miranda Aldhouse-Green believes that this may either

Detail from The Gundestrup Cauldron showing a tall figure holding a man over a vat as if to drown him.

represent an episode of human sacrifice or a mythical scene associated with reincarnation, with foot soldiers transformed into cavalrymen. Either way the victim is being deliberately drowned.

A number of classical sources refer to ritual killing and human sacrifice for a variety of reasons. We must bear in mind, however, that these were written by so called 'civilized' Romans who (conveniently forgetting their own taste for sacrifice in the Arena in the name of sport) were trying to justify their conquest of the 'barbarian world' and are likely to have been highly exaggerated. They must therefore not be relied on as absolute fact.

In his *Gallic Wars* Caesar notes of the tribes of Gaul 'as well as performing regular state sacrifices, some tribes chose to sacrifice those caught in the act of theft or some other offence on the grounds that the gods preferred such persons to innocent men, although if there were a dearth of criminals, the innocent would be sacrificed without hesitation'. Strabo, on the other hand, states that victims were stabbed in the back with a dagger so that the future could be foretold from their convulsions. Priestesses would cut the throat of prisoners of war while dangling them over a huge bronze cauldron, and others would inspect the entrails to look for signs of victory. According to Diodorus Siculus criminals were imprisoned for five years and then impaled to honour the gods. Prisoners of war and even animals were also sacrificed.

So a violent death could either be the result of a ritual killing or a criminal execution. As we have seen many of the prehistoric bog bodies had received a number of gruesome injuries such as those described above. Mike Parker Pearson points out that the dominant method of body disposal during the Iron Age appears to have been cremation, with the body placed in a pot and buried under a small mound on high, dry land, so whatever the reason for execution, this method of burial was in complete contrast to the norm.

Another interesting factor is that many ancient bog bodies show signs of some kind of deformity, such as Lindow III with his extra thumb. For example, in Holland a bog body known as Yde girl had a deformed spine, while two males from Dojnnge had one arm longer than the other. Some believe that these individuals were considered to be 'touched by the gods' and carefully raised for the sole purpose of being sacrificed. This does not seem to be the case with Lindow Man as he appears to have been fit and healthy, but we must bear in mind that one of his feet has never been found and one of his hands was badly damaged by the peat cutter. Intriguingly two of the incredibly rare footprints carved into the remains of the Neolithic chambered tomb known as The Calderstones near Liverpool, discussed earlier, have an unusual number of toes. One of the footprints has four toes and the other six.

The sacrifice of objects of special value into watery places was carried out from the Neolithic period onwards, but became common practice during the Iron Age. Even then the ritual killing of humans was quite rare, but numerous gifts of weapons and other metalwork, figurines, clothing and even human hair have been discovered in rivers, lakes and marshes in recent years. Iron Age expert, Miranda Aldhouse-Green, believes that something was 'given to the gods in order to elicit benefits to the donor and thus to engender feelings of obligation between the deity and human'. In order for the gift to be significant it must be removed from the human world – in the case of metalwork it could be damaged rendering it useless; in the case of humans – death. A man or woman of status may have been the most valuable offering certain prehistoric communities could make to the gods. Curiously well-preserved bog bodies do not occur in the same wetlands as other votive artefacts in Britain. Peat bogs, both wet and dry, may have been associated with the 'other world', a place beyond human control. The question is did the people who placed the bodies in the bogs intend them to be preserved or was it just an accident?

An excavation on a number of house platforms at Cladh Hallan on South Uist in the Outer Hebrides, carried out recently by Mike Parker Pearson and a team of archaeologists from Sheffield University, may reveal the answer. Here houses had been built on the same site for several hundred years, but when the archaeologists came down onto the last level, they discovered that under each house lay a body. This was quite unusual in itself, but when the radiocarbon dates came back, the human remains appeared to predate the construction of the first houses by hundreds of years. Furthermore, the bodies were not just skeletons when they were interred, as the bones had not fallen apart – mummification was the only answer.

Various theories were proposed as to how the bodies had been preserved including smoking and wind drying, but the most likely answer seemed that they had been temporarily immersed in a peat bog, for perhaps between 6 and 18 months. Bone deteriorates in bog acid and tests on the skeletons revealed that the outer few millimetres had started to decay proving this was exactly the case. Other later prehistoric sites in Scotland and Ireland have revealed that butter and tallow were often immersed in the bog in order to preserve them. This would seem to indicate that the preservative powers of the peat bogs had been known for thousands of years, so perhaps the assassins did intend for their victims to somehow cheat death and survive into the future.

Times of Trouble

Bold statements seem to have gone hand in hand with times of trouble and uncertainty in the prehistoric period. In the Neolithic, people placed the bones of certain members of their ancestors in huge communal tombs and periodically removed and added to them, during times of change. In the Bronze Age, communities constructed barrows as territory markers on the edge of their boundaries and added secondary interments at various later dates, perhaps during times of conflict. In the Iron Age they sacrificed things of great value into watery places, the gateways between their world and that of the spirits.

There are many theories as to why people practised human sacrifice particularly in later prehistory. It may have been down to the deterioration in the climate, which in turn led to crop failure and starvation. Evidence from Lindow indicates that the peat was much more waterlogged at the time when the bodies were buried. The diet of both Tollund Man and Grauballe Man seems to suggest communities on the verge of famine. Could they have been sacrificed in order to try and placate the spirits of the harvest?

Another explanation, notably for Lindow Man, could be ascribed to the Roman invasion. In 43AD the Emperor Claudius made inroads into Britain but his campaigns mainly concentrated on the south and east, only going as far north as the line of the Fosse Way (the road running roughly diagonally from the Severn to the Trent) in the Midlands. In the north the native tribes were established as 'client kings', loyal to Rome but not directly under Roman control. A legionary fortress was established in Chester (*Deva*) and auxiliary forts in Northwich,

Middlewich and Manchester perhaps sometime during the 50sAD. Lindow would have been on the fringes of Roman rule some distance away from the military bases, but close enough to feel under pressure from the invading forces.

In 60AD the Roman Governor of Britain, Gaius Suetonius Paulinus, took the Roman army to the island of Anglesey (*Mona*) and according to Tacitus completely eradicated all traces of the 'old religion' or Druidism from the sacred groves there. While he was away, the Britons in the south rebelled under Queen Boudica and a serious revolt ensued. This was eventually quelled by Roman forces with Boudica taking her own life. A period of consolidation then followed with tribe after tribe slowly succumbing to the influence of Rome. In 70 and 71AD the Roman Governors, Vettius Bolanus and his successor Petilius Cerealis, subdued the Brigantes tribe in the Pennine region, establishing a fortress at York (*Eboracum*) in 71AD. Tacitus comments on this conflict, 'After a series of battles – some of them by no means bloodless – Petilius had overrun, if not actually conquered, the major part of their territory'. There can be no doubt that for the people of Cheshire this must have been a very disturbing time and one which required desperate measures.

The Lindow Legacy

The remains of Lindow Man, which have since been soaked in a chemical solution and freeze dried, now lie in The British Museum in London. One of only four objects permanently on display (the others being the Rosetta Stone, The Portland Vase and the Parthenon Sculptures) Pete Marsh is one of the Museum's most visited exhibits, and is described by their own book as 'a famous object' attracting great public interest.

In light of all this evidence there can be no doubt that Cheshire was highly significant during prehistoric times. In contrast to the opinions of the author in 1940, referred to in the introduction, it is now possible to say that Cheshire was very important. It has a varied range of prehistoric pottery, many habitation sites, numerous burial sites and a number of notable monuments; in short all of the things which suggest settlement and 'wealth'.

7 Cheshire Sites Gazetteer

Included here is a list of all the prehistoric sites mentioned in the text along with several others of note which have long since disappeared or are now badly eroded. It is by no means an exhaustive gazetteer of every prehistoric site in and around Cheshire and those wishing to discover more should consult the relevant *County Sites and Monuments Records* (see list of useful addresses at the back of the book). Directions are included here for those sites which are easily accessible or visible from the nearby roads and footpaths. Please note that some of these ancient monuments are located on private land. Many can be easily viewed from a distance, but please ensure you ask permission from the landowner before taking a closer look.

Chester

Abbey Green Iron Age plough marks and pottery: SJ405667. Now buried under modern buildings in the City of Chester.

Bache Pool Mesolithic Camp Site: SJ404683 (destroyed).

Brookhouse Farm, Bruen Stapleford Late Bronze Age/Iron Age Settlement: SJ497639. Visible only as a cropmark.

Carden Park Mesolithic Rock Shelter: SJ464537. This can be accessed via a short walk on the public footpath from Higher Carden (SJ466539) where there is a convenient lay-by for parking.

Castle Hill, Oldcastle possible Iron Age Enclosure: SJ468441. Located on private land close to Malpas and inaccessible.

Churton Neolithic Long Mortuary Enclosure: SJ411558. This is visible only as a cropmark in certain conditions.

Poulton Bronze Age Cemetery: SJ404584. Situated on private land in the grounds of what used to be the medieval Abbey. The area is being excavated by the Poulton Research Project – further details can be found on their website http://srs.dl.ac.uk/arch/poulton.

Congleton Borough

Astbury Churchyard Bronze Age Round Barrow: SJ845616 (destroyed). This is now the site of a modern graveyard adjacent to the A34 on the opposite side of the road from Astbury Church. The urn is on display in the Congleton Museum.

Dark Valley Bronze Age Barrow Cemetery: SJ788706.

Jodrell Bank Bronze Age Barrow Cemetery: (i)SJ791704 (ii)SJ794703 (iii)SJ796701 (destroyed) (iv)SJ797699 (v)SJ798698 and (vi)SJ799697. The barrows are in view of the Radio Telescope in the stretch of the A535 Holmes Chapel to Chelford road between Twemlow Green and Jodrell Bank. A footpath to one and two leads across the fields opposite Terra Nova School at SJ795702. The other three surviving barrows are located on private land in the grounds of the school and neighbouring fields.

Loachbrook Farm or Somerford possible Neolithic Long Barrow: SJ830634. This is situated on private land but can be easily viewed from the nearby road known locally as Sandy Lane, which joins the A54 and A534 at Somerford near Congleton.

Somerford Round Barrow: SJ811645 (destroyed).

Swettenham Hall Bronze Age Round Barrow: SJ813667. This badly damaged mound, marked on the OS Map as a 'tumulus', is located on private land in the grounds of Swettenham Hall but can be easily viewed from the entrance at SJ814667.

Crewe & Nantwich Borough

Beeston Neolithic Settlement, possible Bronze Age Round Barrows, Metalworking site and Iron Age Hillfort: SJ538592. Beeston Castle is in the care of English Heritage and there is a charge for entry (see the English Heritage website for further details http://www.english-heritage.org.uk). A car park is located close by at SJ540590 and the Castle is well signposted from the main road (A49).

Bridgemere Site of Bronze Age Metalwork Hoard, possible Round Barrow: SJ716453 (destroyed).

Church Lawton Bronze Age Barrow Cemetery and Stone Circle: (i) SJ809559 (now destroyed) (ii) SJ808558, (iii) SJ809557 (with stone circle but this is not visible). Church Lawton II and III are located on the junction of the A50, A5011 and B5077 near Alsager. Heading towards Alsager II can be seen in a field on the right just past the crossroads and III on the left, taking the B5077.

Maiden Castle Iron Age Hillfort: SJ498529. In the care of The National Trust, this hillfort near Bickerton can be accessed via a pleasant walk from the car park at SJ494525. The area has a sign posted nature trail. Care should be taken as there are very steep drops and slippery rocks in some places.

Ellesmere Port & Neston

Burton Point Iron Age Promontory Fort: SJ303735. This fort is inaccessible and located on private land close to a danger area and shooting range overlooking the salt flats close to the village of Burton near Neston.

Macclesfield Borough

Alderley Edge, Castle Rock possible Mesolithic Flint Working Site and Neolithic Settlement: SJ856779. Castle Rock has fantastic views across the Cheshire Plain and is easily accessible via a short walk along the footpath from the lay-by of the B5087 from Alderley to Macclesfield at SJ855778.

Andrew Knobb Bronze Age Round Barrow: SJ959793 (destroyed).

Armada Beacon, Alderley Edge Bronze Age Round Barrow: SJ858777. Park in the main National Trust car park at SJ860773 and follow the path to the north between the Information Centre and the Warden's Cottage past the Engine Vein and on ahead into the woods. Keep going straight and you will soon come to the barrow, which is capped by a stone plinth.

Arthill Heath Farm Iron Age Enclosure: SJ728859. This settlement is visible only as a cropmark on a farm near Little Bollington.

Astle Park Bronze Age Round Barrow: SJ811738. Situated on private land in the grounds of Astle Hall near Chelford.

Bartomley Farm Neolithic Long Barrow: SJ964656. Follow the footpath which leads from the back of the Ship Inn in Wincle (SJ961653) across the field, passing a hill which looks remarkably like a miniature Silbury Hill, through the trees. The path goes down over a stream and then up the other side. Once you have crossed the stile at the top, the mound can be seen to the right in the field, just before the house on the left.

Bartomley Farm Bronze Age Round Barrow: SJ964656. The *County Sites and Monuments Record* puts this at the same grid reference as the supposed long barrow above.

Bearhurst Farm Bronze Age Round Barrow: SJ873720. The barrow marked on the OS Map as a 'tumulus' is located in a private field close to the east of Bearhurst Lane (the road linking Pexhill Road to School Lane in Henbury). Unfortunately it is not visible from the lane due to the height of the bank and hedge.

Birtles Hall Bronze Age Round Barrows: SJ856745. Three possible barrows lie on private land in the grounds of Birtles Hall near Monk's Heath in Over Alderley.

Robin Hood's Tump Bronze Age Round Barrow: SJ574599. Marked on the OS Map as a 'tumulus', this mound close to Alpraham can be viewed easily from the nearby minor road known locally as Vale Road (off the A51(T)).

Black Rock Farm Bronze Age Round Barrow: SJ958766. Located in the Parish of Rainow adjacent to a public footpath, one of the best ways to see this barrow, marked on the OS Map as a 'tumulus', is to turn off the B5470 Macclesfield Road on to Smith Lane a little way north of the hamlet of Ginclough. Once you are on this lane stop (safely) and look back down the lane, over the main road to the field beyond. To the left of a dry-stone wall you will see the barrow interrupting the view across the Cheshire Plain.

Blue Boar Farm Bronze Age Round Barrow: SJ970763. From Black Rock Farm continue along Smith Lane in an easterly direction. After the junction with Pike Road, you will see Blue Boar Farm to the left (north). The barrow lies 300m due south of the farm on private land, but can be viewed from the field entrance, approximately 100m east of the farm, looking south.

Broad Oak Farm Bronze Age Round Barrow: SJ921699. This barrow, with a distinctive oak tree on top of it, can be seen from the Leek Old Road close to the possible remains of the henge. Please note this site is on private land.

Brock Low Possible Bronze Age Round Barrow: SJ971749. Brock Low in the Parish of Rainow is best accessed from the footpath from the Lamaload Reservoir car park (SJ977733) which can be reached by taking the left hand turning (north) off The Cat & Fiddle road A537 (from Macclesfield to Buxton) at SJ977733 and following the country lane for approximately 2 kilometres. The mound, located above the reservoir, can also be easily viewed from this car park.

Brynlow (or Brindlow) Bronze Age Copper Mine: SJ855773. The prehistoric finds discovered here in the 19th century, including an oak shovel radiocarbon dated to the Bronze Age, are now on display in Manchester Museum.

Butley Cairn Cemetery and possible Stone Circle: SJ907784 (surviving barrow). The remains of a barrow, which may have been one of these cairns, still stands in the field at the junction of Manchester Road (A523T) and Bonis Hall Lane (B5385) near to Macclesfield. Others believe, however, that the cemetery may have been located in a nearby sand quarry at SJ908780.

Capesthorne Hall north-east Bronze Age Bowl Barrow: SJ843729. This barrow surmounted by a pedestal can be seen in the grounds of Capesthorne Hall to the west of the A34, close to the East Lodge.

Capesthorne Hall north-west Bronze Age Bowl Barrow: SJ838730. Located within the grounds of Capesthorne on private land to the rear of the Hall itself.

Capesthorne Hall south-east Bronze Age Bowl Barrow: SJ845725. This barrow is marked on the OS Map and located in a woodland to the west of the A34.

Cessbank Common Bronze Age Round Barrow: SJ958681. Follow the directions for The Bullstones (see above) but take the footpath slightly to the north of the Bullstones path opposite the lane. Follow it along the metalled track until you come to a grassy hump surmounted by a gravestone.

Charity Lane Bronze Age Round Barrows: (i)SJ970724 (ii)SJ967726 (iii)SJ967726. Three possible barrows are located on private land adjacent to this footpath which runs down to Macclesfield Forest from Rainow. They are best approached from the Macclesfield Forest end in Forest Chapel where there is a car park at SJ974721.

Charles Head Bronze Age Round Barrow: SJ976787. Sited on private land belonging to Charles Head Farm in Rainow.

Clulow Cross Mound possible Bronze Age Round Barrow: SJ952673. Clulow Cross (or Cleulow) stands in a small plantation at the junction of the A54 Congleton to Buxton Road and the minor crossroads leading to Sutton (SJ953672). There is no formal access but it can easily be seen from the road.

Conical Reservoir Mound possible Bronze Age Round Barrow: SJ948717. Going from the village of Langley (to the south of Macclesfield) up into Macclesfield Forest along the road known locally as Clarke Lane, the Conical Mound can be seen to the left (north) of the road between Bottoms Reservoir and Teggsnose Reservoir, opposite the little row of cottages.

Dickens Wood Mines Bronze Age Copper Mine: SJ863778.

Eddisbury, Rainow possible Iron Age Enclosure: SJ938732. This is situated on National Trust land to the south-east of the main Macclesfield to Buxton Road (A537) just after the junction with the Old Buxton Road in Macclesfield.

Engine Vein Bronze Age Copper Mine: SJ859775. Parking is available in the main National Trust car park at SJ859772. The easiest way to reach this mine is to take the path to the north between the Information Centre and the Warden's Cottage. Follow this for 200m or so through the woods and you will come to the western end of the Engine Vein. The mines are leased by the Derbyshire Caving Club who hold regular Open Days with guided tours – see their website (www.derbyscc.org.uk/alderley/work_open_days.htm) for further information.

Fairy Brow, Little Bollington Bronze Age Round Barrow: SJ730865.

Further Harrop Bronze Age Round Barrow: SJ971791. Marked on the OS Map this barrow is located on private land

but easily visible from Bakestonedale Road (towards the eastern end near the junction with B5470 Macclesfield Road) and can be approached from Pott Shrigley. It can be viewed from the field entrance 400m east of Brink Farm.

Ginclough Bronze Age Standing Stone: SJ956764. Travellers who regularly pass along the B5470 (Macclesfield Road) in Rainow, may be completely unaware that just south of the hamlet of Ginclough is a standing stone right next to the road. It is not easy to see as its crown only just peeps over a dry-stone wall so if you blink you will miss it!

Great Low possible Iron Age Hillfort: SJ957770 (destroyed). The *CSMR* lists this hill known as 'Big Low' in Rainow near Macclesfield as the site of a possible hillfort.

Henbury Three Bronze Age Round barrows: SJ872713 (destroyed).

High Low Bronze Age Round Barrow: SJ951715. Going from the village of Langley up into Macclesfield Forest along Clarke Lane, High Low can be seen to the left (north) of the road in a field on private land as you go up the hill after the Conical Mound (see above) and just before you come to the farm of the same name, close to the Leather's Smithy public house.

Higher Ridgegate Stone: SJ955717. The stone can be viewed from a field entrance on the lane which forks left (off Clarke Lane) at the Leather's Smithy near Ridgegate Reservoir in Macclesfield Forest. Please note this site is on private land.

Knights Low Wood Bronze Age Bowl Barrows: SJ964815 (Western and Eastern), SJ964817 (east and west of path, barrow in wood), SJ962818 (north-west). The barrows in Knights Low Wood are very hard to distinguish and not really worth visiting specifically to try and find them. However, the walk through the woodland is very pleasant. It is best reached by parking on the roadside near the Bowstones at SJ974813 and following the footpath (Gritstone Trail) down the hill and into the woods.

Leek Old Road Neolithic Henge: SJ920696. Slight traces of the earthworks can be seen in a field in Oakgrove to the east of the old Macclesfield to Leek turnpike road, which lies to the rear of the Fools Nook Inn in Gawsworth off the A523. The site lies on private land but can be easily seen from the road.

Legh Oaks Farm Iron Age/Romano-British Enclosures: SJ690832. Visible only as cropmarks.

Lindow Moss Site of ancient Bog Bodies: SJ820805. Lindow Man was found at SJ820806 and Lindow III at SJ822807. A possible trackway was also uncovered in the 19th century at SJ810800. The area of peat in which the bodies were found has now almost completely disappeared but a public footpath provides a pleasant walk in the vicinity. Parking is available on the road near to the Nursery and the path starts at SJ823802.

Little Low possible Bronze Age Round Barrow: SJ954777.

Longutter possible Stone Circle: SJ955674. Lying on private land close to Clulow Cross in Wincle.

Macclesfield Cemetery, Mount Pleasant Bronze Age Round Barrow: SJ908745 (destroyed in the 19th century during the building of the modern cemetery).

Macclesfield Common Bronze Age Round Barrow (destroyed). The *CSMR* states it may have been located at SJ938732 on the western flank of Eddisbury Hill, but as quarrying has taken place in the area, no traces exist. The site now has a telegraph pole on it!

Minn End Lane Bronze Age Standing Stones: (i) SJ939659 (ii) and (iii) SJ940660 (iv) and (v) SJ940662. The stones are best approached on foot along Minn End Lane (an unclassified track) which follows the spine, separating Bosley Minn from Wincle Minn. If you are looking for the shortest route then Minn End Lane should be accessed from the south (having turned off the A523(T) Macclesfield to Leek road at SJ928642). The lane can be taken as far as the properties in the Hawkslee area where (with permission) you may be able to park. Follow the winding path north for around 500m until you come to an iron gate. The first leaning standing stone is located a few metres on, to the left of the path – you can't miss it! To find the other two genuine standing stones continue along the metalled lane (passing the two obvious more modern looking gate posts which you will shortly encounter) until you come across another two leaning stones on your left, just before the second iron gate. These stones are again unmissable.

Mottram St Andrew Bronze Age Copper Mines: SJ874784. These are inaccessible due to flooding.

Nab Head Bronze Age Round Barrow: SJ940788. Nab Head is easy to reach as access to the summit has been formalised recently. As a result the public right of way is only marked on the 'new' Explorer series OS map (number 268). There is only one way to get to the barrow. If you are driving parking is available on Cockshead Hey Road (off Shrigley Road at the Bollington end SJ940783). The path can be followed through Cockshead Hey Farm (it is signposted and there are a couple of stiles) up the slope for 600m until you reach the stone pillar that marks the high point of the hill. The damaged barrow surrounds the trig point.

Nab Wood Bronze Age Round Barrow: SJ939791. This barrow is located on private land and is inaccessible.

Nether Knutsford Bronze Age Round Barrow: SJ756785.

New Farm, Henbury Bronze Age Stone Circle: SJ887728. The site of the circle can be accessed in either one of two ways. The first, which is the easiest for parking but a slightly longer walk, is to take the Gawsworth Road from Broken Cross to the west of Macclesfield until you come to open countryside with a small row of houses on the right. Take the footpath at SJ891725 and follow this across the field and over a small bridge for approximately 700m. Once you have crossed the rickety wooden footbridge, you will find yourself in the field where the circle once stood. Some of the stones, which may once have formed the circle, can be seen along the hedge line. One of particular note is located close to the fence a few tens of metres to the right of the stile on Lower Pexhill road. The alternative route is to take the B5392, Lower Pexhill Road, from Broken Cross and access the field via the footpath from this end. However, parking can be difficult from here. Please note the site of the circle itself is located on private land.

Oversley Farm, Manchester Airport Neolithic to Iron Age Settlement Site with Drove Way: SJ816834. This is now under Manchester Airport's second runway development.

Rains Low Bronze Age Round Barrow: SJ976717. This barrow located deep within Macclesfield Forest is not worth a special visit but from High Low (see page 172) continue along Clarke Lane and take the left hand fork (i.e. straight on) at the Leather's Smithy and drive up through the Forest for circa 2.5km, bearing round to the right when you come to the small hamlet of Forest Chapel. The site is on private land but can be seen in the field to the right of the road after approximately 300m.

Reed Hill Bronze Age Round Barrow: SJ978798. There is no formal access to Reed Hill but it is best viewed from the minor road leading to The Bowstones (located off Higher Lane opposite the Hilton Moorside Grange Hotel) at approx SJ974813. It is marked on the OS Map as a 'cairn'.

Rostherne Celtic Head: SJ743837. This carving can be found in Rostherne Churchyard to the rear of the church (on the Mere side) in the corner of a low wall.

Sodger's Hump or Soldier's Tump Bronze Age Round Barrow: SJ841739. Heading from Macclesfield to Chelford on the A537, the first major crossroads you will come to is Monk's Heath. Sodger's Hump (located on private land) can be seen to the left of the road from the lay-by just after the crossroad (opposite the garage/petrol station).

Sponds Hill North and South Bronze Age Round Barrows: SJ969802. To visit the Sponds Hill barrows, park at The Bowstones on the minor road (located off Higher Lane opposite the Hilton Moorside Grange Hotel) at approx SJ974813 and take the Gritstone Trail south for around a kilometre to the summit of the hill.

Sutton Hall Bronze Age Round Barrow: SJ924713. From Macclesfield take the road known as Byrons Lane off the Macclesfield to Leek Road (A523) towards Sutton. Just before you reach the canal bridge in Gurnet, take the right hand turn into Bullocks Lane. The barrow (marked on the OS Map as a 'cairn' and located on private land) can either be viewed from the road (from just south of Sutton Hall) or from a public footpath which skirts the field to the east of the site at SJ924715.

Tatton possible Neolithic Long Barrow: SJ748808. Located within the grounds of Tatton Park in the care of The National Trust.

Tatton Mere Mesolithic Campsite: SJ757803.

Tatton Park Neolithic Settlement: SJ757814 and SJ754811. Located within the grounds of Tatton Park close to the Old Hall, in the care of The National Trust

Tegg's Nose Farm Bronze Age Round Barrow: SJ944727.

Teggsnose Reservoir Bronze Age Burial, possible site of Round Barrow: SJ953719. An urn and a flint arrowhead were unearthed here during work in the 19th century.

The Bridestones Neolithic Chambered Cairn: SJ906622. Located on the Cheshire/Staffordshire border, near

Congleton, the burial chamber can be found just off the country lane, which links the A523 (Macclesfield to Leek road) to the A527 (Congleton to Biddulph road), known locally as Dial Lane. Parking is available on the roadside verge and the stones are reached by taking a short walk along the drive leading to Bridestones Farm. The monument can be found to the left in a small fenced area through the wooden gate. Please note that the drive ahead is private land.

The Bullstones Bronze Age Stone Circle: SJ956676. From the A54 Congleton to Buxton Road (Axe Edge), heading towards Buxton, turn left onto the minor road just after The Fourways Motel in Wincle (SJ953672). Follow this lane for approximately 700m until you come to an informal lay-by opposite the junction with Withenshaw Lane. Park here and take the southernmost footpath across the fields (not the metalled road). After crossing two stiles, the centre stone will be visible on the horizon. Please note the site is on private land and permission must be sought from the landowner before visiting. It can be viewed from a distance from this footpath or from the lane at SJ954676.

The Druid's Circle, Alderley Edge, recent folly: SJ860778. This relatively modern stone circle is located in the woods to the east of the Armada Beacon (see directions on page 171).

The Golden Stone possible Bronze Age Standing Stone: SJ862776. Park in the National Trust car park at Alderley Edge (and take the path from The Wizard Inn past the warden's cottage and the eastern end of the Engine Vein. At the end, follow the track round to the right (to the south-east) towards Edge House Farm and you will see the Golden Stone to the left of the path after a few metres.

The Highway Man Stone: SJ967768. From the B5470 (Macclesfield to Whaley Bridge Road) turn right into the lane known as Pike Road, just before the Highway Man pub. Continue along here for around 500m and as the road starts bear round to the right at the top of the hill; you will see the stone in a field to your left. Please note this is located on private land.

The Murder Stone Bronze Age Standing Stone: SJ985811. This stone is situated on private land close to Cornfield Farm. It is visible from the B5470 'Macclesfield Road' near Whaley Bridge and from the public footpath (SJ985809) skirting the stone to the west.

The Plague Stone (or Greenway Cross) Christianised Bronze Age Standing Stone: SJ956692. The Plague Stone, marked on the OS Map as a 'cross', can be found on the verge to the north-east of the minor road known as Higher Greenway Lane at Sutton End near Wilboarclough. It is located close to The Hanging Gate public house (SJ951696), which has a fantastic view across the Cheshire Plain to Wales.

Toot Hill Tumulus (Warilow) Bronze Age Round Barrow: SJ969718. Located on private land in Macclesfield Forest.

Toot Hill Standing Stone: SJ970722. Located on private land in Macclesfield Forest.

Tytherington, North of Beech Hall School Bronze Age Round Barrow: SJ914749. This barrow can be found in the cul-de-sac of Lavenham Close on the Tytherington Estate, to the rear of Beech Hall School.

Withington Hall Bronze Age Barrow Cemetery: (i)SJ807724 (ii)SJ807723 (iii)SJ807722 and (iv)SJ807721. Going down the A535 Holmes Chapel to Chelford road from Jodrell Bank, the Withington barrows are located approximately 3 kilometres away, just past Withington Green. They can be seen from the lay-by after the last right-angled bend at SJ807719.

Woodhouse End possible Neolithic Settlement and Bronze Age Beaker Barrow: SJ914695. Woodhouse End lies close to the A523 Macclesfield to Leek road. It is located on private land but easily visible from the car park of the Fools Nook Inn, looking across the main road and the canal to the other side of the valley, once the leaves have dropped. For the best view of the mound and the site of the former lake, park at the side of the road (known locally as Woodhouse Lane) which crosses the canal opposite the Fool's Nook (SJ916694) and walk back along the towpath.

Yearnslow Bronze Age Round Barrow: SJ964759. This is located on private land close to the public footpath below Smith Lane (linking the B5470 Macclesfield Road to the minor road known as Ewrin Lane) above Lamaload Reservoir. To enjoy it in its wider landscape, drive along Smith Lane from the hamlet of Ginclough in Rainow (see page 172) for approximately 500m until you reach a lay-by forming part of the quarry entrance at Wimberry Moss. Looking over the wall to the south of the lane, Yearnslow can be seen to the south under the dry-stone wall on the horizon.

Yearnslow Stone, possible Standing Stone: SJ965762. This stone is adjacent to the public footpath (below Smith Lane) mentioned above.

Vale Royal Borough

Bradley Iron Age Promontory Fort: SJ539768. The few remaining earthworks of this settlement can be seen from the public footpath leading from the 'no through road' at the eastern end of Bradley village at SJ538769. The earthworks are on private land but can be easily viewed from the gate to the east of the path at the top of the slope.

Castle Cob Bronze Age Round Barrow: SJ534734. Situated in a private garden, this barrow is largely destroyed, surmounted by a water tank and a summerhouse, close to the village of Kingsley.

Castle Ditch, Eddisbury Iron Age Hillfort: SJ553693. This hillfort is located on private land but some of the earthworks of the ramparts can be viewed from the minor road to the south, known locally as Eddisbury Hill (off Stoney Lane), close to Eddisbury Hill Farm at SJ553691.

Delamere Bronze Age Stone Circle: SJ536688. The site of the stone circle is located just off a small lane, known as Morreys Lane, to the north of the A54(T) Northwich to Chester Road. If anything remains it is currently on private land belonging to a local nursery.

Delamere, Monarchy Hall Bronze Age Round Barrows: SJ551664 (destroyed).

Forest Farm Bronze Age Round Barrow: SJ563670. Located on private land close to The Seven Lows barrow cemetery near Delamere.

Gallowsclough Cob Bronze Age Round Barrow: SJ570713. Again marked on the OS Map, the very slight traces of this mound lie close to a hedge on Gallowsclough Lane, near Norley to the north of the Chester to Northwich road (A54). Please note this site is on private land.

Glead Hill Cob (or Houndslow) Bronze Age Round Barrow: SJ538726 (destroyed). This barrow close to Kingsley and Delamere Forest was levelled during the building work at Houndslough Farm in the 19th century.

Helsby Hill Iron Age Hillfort: SJ493754. In the care of The National Trust this settlement near Helsby can be accessed via various public footpaths. The easiest approach is from the east at SJ494752. There is also a fantastic view of the fort from the services at junction 14 of the M56 motorway.

High Billinge Bronze Age Round Bowl Barrow: SJ554662. Marked on the OS Map as a 'tumulus', this barrow is situated on private land but can be easily viewed from the nearby Quarry Bank Road close to High Billinge House at SJ556661.

Kelsall Possible Iron Age Field Systems: SJ529700.

Kelsborrow Iron Age Promontory Fort: SJ532675. There is no access to the fort itself but a public footpath, accessed at SJ532679, skirts the base of the hill.

Moultonbank Farm Bronze Age Round Barrow: SJ653694. Situated on private land near the village of Moulton.

Oak Mere Iron Age Enclosure: SJ576678. This waterside enclosure is located on private land to the west of the Horse Training Ground near Delamere. The Mere is encircled by trees, making it impossible to see from the neighbouring roads.

Peckforton Mere Iron Age Enclosure: SJ543577. Located on private land and hidden from the nearby public footpaths by a plantation of trees.

Robin Hoods Butts Bronze Age Round Barrow: SJ662778 (destroyed).

Tarporley Bronze Age Round Barrow: SJ550633 (destroyed).

The Seven Lows Bronze Age Barrow Cemetery: (i)SJ567671 (ii)SJ567670 (destroyed) (iii)SJ567671 (destroyed) (iv)SJ567670 (v)SJ56670 (vi)SJ567671 and (vii)SJ566671 (destroyed). The four remaining mounds can be viewed today from B5152 (the road linking the A54 Northwich to Chester road with the A49T Warrington to Whitchurch road) near Ottersbank Farm. However it is not worth making a special visit!

Tiverton Bronze Age Round Barrow: SJ550600 (destroyed).

Whitley Bronze Age Round Barrow 120m east of the village: SJ617793. This barrow is located on private land, close to the road near Lower Whitley but on a recent visit the authors failed to find it.

Woodhouses Iron Age Hillfort: SJ511757. There are several footpaths in the area but the easiest way to access the site is via the footpath to the east from Manley Road (SJ519753). This takes you on a gently sloping walk through Snidley Moor Wood. Take care if you have small children as the path can become very muddy and slippery.

Sites close to the modern County Borders

High Peak (Derbyshire)

Foxlow Edge Bronze Age Standing Stone: SK004759. The standing stone on Foxlow Edge stands close to the ruins of Errwood Hall. Parking is available for several cars in a lay-by on a lane known locally as 'The Street' at SK002761. From here the stone is visible to the south-east but to reach it you need to take the path that leaves the lay-by. After 200m when the path forks, follow the left route up to Foxlow Edge and you will come to the stone, after 300m or so, to the left of the path.

Liverpool (Merseyside)

Robin Hood's Stone Standing Stone, possibly one of The Calderstones: SJ399863. This stone is located at the junction of Booker Avenue and Acherfield Road in Allerton, not far from The Calderstones.

The Calderstones Neolithic Chambered Tomb: SJ405875. The Calderstones now reside in a greenhouse in Calderstones Park in Allerton on the outskirts of Liverpool. The greenhouses are locked so permission to visit the stones should be sought in advance from the Park Rangers Office by telephoning 0151 225 5910 or by e-mailing park.rangers@liverpool.gov.uk

Salford (Greater Manchester)

Great Woolden Hall Farm Iron Age Enclosure: SJ691935. This settlement close to the village of Glazebrook near Irlam is visible only as a cropmark. A promontory fort lies close by at SJ691936.

Worsley Romano-British Bog Body: SJ710970. The remains of a human head were found in a bog at Astley Moss close to Chat Moss near Worsley in the 1950s.

Stockport (Greater Manchester)

Brown Low Bronze Age Round Cairn: SJ988909. This tree-covered mound on private land can be viewed from the nearby public footpath accessed from Sandhill Lane (SJ987904).

Ludworth Intakes Bronze Age Round Cairn: SJ990913. This mound, marked on the OS Map as a 'cairn' and dissected by a dry-stone wall, can be also be viewed from the nearby public footpath, accessed from Sandhill Lane (SJ987904). Please note this site is on private land.

Mellor Iron Age Hillfort: SJ982889. The hillfort is located on private land belonging to Mellor Church and Vicarage, but The Mellor Trust (see addresses on page 180) have an annual open weekend which is well worth visiting.

Warrington

Grappenhall Two Bronze Age Kerb Cairns associated with a cremation cemetery: SJ637866 and SJ638865 (destroyed). These are now buried under a housing estate to the south of Warrington. The finds are in Warrington Museum.

Warrington Possible Crannogs: SJ611882 and SJ607864. Discovered on the site of the former Thomas Lockyers Factory, these are now believed to be from the post-medieval period.

Winwick Bronze Age Round Barrow: SJ613932. Marked on the OS Map as a 'tumulus', this mound lies close to the M6 Motorway on the outskirts of Winwick.

Wirral (Merseyside)

Greasby Mesolithic Settlement Site: SJ250870. The site of what is believed to be a Middle Stone Age shelter is now located in a built up area close to Hoylake.

Great Meols site of Mesolithic Forest and Iron Age Trading Port/Settlement: SJ231906. Various Iron Age artefacts have been discovered in and around the area of Meols to the north of Hoylake on The Wirral, particularly in the area around Dove Point.

Irby Late Bronze Age/Iron Age Settlement: SJ254837. Located in the gardens of private houses on Mill Road.

West Kirby Site of Bronze Age Cremations, possible Round Barrow: SJ221867. An urn was discovered in the garden of a private house on Grange Hill.

8 Glossary

adze A hand tool with a blade attached at right angles to a wooden handle, used for dressing timber.

antiquarian An amateur archaeologist who excavated many important monuments in the past, often hurriedly.

azurite A type of copper ore which is characteristically blue in colour.

barrow A man-made burial mound usually constructed from earth (but commonly from stone in the upland areas). Long barrows are typically Neolithic and round barrows usually Bronze Age.

BC Dating before the time of Christ.

Beaker burials Burials of a single crouched inhumation or cremation accompanied by a special type of decorated drinking cup, known as a Beaker, and a variety of rich grave goods, common in the Early Bronze Age from circa 2300BC onwards.

Beaker A characteristically fine, thin-walled, well-fired drinking vessel, usually red in colour and covered with various zones of complicated geometric decoration over the majority of the exterior surface.

berm An artificial ridge or embankment. A term often used to describe the ledge between the ditch and rampart of a hillfort.

Bronze Age Dates vary according to place and culture (and the books you read), but in the British Isles it is generally accepted to encompass the period from circa 2300BC to circa 800BC with Early Bronze Age being circa 2300BC to 1800BC, Middle Bronze Age circa 1800BC to 1300BC and Late Bronze Age circa 1300BC to 800BC. These dates are only a rough guide. As to exactly when the Neolithic ended and the Bronze Age began no one is really certain. In fact it has now even been suggested that in certain areas of mainland Europe there may have been a brief 'Copper Age' (Chalcolithic) in between.

cairn A mound of stones, sometimes as a result of clearing the land, but usually covering a burial. Cairns can either be circular (round cairn) or long (long cairn) in shape, or covering a tomb (chambered cairn).

calcinated A substance which has been oxidised as a result of heating.

capstone A stone forming the roof of a burial chamber.

causewayed enclosure (also known as causewayed camp) An Early and Middle Neolithic roughly circular area enclosed by banks and ditches. Usually situated both in valley bottoms and on hilltops, they are believed to have been areas where trade occurred and rituals were carried out.

Chalcolithic The 'Copper Age' which occurred in certain areas of Europe circa 3000BC, between the Neolithic and Bronze Ages.

chambered tomb Any burial tomb with a chamber, usually constructed from stone, and dating to the Neolithic. Bones and other interments were often added over a long period of time and often brought out for ritual and ceremonial purposes.

chert A black or grey variety of quartz that resembles flint.

cinerary urn An urn in which the cremated ashes of the dead were placed.

cist A small rectangular grave pit, lined with stone slabs and covered with a capstone.

Collared urns Containers which were used regularly after 2000BC as grave goods, either accompanying inhumations or holding cremated ashes.

cremation Burnt human remains. Not surviving as ashes in the sense we know them today, but as burnt fragments of bone.

cropmarks Light and dark marks in growing crops visible from the air, reflecting differences in the soil beneath. Parched lines indicate stone walls whereas greener crops grow where there is more water such as in pits, ditches and gulleys.

cupmark A small, man-made, eggcup shaped hollow ground into stone and sometimes surrounded by a ring (ringmark). It is the most common feature in prehistoric rock art.

dirk A short dagger.

earthworks Banks and ditches, mounds and hollows made from earth, clay, soil or turf.

equinox The days when day and night are of equal length, exactly half way between the solstices. The vernal equinox usually occurs around the 21st March, while the autumnal equinox is around the 21st September.

excarnation platform An area where dead bodies were exposed to remove the flesh from the bones before burial. Similar practices are still carried out today in certain areas of the East.

fieldwalking A method of looking for sites and finds by walking over the ground in a systematic manner. The area to be examined is usually divided into a grid so that finds can be plotted into the relevant area and an overall plan of the scatter of artefacts can be drawn up.

flint A very hard silica-based rock, often used for arrowheads, blades and other cutting tools, as well as lighting fires.

Food Vessel An Early Bronze Age decorated pot often found accompanying a burial.

forecourt The area of a barrow, often paved, where rituals were carried out.

grave goods Items such as pottery, tools, weapons and jewellery placed with a burial or inhumation as an accompaniment to the next world.

Grimston ware A type of Early Neolithic pottery. Dating from circa 3300BC onwards it is characteristically plain, fine and hard with a round base, sometimes burnished and tempered with grit.

Grooved ware A flat-bottomed, bucket or flower-pot shaped pottery, characteristically thick and decorated with grooved lines. Dating to the Late Neolithic and Early Bronze Age (circa 3000 to 2000BC).

haft The handle of a dagger, knife or axe.

halberd A combined spear and battle axe of Bronze Age date.

henge A later Neolithic circular earthen banked enclosure usually with an internal ditch and one or more entrances, which may or may not have internal settings of timber or stone.

hillfort A hilltop defended by a wall, earthen bank or timber palisade and a ditch, dating from the Late Bronze Age to Iron Age.

hoard A store of coins or other metal objects of worth, which were hidden and never reclaimed by the owner.

inhumation An uncremated human burial where the skeleton is placed either in a crouched position or lying flat.

Iron Age Most of the last millennium BC, apart from the first few hundred years when iron became the primary metal for weapons and tools.

kerb Stones forming a retaining wall around a mound, which may be internal or external.

La Tène A style of Iron Age metalwork and associated culture named after a site in Switzerland. Artwork is characterised by geometric motifs and dates to between the 5th and 1st centuries BC.

long barrow (see barrow)

macehead A stone tool similar to an axe head but with rounder ends.

malachite A type of copper ore which is characteristically green in colour.

megalithic Made from large stones.

Mesolithic The Middle Stone Age which began after the last Ice Age. The period is generally divided into two phases: Early Mesolithic (circa 8500 to 6500BC) when Britain was still connected to the Continent and Late Mesolithic (circa 6500 to 4500BC) when it became an island.

microliths Small flint tools, pointed or triangular in shape, common in the Mesolithic.

monolith A single stone.

mortuary house A house of the dead, usually a sub-rectangular wooden structure enclosed by a bank and ditch, perhaps where bodies were exposed in order to remove the flesh before burial. Many were the starting point for barrows.

Neolithic The New Stone Age circa 4500BC to circa 2300BC with Early Neolithic being circa 4500BC to 3500BC, Middle Neolithic circa 3500BC to 2800BC and Late Neolithic circa 2800BC to 2300BC. These dates are only a rough guide. As to exactly when the Neolithic ended and the Bronze Age began no one is really certain, it varies according to which book you read. In fact it has now even been suggested that in certain areas of mainland Europe there may have been a brief 'Copper Age' (Chalcolithic) in between.

orthostat A standing stone, usually part of a stone circle or other monument.

palisade A strong fence made of stakes driven into the ground for defensive purposes.

Peterborough ware A Neolithic coarse, thick, round-bottomed pottery profusely decorated with a range of designs using stamps, combs, cord, fingers and bird bones.

portal stone A stone in the entrance of a stone circle or henge, or forming the entrance to a burial chamber.

potboilers Stones which were warmed in a fire and then dropped into water to heat it.

pygmy cup A specific type of urn dating to the Late Neolithic and Early Bronze Age. Used for funerary purposes, it may perhaps have contained incense.

pyrites A yellow mineral found in association with a number of metals, especially copper and tin.

quern A stone handmill used for grinding corn.

radiocarbon An archaeological dating method measuring the decay of radioactive carbon 14.

rampart The surrounding embankment of a fort, including walls and fences that are built on the bank.

revetted A wall or embankment faced with stones.

rill A small groove or gully eroded by water.

ringmark (see cupmark)

Romano-British Native Britons and artefacts from the time of the Roman occupation, i.e. from 43AD (when the Emperor Claudius invaded) to the 5th century AD when links with the Roman Empire were severed.

rock shelter A cave where the mouth has been weathered to create an overhang, often used as a dwelling.

round barrow (see barrow)

satellite burials Later interments placed around an earlier primary burial, sometimes in or near a barrow.

scrapers Small flint instruments used for skinning animals and dating to the Neolithic and Bronze Age.

shards (or sherds) Broken fragments of pottery.

solstice The days of the year when the sun is at the maximum in the Northern and Southern hemispheres, i.e. the longest and shortest days of the year. Usually around the 21st June and the 21st December.

sphagnum A type of moss which grows in peat bogs.

tumulus A term often used to describe a round barrow or an artificial mound, the use of which is unsure.

tundra A vast, flat, treeless area characteristic in Arctic regions.

urn A pottery vessel in which human remains are often found.

vitrified Converted to a glass-like substance by heat. A term used to describe the hardening of hillfort defences by burning.

VCP A type of pottery known as 'Very Coarse Pottery', used specifically for the manufacture and transportation of salt.

votive deposits Offerings left as a dedication at special places such as stone circles, henges or watery places.

whetstone A stone used for sharpening edged tools and knives.

wristguard A rectangular guard made from stone, wood or metal, worn on the inner side of the wrist to protect it when drawing a bow, found in both Neolithic and Bronze Age burials.

Useful Addresses and Websites of Interest

Websites of Interest

Cheshire Archaeology – *www.cheshire.gov.uk/archaeology/home.htm*

Chester Archaeological Society – *www.chesterarchaeolsoc.org.uk*

Current Archaeology Magazine – *www.archaeology.co.uk*

Council for British Archaeology – *www.britarch.ac.uk*

The Megalithic Portal – *www.megalithic.co.uk*
The most definitive ancient site guide on the web - a superb photographic guide to ancient sites developed by Andy Burnham, including the latest prehistory news stories, a huge searchable database of ancient sites both in the UK, Ireland and Europe, and 'The Megalith Map' allowing you to search for sites by Ordnance Survey grid squares.

Peak District National Park – *www.peakdistrict.org*

Portable Antiquities Scheme – www.finds.org.uk

Applepot – *www.applepot.co.uk*

Useful Addresses

Archaeology Contacts

Cheshire County Council
Archaeological Services
Environmental Planning
Backford Hall
Backford
Chester CH1 6PZ
Tel: 01244 603160
Fax: 01244 603360
e-mail: archaeology@cheshire.gov.uk

English Heritage
Hazelrigg House,
33 Marefair, Northampton,
Northants, NN1 1SR
www.english-heritage.org.uk

**Greater Manchester
Archaeology Unit**
Architecture Building
Oxford Road
Manchester M13 9PL
Tel: 0161 275 2314
Fax: 0161 275 2315
www.art.man.ac.uk/
FieldArchaeologyCentre/gmau.htm

Mellor Archaeological Trust
The Old Vicarage
Mellor
SK6 5LX
Tel: 0161 427 1149

Merseyside Archaeological Services
Liverpool Museum
William Brown Street
Liverpool, L3 8EN
Tel: 0151 478 4207
Fax: 0151 478 4390
www.liverpoolmuseum.org.uk

Peak District National Park Authority
Archaeological Services
Aldern House
Baslow Road
Bakewell
Derbyshire DE45 1AE
Tel: 01629 816200
Fax: 01629 816310
e-mail: archaeology@peakdistrict-npa.gov.uk

Museums Displaying or Housing Prehistoric Artefacts

Congleton Museum
Market Square,
Congleton
CW12 1ET
Tel: 01260 276360
www.comcarenet.com/museum

Manchester Museum
University of Manchester,
Oxford Road,
M13 9PL
Tel: 0161 2752634
www.museum.man.ac.uk

The British Museum
Great Russell Street,
London
WC1B 3DG
Tel: 0207 323 8299
www.thebritishmuseum.ac.uk

The Grosvenor Museum
27 Grosvenor Street,
Chester
CH1 2DD
Tel: 01244 402008
www.chestercc.gov.uk/heritage/
museum/home.html

Warrington Museum
Bold Street,
Warrington,
WA1 1JG
Tel: 01925 442392
Fax: 01925 442399
www.warrington.gov.uk/entertain-ment/Museum/home.htm

180

References and Further Reading

Abbreviations

JCAS	*Journal of the Chester Archaeological Society.*
SMR	*Sites and Monuments Record*
THSLC	*Transactions of the Historic Society of Lancashire and Cheshire.*
TLCAS	*Transactions of the Lancashire and Cheshire Antiquarian Society.*

Introduction

Cheshire Archaeology News issue 7, (2000). [Monuments at Risk Survey].

Morgan, P. and V. "Rock Around the Peak – Megalithic Monuments of the Peak District", Sigma Press, Wilmslow (2001).

Proceedings of the Macclesfield Scientific Society (1877-1878).

Rowley, G. "The Excavation of a Barrow at Woodhouse End, Gawsworth, Near Macclesfield", *JCAS* volume 60 (1977).

Sainter, Dr J.D. "The Jottings of Some Geological, Archaeological, Botanical, Ornithological, and Zoological Rambles Round Macclesfield", Swinnerton and Brown Printers, Macclesfield (1878).

Varley, W.J. and Jackson, J.W. "Prehistoric Cheshire", Cheshire Rural Community Council (1940).

Landscape

Leah, M.D, Wells, C.E., Applebly, C., Huckerby, E. "The Wetlands of Cheshire, North West Wetlands Survey 4", Lancaster Imprints, Lancaster Archaeological Unit (1997).

Longley, D.M. "Prehistory" in C.R. Elrington (ed) "The Victoria History of the County of Chester", volume 1, Oxford University Press, pg1-4 (1987).

Varley, W.J. "Cheshire Before the Romans", Cheshire Community Council (1964).

Whitten, D.G.A. and Brooks, J.R.V. "The Penguin Dictionary of Geology", Penguin (1972).

The Mesolithic

Adams, Dr M. "Burbo Offshore Windfarm Archaeological Report", Liverpool Museum Field Archaeology Unit (August 2002).

Carrington, P. "Chester", English Heritage and BT Batsford (1994).

Cheshire Archaeology News (Spring 1999).

Coles, B., Friell, G., Huckerby, E., Middleton, R., Newman, R.M., Wells, C.E. and Wilmott, A. "The Wetlands of Merseyside", Lancaster Imprints 2 (1994).

Darvill, T. "Prehistoric Britain", B.T. Batsford Ltd, London (1987).

Ellis, P. (ed) "Beeston Castle, Cheshire – Excavations by Laurence Keen and Peter Hough, 1968-85", English Heritage Archaeological Report 23 (1993).

Griffiths, D. "Great Sites: Meols", *British Archaeology Magazine* issue 62 (December 2001).

Higham, N.J. and Cane, T. "The Tatton Park Project, Part 1: Prehistoric to Sub-Roman Settlement and Land Use", *JCAS* volume 74, (1996-97).

Leah, M.D, Wells, C.E., Applebly, C. and Huckerby, E. "The Wetlands of Cheshire, North West Wetlands Survey 4", Lancaster Imprints, Lancaster Archaeological Unit (1997).

Matthews, K. "The Mesolithic Occupation" Retrieved (02/07/2003) from:
http://users.lunet.ac.uk/kmatthews/carden3.html

Mellor Archaeological Trust "The Hillfort at Mellor, Excavations 1998-2002" (2003).

Penney, S. "A Mesolithic Flint Site at Alford", *Cheshire Past* issue 2 (1993).

Richards, J. "Britain's Oldest House? A Journey into the Stone Age" Retrieved (13/06/03) from:
http://www.bbc.co.uk/history/archaeology/oldest_house_01.shtml

181

Sainter, Dr J.D. "The Jottings of Some Geological, Archaeological, Botanical, Ornithological, and Zoological Rambles Round Macclesfield", Swinnerton and Brown Printers, Macclesfield (1878).

Stokes, P. "Divers find Stone Age Site in North Sea", *The Daily Telegraph* (12/09/2003).

The Neolithic

Introduction

Barnatt, J. "The Henges, Stone Circles and Ringcairns of the Peak District", Sheffield University Press (1990).

Barnatt, J. and Smith, K. "Peak District Landscapes Through Time", English Heritage and B.T. Batsford, London (1997).

Coles, B., Friell, G., Huckerby, E., Middleton, R., Newman, R.M., Wells, C.E. and Wilmott, A. "The Wetlands of Merseyside", Lancaster Imprints 2 (1994).

Higham, H.J. "The Origins of Cheshire", Manchester University Press (1993).

Leah, M.D, Wells, C.E., Appleby, C. and Huckerby, E. "The Wetlands of Cheshire, North West Wetlands Survey 4", Lancaster Imprints, Lancaster Archaeological Unit (1997).

Morgan, P. and V. "Rock Around the Peak – Megalithic Monuments of the Peak District", Sigma Press, Wilmslow (2001).

Pollard, J. "Neolithic Britain", Shire Archaeology, Princes Risborough, (1997).

Rowley, G. "Macclesfield in Prehistory" (1982).

Life and Settlement

Cheshire County Sites and Monuments Record (Alderley Edge – Castle Rock Field) *SMR* 1440/0/1 (Alderley Edge - White Barn Farm) *SMR* 1440/0/7 (Tatton) *SMR* 1296, 1312.

Adkins, L. and R. "The Handbook of British Archaeology", Constable, London (1982).

Ellis, P. (ed) "Beeston Castle, Cheshire – Excavations by Laurence Keen and Peter Hough, 1968-85", English Heritage Archaeological Report 23 (1993).

Gibson, A. "Stonehenge and Timber Circles", Tempus Publishing, Stroud (2000).

Herepath, N. "Report on the Stone Axe found at Langley, Derbyshire", Liverpool Museum (November 2000).

Higham, N.J., Cane, T. "The Tatton Park Project, Part 1: Prehistoric to Sub-Roman Settlement and Land Use", *JCAS* volume 74, (1996-97).

Leah, M.D, Wells, C.E., Appleby, C. and Huckerby, E. "The Wetlands of Cheshire, North West Wetlands Survey 4", Lancaster Imprints, Lancaster Archaeological Unit (1997).

Longley, D.M. "Prehistory" in C.R. Elrington (ed) "The Victoria History of the County of Chester", volume 1, Oxford University Press, pg40-56 (1987).

Mullin, D. "Grimston Ware – Examples of Early Neolithic Pottery from North and East Cheshire", *JCAS* volume 77 (2002).

Pryor, F. "Britain BC", Harper Collins, London (2003).

Roeder, C. and Graves, F.S. "Recent Archaeological Discoveries at Alderley Edge", *TLCAS* volume 23 (1905).

Rowley, G. "The Excavation of a Barrow at Woodhouse End, Gawsworth, Near Macclesfield", *JCAS* volume 60 (1977).

Rowley, G. "Macclesfield in Prehistory" (1982).

Russell, M. "Flint Mines in Neolithic Britain", Tempus Publishing, Stroud (2000).

Macclesfield Community News (December 2000).

Monuments of the Living

Burl, A. "Prehistoric Henges", Shire Publications, Princes Risborough (1997).

Burl, A. "The Stone Circles of Britain, Ireland and Brittany", Yale University Press (2000).

Longley, D.M. "Prehistory" in C.R. Elrington (ed) "The Victoria History of the County of Chester", volume 1, Oxford University Press, pg40-42 (1987).

Matthews, K. "The Late Neolithic/Bronze Age Transition in the Carden Region". Retrieved (14/10/2003) from: http://users.breathe.com/kmatthews/chalco.html

Mercer, R.J. "Causewayed Enclosures", Shire Publications, Princes Risborough (1990).

Rowley, G. "Macclesfield in Prehistory" (1982).

Souden, D. "Stonehenge, Mysteries of the stones and Land scape", Collins and Brown in association with English Heritage, London (1997).

Monuments of the Dead

Cheshire County Sites and Monuments Record (Bridestones) *SMR* 154 (Somerford) *SMR* 823.

Barnatt, J. "The Bullstones ", Personal Communication (2002).

Beckensall, S. "British Prehistoric Rock Art", Tempus Publishing Ltd, Stroud (1999).

Brocklehurst, Sir P. "Swythamley and Its Neighbourhood", Appendix 1 - The Origin of the Bridestones - a local legend, Swinnerton and Brown, Macclesfield (1874).

Burl, A. "The Stone Circles of Britain, Ireland and Brittany", Yale University Press (2000).

Cheshire Archaeological Bulletin volume 3, pg 60 (Loachbrook Farm).

Congleton Chronicle "Excavations at the Bridestones - Important Discoveries" (12th June 1936).

Cooper, T. "Remarks respecting the Ancient British and Roman Encampments and The Bridestones at or near Congleton, Cheshire, and other matters of Antiquarian Interest in the Neighbourhood" (1893).

Cowell, R.W. and Warhurst, M. "The Calderstones", Merseyside Archaeological Society (1984).

Crosby, A. "A History of Cheshire", Phillimore and Co. Ltd, Chichester (1996).

Darvill, T.C. "The Megalithic Chambered Tombs of the Cotswold-Severn Region", Vorda (1982).

Dunlop, M. "A Preliminary Survey of the Bridestones, Congleton, and Related Monuments", *TLCAS* volume 38 (1938).

Forde-Johnson, J.L. "The Calderstones, Liverpool" extracted from Powell, T.G.E. and Daniel, G.E. "Barclodiad y Gawres" Liverpool University Press (1956).

Forde-Johnson, J.L. "Megalithic Art in the North West of Britain: The Calderstones, Liverpool", *Proceedings of the Prehistoric Society* volume 23 (1957).

Grinsell, L.V. "The Ancient Burial Mounds of England", Methuen and Co, London (1953).

Herdman, W.A. "A Contribution to the History of the Calderstones, near Liverpool", *Transactions of the Liverpool Biological Society* (1896).

Higham, H.J. "The Origins of Cheshire", Manchester University Press (1993).

Higham, N.J. and Cane, T. "The Tatton Park Project, Part 1: Prehistoric to Sub-Roman Settlement and Land Use", *JCAS* volume 74 (1996-97).

Kilburn, K. "Archaeoastronomy" Retrieved (05/04/2003) from: http://www.leekonline.co.uk/sunset/index.htm

Kilburn, K. "The Bridestones Legacy" (forthcoming).

Longley, D.M. "Prehistory" in C.R. Elrington (ed) "The Victoria History of the County of Chester", volume 1, Oxford University Press, pg42-47 (1987).

Mercer, R. "Prehistory" in "Historical Atlas of Britain, Prehistoric to Medieval" edited by N. Saul, Bramley Books, Godalming, (1998).

Morris, R.W.B. "The Prehistoric rock art of Great Britain: a survey of all sites bearing motifs more complex than simple cup-marks", *Proceedings of the Prehistoric Society* volume 55 (1989).

Mullin, D. "The Loachbrook Farm Mound: Neolithic Long Barrow or cattle plague burial mound?", *TLCAS* volume 98 (2002).

Nevell, M. "The Bridestones: A Neolithic Tomb in Cheshire", *Cheshire History 25* (Spring 1990).

Ormerod, G. "The History of the County Palatine and City of Chester", 2nd Edition (1882).

Parker Pearson, M. "The Archaeology of Death and Burial", Sutton Publishing Ltd, Stroud (1999).

Pickford, D. "The Bridestones", Bawdstone Press (1998).

Romilly Allen, J. "The Calderstones" *Journal of British Archaeological Society* volume 39 (1883) and volume 44 (1888).

Rowley, G. "The Excavation of a Barrow at Woodhouse End, Gawsworth, Near Macclesfield", *JCAS* volume 60 (1977).

Rowley, G. "Macclesfield in Prehistory" (1982).

Royden, M. "The Calderstones" Retrieved (12/09/2003) from: http://www.btinternet.com/~m.royden/mrlhp/local/calders/calders.htm

Sainter, Dr J.D. "The Jottings of Some Geological, Archaeological, Botanical, Ornithological, and Zoological Rambles Round Macclesfield", Swinnerton and Brown Printers, Macclesfield (1878).

Scott, J.G. "Megalithic Enquiries in the West of Britain", Liverpool University Press (1969).

Shone, W. "Prehistoric Man in Cheshire", Simpkin, Marshall, Hamilton, Kent and Co. Ltd (1911).

Simms, Mr B.B. "The story of the Bridestones - Their Origin, The People who Erected them and Cultural Associations", *Congleton Chronicle* (1936).

Souden, D. "Stonehenge, Mysteries of the Stones and Landscape", Collins and Brown in association with English Heritage, London (1997).

Spindler, K. "The Man in the Ice", Weidenfield and Nicolson, London (1993).

Turner, R.C. and Scaife, R.G. (ed) "Bog Bodies – New Discoveries and Perspectives", British Museum Press, London (1995).

Varley, W.J. and Jackson, J.W. "Prehistoric Cheshire", Cheshire Rural Community Council (1940).

Varley, W.J. "Cheshire Before the Romans", Cheshire Community Council (1964).

Ward, J. "The Borough of Stoke Upon Trent" (1843, republished 1969).

The Bronze Age

Introduction

Baillie, M.G.L. "Dendrochronology and the Chronology of the Irish Bronze Age" in "Ireland in the Bronze Age" edited by J. Waddell and E. Shee-Twohig, Stationery Office, Dublin, 30-37 (1995).

Bentley Smith, D. "Past Times – Oversley Farm", *Macclesfield Community News* (April 1998).

Cheshire County Sites and Monuments Record (Macclesfield Cemetery Quern) *SMR* 1551/0/2.

Current Archaeology volume 172 "Wetlands Special" (February 2001).

Dineley, M. "Finding Magic in Stone Age real ale", British Archaeology No.19 (November 1996).

Garner, D. "The Bronze Age of Manchester Airport: Runway 2" in Brück, J (ed), "Bronze Age Landscapes - Transition and Transformation", Oxbow Books, Oxford (2001).

Grattan, J.P. and Gillberton, D.D. "Prehistoric "Settlement Crisis", environmental change in the British Isles, and volcanic eruptions in Iceland: An exploration of plausible linkages", Geological Society of America Special Paper 345 (2000).

Jackson, J.W. "The Prehistoric Archaeology of Lancashire and Cheshire – Presidential Address 26th January, 1924", *TLCAS* volume 50 (1934/35).

Longley, D.M. "Prehistory" in C.R. Elrington (ed) "The Victoria History of the County of Chester", volume 1, Oxford University Press, pg56-103 (1987).

Matthews, K. "The Bronze Age at Carden", Retrieved (02/07/2003) from: http://users.lunet.ac.uk/kmatthews/carden5.html

Nevell, M. "Arthill Heath Farm. Trial excavations on a prehistoric settlement 198/-88. Interim report", *Manchester Archaeological Bulletin* volume 3, 4-13 (1988).

Peiser, B.J., Palmer. T and Bailey, M.E (ed) "Natural Catastrophes During Bronze Age Civilisations: Archaeological, geological, astronomical and cultural perspectives", British Archaeological Reports - S728, Archaeopress, Oxford (1998).

Roberts, N. "The Bronze Age – A Time of Change", Signal House Publications, Shropshire (1994).

Sainter, Dr J.D. "The Jottings of Some Geological, Archaeological, Botanical, Ornithological, and Zoological Rambles Round Macclesfield", Swinnerton and Brown Printers, Macclesfield (1878).

Shone, W. "Prehistoric Man in Cheshire." Simpkin, Marshall, Hamilton, Kent and Co. Ltd (1911).

Wilson, D. "Withington", *Current Archaeology* volume 76 (1981).

Copper Mining and Metalwork

Cheshire County Sites and Monuments Record (Alderley Mines) *SMR* 1440/0/0 (Flint Block) *SMR* 1440/0/5 (BA Hammer Stone) *SMR* 1440/0/8 (BA Hammer Stones) (BA Hammer) *SMR* 1440/0/9 1440/0/10 (BA Axe Hammer) *SMR* 1440/0/11 (BA Stone axe hammer) *SMR* 1440/0/12 (BA Sword) *SMR* 1440/0/13 (Alderley Shovel) *SMR* 1440/0/14 (Engine Vein) *SMR* 1440/1 (Brindlow) *SMR* 1440/2 (Windmill Wood) *SMR* 1440/3 (Dickens Wood) *SMR* 1440/4 (West Mine) *SMR* 1440/5.

Alcock, L. "The Excavation of Cadbury Castle 1966-1970", Thames and Hudson (1972).

Braithwaite, B. and Christie, T. "Mineral Commodity Report 11 – Tin", Institute of Geological and Nuclear Sciences Ltd, Retrieved (28/10/2003) from: http://www.med.govt.nz/crown_minerals/minerals/docs/comreports/report11_tin.pdf

Budd, P. "Meet the Metal Makers" *British Archaeology*, no56 (2000).

Coles, B., Friell, G., Huckerby, E., Middleton, R., Newman, R.M., Wells, C.E. and Wilmott, A. "The Wetlands of Merseyside", Lancaster Imprints 2 (1994).

Ellis, P. (ed) "Beeston Castle, Cheshire – Excavations by Laurence Keen and Peter Hough, 1968-85", English Heritage Archaeological Report 23 (1993).

Encyclopaedia Britannica "The new Encyclopaedia Britannica Micropaedia Ready Reference", Chicago Encyclopaedia Britannica (1988).

Leah, M.D, Wells, C.E., Applebly, C. and Huckerby, E. "The Wetlands of Cheshire, North West Wetlands Survey 4", Lancaster Imprints, Lancaster Archaeological Unit (1997).

Longley, D.M. "Prehistory" in C.R. Elrington (ed) "The Victoria History of the County of Chester", volume 1, Oxford University Press, pg78, 90 (1987).

O'Brien, W. "Bronze Age Copper Mining", Shire Publications (1996).

Roeder, C. "Prehistoric and Subsequent Mining at Alderley Edge, with a sketch of the Archaeological Features of the Neighbourhood", *TLCAS* volume 19 (1901).

Roeder, C. and Graves, F.S "Recent Archaeological Discoveries at Alderley Edge", *TLCAS* volume 23 (1905).

Sainter, Dr J.D. "The Jottings of Some Geological, Archaeological, Botanical, Ornithological, and Zoological Rambles Round Macclesfield", Swinnerton and Brown Printers, Macclesfield (1878).

Sainter, J.D. "Scientific Rambles Round Macclesfield", Silk Press reprint (1999).

Shone, W. "Prehistoric Man in Cheshire", Simpkin, Marshall, Hamilton, Kent and Co Ltd, London (1911).

Timberlake, S. "Mining and prospection for metals in Early Bronze Age Britain – making claims within the archaeological landscape" In Brück, J (ed), "Bronze Age Landscapes. Transition and transformation", pg 179-192, Oxbow Books, Oxford (2001).

Tindall, A. "Two Middle Bronze Age Axes from Cheshire", *Cheshire Past* issue 1 (1992).

Tindall, A. "Some Bronze Age Axes from Cheshire", *Cheshire Past* issue 2 (1993).

Turner, R.C. "The Bridgemere Bronze Hoard", *Cheshire Archaeological Bulletin* 10 (1984/5).

Vint, J. "The Congleton Late Bronze Age Hoard", *Cheshire Past* issue 1 (1992).

Warrington, G. "The Copper Mines of Alderley Edge and Mottram St Andrew", Cheshire' *JCAS* volume 64 (1981).

Williams, C.J. "Great Orme Mines", British Mining No.52, Northern Mine Research Society, Keighley (1995).

Wilson, G.V. with contributions by J.S.Flett, LL.D, FRS, "Memoirs of the Geological Survey – Volume XVII – The Lead, Zinc, Copper and Nickel ores of Scotland", Special Reports on the Mineral Resources of Great Britain, HMSO Edinburgh (1921).

Yannopoulos, J.C. and Agarwal, J.C. "Extractive Metallurgy of Copper volume 1" (1976).

Stone Circles

Cheshire County Sites and Monuments Record (Bullstones) *SMR* 1522, (New Farm, Henbury) *SMR* 1376/1.

Bamford, P. "Cheshire Curiosities", Dove Cote Press (1992).

Barnatt, J. "The Bullstones", Personal Communication (2001).

Burl, A. "A Guide to the Stone Circles of Britain, Ireland and Brittany", Yale University Press (1995).

Burl, A. "The Stone Circles of Britain, Ireland and Brittany", Yale University Press (2000).

Longley, D.M. "Prehistory" in C.R. Elrington (ed) "The Victoria History of the County of Chester", volume 1, Oxford University Press, pg.38-65 (1987).

Morgan, V. and P. "Rock Around the Peak – Megalithic Monuments of the Peak District", Sigma Press (2001).

Rowley, G. "Excavation of a circle at New Farm, Henbury", *TLCAS* volume 78 (1975).

Rowley, G. "Macclesfield in Prehistory" (1982).

Sainter, Dr J.D. "The Jottings of Some Geological, Archaeological, Botanical, Ornithological, and Zoological Rambles Round Macclesfield", Swinnerton and Brown Printers, Macclesfield (1878).

Skinner, T. "Garner's Edge", *Cheshire Life,* pg40-43 (March 1991).

Barrows and Cairns

Cheshire County Sites and Monuments Record (Alderley Edge – Armada Beacon) *SMR* 2849 (Andrew Knobb, Bollington) *SMR* 1595 (Astbury Churchyard) *SMR* 1129, 1130 (Bearhurst Farm, Henbury) *SMR* 1369, 1370/1/1, 1370/1/2 (Beech Hall) *SMR* 1552/1/1, 1552/1/2 (Birtles Hall) *SMR* 1364/1/1 (Blackrock Farm, Rainow) *SMR* 1599 (Blue Boar Farm, Rainow) *SMR* 1601 (Bonis Hall Lane – Butley) *SMR* 1557/1 (Brock Low) *SMR*1569 (Capesthorne Hall) *SMR* 1352, 1349, 1342 (Cessbank, Wincle) *SMR* 1523 (Charles Head, Rainow) *SMR* 1604/0/1 (Church Lawton) *SMR* 133/1/1, 133/1/2, 133/1/3 (Dark Valley) *SMR* 2639/1, 2639/1/1 (Delamere – Fishpool Lane) *SMR* 841 (Further Harrop) *SMR* 1603 (Gallowsclough Cob) *SMR* 923 (High Billinge) *SMR* 858 (High Low) *SMR* 1541 (Knight's Low Wood, Lyme) *SMR* 1632/1/2, 1632/1/1, 1628/1/1, 1628/1/2, 1628/1/3, 1629 (Langley Conical Mound) *SMR* 1540 (Macclesfield Cemetery) *SMR* 1551/0/1 (Macclesfield Common) *SMR* 1554/1/4 (Nab Head) *SMR* 1585 (Reed Hill) *SMR* 1597 (Monarchy Hall) *SMR* 856 (Seven Lows) *SMR* 840/1/0, 840/1/1, 840/1/2, 840/1/3, 840/1/4, 840/1/5, 840/1/6, 840/1/7 (Robin Hood's Butts) *SMR* 808 (Soldier's Tump) *SMR* 1337 (Somerford) *SMR* 1131 (Sponds Hill, Lyme) *SMR* 1627/1/1, 1627/1/2 (Sutton Hall) *SMR* 1539 (Swettenham Hall) *SMR* 1138 (Swythamley) *SMR* 1535 (Toot Hill) *SMR* 1567 (Twemlow Hall) *SMR* 1056/1/1, 1056/1/2 (Whiteley) *SMR* 1028 (Wilmslow Urns) *SMR* 1493/0/3, 1493/0/1, 1493/0/2 (Withington) *SMR* 1343, 1340/1/1, 1340/1/2, 1340/1/4, 1340/1/0, 1340/1/3 (Woodhouse End) *SMR* 1511 (Yearnslow, Rainow) *SMR* 1600.

Adkins, L. and R. "Handbook of British Archaeology", Constable, London (1998).

Andrew, W.J. "Excavation of the Tumulus on Sponds Hill, East Cheshire" *TLCAS* volume 30 (1912).

Ashmole Mss. No.854, Fo.322 Bodleian Library (unknown author) [Robin Hood's Butts tumulus].

Bamford, P. "Cheshire Curiosities", Dovecote Press (1992).

Barnatt, J. and Collis, J. "Barrows in the Peak District – Recent Research", J.R.Collis Publications (1996).

Bateman, T. "Ten Years Digging in Celtic and Saxon Grave Hills" (1861).

BBCi "The Nebra Sky Disk" retrieved (30/01/2004) from: http://www.bbc.co.uk/dna/h2g2/A2167922

Brocklehurst, Sir. P. "Swythamley and Its Neighbourhood", Swinnerton and Brown Printers, Macclesfield (1874).

Bu'Lock, J.D. "The Bronze Age in the North-West", *TLCAS* volume 71 (1961).

Cheshire Archaeology News issue 7, (2000). [Monuments at Risk Survey].

Coles, B., Friell, G., Huckerby, E., Middleton, R., Newman, R.M., Wells, C.E. and Wilmott, A. "The Wetlands of Merseyside", Lancaster Imprints 2 (1994).

Cumming Walters, J. and Greenwood, F. "Romantic Cheshire", Hodder and Stoughton, London (1931 reprint).

Earwaker, J.P. "East Cheshire Past and Present" volume 2 (1880).

Ellis, P. (ed) "Beeston Castle, Cheshire – Excavations by Laurence Keen and Peter Hough, 1968-85", English Heritage Archaeological Report 23 (1993).

Forde-Johnston, J. "The excavation of a round barrow at Gallowsclough Hill, Delamere Forest, Cheshire", *TLCAS* volume 70 (1960).

Foote Gower, Dr (Addl. MSS Brit. Museum, Vol II, 338, FO72).

Goodrick, G. and Harding, J. "Virtual Reality at the Neolithic Monument Complex of Thornborough, North Yorkshire". in J.A. Barcelo et al (eds) "Virtual Reality in Archaeology", British Archaeological Reports International series 5843, Oxford (2000).

Grinsell, L.V. "The Ancient Burial Mounds of England", Methuen and Co, London (1953).

Harding, J. "The Neolithic and Bronze Age Monument Complex of Thornborough, North Yorkshire, and its landscape context - desk top assessment"" Retrieved 30/01/2004 from: http://thornborough.ncl.ac.uk/desktop_assessment/desktop_contents.htm

Heathcote, J.P. "Birchover Its Prehistoric and Druidical Remains" (1934).

Journal of the Chester Archaeological Society "Miscellanea", volume 47, pg33 (1960) [stone axe-hammer from Old Withington].

Journal of the Chester Archaeological Society "Miscellanea - Bronze Age Burial from Beech Hall, Macclesfield" volume 48, pg43-45 (1961).

Kilburn, K. "Archaeoastronomy" Retrieved (05/04/2003) from: http://www.leekonline.co.uk/sunset/index.htm

Kilburn. K "The Bridestones Legacy" (forthcoming).

Leah, M.D, Wells, C.E., Applebly, C. and Huckerby, E. "The Wetlands of Cheshire, North West Wetlands Survey 4", Lancaster Imprints, Lancaster Archaeological Unit (1997).

Lees-Milne, J. "Little Moreton Hall, Cheshire", National Trust (1974).

Leland, J. "The Itinerary" (1745 edition).

Lempriere, J. "Lempriere's Classical Dictionary", Bracken Books, London (1990).

Longley, D.M. "Prehistory" in C.R. Elrington (ed) "The Victoria History of the County of Chester", volume 1, Oxford University Press, pg56-73, 82-86 (1987).

Marriott, Rev. W. "Antiquities of Lyme" (1810).

McNeil, R. "Notes on Church Lawton North and South", *Cheshire Archaeological Bulletin*, volume 8 (1982).

Moore, Sir P. "The Observer's Year", Springer, London (1998).

Morgan, V. and P. "Rock Around the Peak – Megalithic Monuments of the Peak District", Sigma Press (2001).

Moss, J.M. "A rambling survey amongst the tumuli and Saxon settlements in the neighbourhood of Macclesfield", *Proceedings of the Macclesfield Scientific Society* (1877-1878).

Ormerod, G. "The History of Cheshire", 2nd Edition (1882).

Parker Pearson, M. "The Archaeology of Death and Burial", Sutton Publishing Ltd, Stroud (1999).

The Poulton Research Project "Late Bronze Age/Iron Age Ring Ditch", Retrieved (07/07/2003) from The Poulton Research Project website: http://srs.dl.ac.uk/arch/poulton/ditches-1.shtml

Pryor, F. "Seahenge – New Discoveries in Prehistoric Britain", Harper Collins (2001).

Ray, K. "From Remote times to the Bronze Age c. 500,000 BC to 600BC" in P.C.Jupp and C.Gittings (ed) "Death in England", Manchester University Press (1999).

Ridgway, M.H. "Bronze Age Urn from Astbury, Cheshire", *TLCAS* volume 59 (1956).

Roeder, C. "Prehistoric and Subsequent Mining at Alderley Edge, with a sketch of the Archaeological Features of the Neighbourhood", *TLCAS* volume 19 (1901).

Roeder, C. and Graves, F.S. "Recent Archaeological Discoveries at Alderley Edge", *TLCAS* volume 23 (1905).

Roeder, C. "Prehistoric Glimpses of Eddisbury Hundred (Cheshire)" *TLCAS* volume 26 (1909).

Rowley, G. "The Excavation of a Barrow at Woodhouse End, Gawsworth, Near Macclesfield", *JCAS* volume 60 (1977).

Rowley, G. "Macclesfield in Prehistory" (1982).

Sainter, Dr J.D. "The Jottings of Some Geological, Archaeological, Botanical, Ornithological, and Zoological Rambles Round Macclesfield", Swinnerton and Brown Printers, Macclesfield (1878).

Shone, W. "Prehistoric Man in Cheshire", Simpkin, Marshall, Hamilton, Kent and Co Ltd, London (1911).

Shrubsole, G.W. "On a Settlement of Prehistoric People in Delamere Forest" *JCAS* volume 4 (1890/1).

Smith, T.J. "Grave Mound Exploration near Macclesfield", *Proceedings of the Macclesfield Scientific Society* (1877-1878).

Thompson, F.H. "Notes on Excavations and Finds in Cheshire During 1960" [Beech Hall School], *TLCAS* volume 70 (1960).

Transactions of the Lancashire and Cheshire Antiquarian Society "Proceedings", volume 1, pg209 [Macclesfield Forest axe]

Twemlow, F.R. "The Twemlows - Their wives and their homes" (1910).

Uhthoff-Kaufman, R.R. "The Archaeology of Jodrell Hall (Terra Nova), Twemlow, Cheshire" (1910).

Varley, W.J. and Jackson, J.W. "Prehistoric Cheshire", Cheshire Rural Community Council (1940).

Varley, W.J. "Cheshire Before the Romans", Cheshire Community Council (1964).

Walker, J.W. "The Tumuli at Twemlow Hall, Cheshire" *THSLC* volume 91 (1939).

Watkin, W.T. "Roman Cheshire", Liverpool (1886).

Wilson, D. "Lower Withington", *Cheshire Archaeological Bulletin*, volume 6.

Wilson, D. "Withington", *Current Archaeology* volume 76 (1981).

Woodward, A. "British Barrows – A Matter of Life and Death", Tempus Publishing, Stroud (2000).

Standing Stones

Cheshire County Sites and Monuments Record (Ginclough) *SMR* 1606 (Minn End Lane) *SMR* 1645, 1646 (Murder Stone) *SMR* 1626 (Toot Hill) *SMR* 1572.

Bamford, P. "Cheshire Curiosities", Dovecote Press (1992).

Cuming Walters, J. and Greenwood, F. "Romantic Cheshire" (1930).

Kilburn, K. "Double Sun Set at Leek, Staffordshire", Retrieved (28/06/01) from: http:// www.leekonline.co.uk/sunset/index.htm

Lynch, F., Aldhouse-Green, S. and Davies, J.L. "Prehistoric Wales", Sutton Publishing (2000).

Marriott, Rev. W. "Antiquities of Lyme" (1810).

McNeil Cooke, I. "Standing Stones of the Land's End – an enquiry into their function", Men-an-Tol Studio (1998).

Merrill, J. N. "Derbyshire Folklore", J.N.M. Publications, Winster (1988).

Mohen, J. "Standing Stones – Stonehenge, Carnac and the World of Megaliths", Thames and Hudson (1999).

Morgan, V. and P. "Rock Around the Peak – Megalithic Monuments of the Peak District", Sigma Press (2001).

Ormerod, G. "The History of Cheshire", 2nd Edition (1882).

Renaud, F. "History of the Parish of Prestbury", Chetham Society (1876).

Timberlake, S. "Mining and prospection for metals in Early Bronze Age Britain – making claims within the archaeological landscape" In Brück, J (ed), "Bronze Age Landscapes. Transition and transformation", pg 179-192, Oxbow Books, Oxford (2001).

Turner, R.C. "Standing Stone – Lyme Handley", *Cheshire Archaeological Bulletin* 9 (1993).

Wroe, P. "Roman Roads in the Peak District", *Derbyshire Archaeological Journal* volume 120 (1982).

The Iron Age

Introduction and Daily Life

Cunliffe, B. "Iron Age Britain", English Heritage and B.T. Batsford Ltd, London (1995)

Elsdon, S.M. "Later Prehistoric Pottery", Shire Publications, Princes Risborough (1989).

Firstbrook, P. "Surviving the Iron Age", BBC Worldwide Ltd, London (2001).

Haselgrove, C. "The Iron Age" in "Archaeology of Britain" edited by J. Hunter and I. Ralston, Routledge, London (1999).

Longley, D.M. "Prehistory" in C.R. Elrington (ed) "The Victoria History of the County of Chester, volume 1, Oxford University Press, pg103-108 (1987).

Todd, M. "Roman Britain", Fontana Press (1981).

Trade and Salt Production

Current Archaeology volume 172 "Wetlands Special" (February 2001).

Laine, T. and Morris, E. (ed) "A Millennium of Saltmaking: Prehistoric and Romano-British salt production in the Fenland", Lincolnshire Archaeological and Heritage Reports Series (2001).

Laing, J. and L. "A Mediterranean Trade with Wirral in the Iron Age", *Cheshire Archaeological Bulletin* 9 (1993).

Matthews. K.J. "The Iron Age of North-West England – A Socio-Economic Model", JCAS volume 76 (2000/2001).

Mellor Archaeological Trust "The Hillfort at Mellor, Excavations 1998-2002" (2003).

Morris, E. "Prehistoric Salt Distributions: two case studies from western Britain", Bulletin of the Board of Celtic Studies 32 (1985).

Petch, D. "Roman Salt Making", A Salt Museum Publication, Cheshire Libraries and Museums.

Price, J. "The Discovery of an Early Saltworking Site near Crewe",. *Cheshire Past* issue 3 (1994).

"Salt in Ancient Times", Retrieved (07/07/2003) from the The Salt Manufacturers' Association website: http://www.saltinfo.com

Tindall, A. "An Iron Age Coin from near Nantwich", *Cheshire Past* issue 2 (1993).

Hillforts and Enclosed Farming Settlements

Bu'Lock, J.D. "Possible Remains of Celtic Fields at Kelsall in Cheshire", *TLCAS* volume 64 (1954).

Bu'Lock, J.D "The Hill-fort at Helsby, Cheshire", *TLCAS* volume 66 (1956).

Cheshire County Sites and Monuments Record (Beeston) *SMR* 1732/1 (Bradley) *SMR* 971/1 (Burton Point) *SMR* 9/1 (Castle Ditch, Eddisbury) *SMR* 866/1 (Castle Hill, Oldcastle) *SMR* 1667/1 (Great Low) *SMR* 1602/1 (Helsby Hill) *SMR* 1007/1 (Kelsborrow) *SMR* 833/1 (Legh Oaks Farm) *SMR* 2062/1, 2062/2 (Maiden Castle) *SMR* 341/1 (Oakmere) *SMR* 848/1 (Peckforton Mere) *SMR* 314 (Warrington Crannogs) *SMR* 498/1, 477/1 (Woodhouses) *SMR* 970/1.

Cocroft, W., Everson, P., Jecock, M. and Wilson-North, W.R. "Castle Ditch Hillfort Eddisbury, Cheshire Reconsidered: the excavations of 1935-38 in the light of a recent field survey" in "From Cornwall to Caithness, some aspects of British Field Archaeology" edited by M. Bowden, D. Mackay and P. Topping, British Archaeological Reports British Series 209, Oxford (1989).

Collens. J. "Flying on the Edge – Aerial Photography and Early Settlement Patterns in Cheshire and Merseyside" in Nevell (ed) (1988).

Crowe, C. "A note on a 'Celtic Head' in the churchyard at Rostherne", *TLCAS* volume 81 (1985)

Current Archaeology volume 189 "Mellor – a new Iron Age Hillfort" (December 2003).

Ellis, P. (ed) "Beeston Castle, Cheshire – Excavations by Laurence Keen and Peter Hough, 1968-85", English Heritage Archaeological Report 23 (1993).

Eve, S. "Warrington Crannogs", Personal Communication (2003).

Fairburn, N., Bonner, D., Carruthers, W.J., Gale, G.R., Matthews, K.J., Morris, E. and Ward, M. "Brook House Farm, Bruen Stapleford – Excavation of a First Millennium BC Settlement", JCAS volume 77 (2002).

Leah, M.D, Wells, C.E., Applebly, C. and Huckerby, E. "The Wetlands of Cheshire, North West Wetlands Survey 4", Lancaster Imprints, Lancaster Archaeological Unit, pg152-154 (1997).

Longley, D.M. "Prehistory" in C.R. Elrington (ed) "The Victoria History of the County of Chester, volume 1, Oxford University Press (1987), pg 109-114.

Matthews. K.J. "The Iron Age of North-West England – A Socio-Economic Model", JCAS volume 76 (2000/2001).

Mellor Archaeological Trust "The Hillfort at Mellor, Excavations 1998-2002" (2003).

Nevell, M.D. (ed) "Living on the edge of Empire: Models, Methodology and Marginality – Late Prehistoric and Romano-British Rural Settlements in North West England", Archaeology North West volume 3, issue 13 (1988).

Nevell, M.D. "Iron Age and Romano-British Rural Settlement in North West England – Marginality and Settlement" in Nevell (ed)(1988).

Nevell, M.D. "Great Woolden Hall Farm – A Model for the Material Culture of Iron Age and Romano-British Rural Settlement in North West England" in Nevell (ed) (1988).

Nevell, M.D. "Great Woolden Hall: excavations on a late prehistoric/Romano-British native site", *Greater Manchester Archaeological Journal* volume 3 (1989).

Nevell, M.D. "Excavations on a Roman-British site at Legh Oaks Farm, Northern Cheshire 1987-88", *Manchester Archaeological Bulletin* volume 4 (1990).

Nevell, M.D. "Legh Oaks Farm, High Legh – The Value of Sample Excavation on Two Sites of the Late Prehistoric and Roman Periods", *JCAS* volume 77 (2002).

Philpott, R.A. and Adams, M.H. "Excavations at an Iron Age and Romano-British Settlement at Irby, Wirral, 1987-96 – An Interim Statement" in Nevell (ed) (1988).

Bog Bodies

Cheshire County Sites and Monuments Record (Lindow) *SMR* 1472/0/0, 1472/0/1, 1472/0/2.

Aldhouse-Green, M. "Dying for the Gods. Human Sacrifice in Iron Age and Roman Europe", Tempus Publishing, Stroud (2002).

Brothwell, D. "The Bog Man and The Archaeology of People", British Museum Press, London (1986).

Burnett, A. and Reeve, J. "Behind the Scenes at the British Museum", British Museum Press, London (2001).

Coles, B., Coles, J., and Jørgensen, M.S. (ed) "Bog Bodies, Sacred Sites and Wetland Archaeology", Wetland Archaeology Research Project (1999).

Current Archaeology volume 172 "Wetlands Special" (February 2001).

Glob, P.V. "The Bog People - Iron Age Man Preserved", Faber and Faber, London (1969).

Hope, V.M. "The Iron and Roman Ages c.600BC to 400AD" in "Death in England – an illustrated history" edited by P.C. Jupp and C. Gittings, Manchester University Press (1999).

Keys, D. "The Mummies of Cladh Hallan" Retrieved (06/05/03) from: http://www.bbc.co.uk/history/archaeology/mummies_cladhhallan_02.shtml

Leah, M.D, Wells, C.E., Applebly, C. and Huckerby, E. "The Wetlands of Cheshire, North West Wetlands Survey 4", Lancaster Imprints, Lancaster Archaeological Unit (1997).

Mabey, R. "Flora Britannica", Sinclair-Stevenson, London (1996).

Norbury, W. "Lindow Common as a Peat Bog - Its Age and Its People", *TLCAS* volume 11 (1884).

Ross, A. and Robins, D. "The Life and Death of a Druid Prince", Rider, London (1989).

Stead, I.M., Bourke, J.B. and Brothwell, D. "Lindow Man - The Body in the Bog", Guild Publishing, London (1986).

Turner, R. "The Lindow Moss Bog Bodies: Further Research", *Cheshire Past* issue 2 (1993).

Turner, R.C. and Scaife, R.G. (ed) "Bog Bodies – New Discoveries and Perspectives", British Museum Press, London (1995).

Index

189